Private Equity Compliance

Founded in 1807, John Wiley & Sons is the oldest independent publishing company in the United States. With offices in North America, Europe, Australia and Asia, Wiley is globally committed to developing and marketing print and electronic products and services for our customers' professional and personal knowledge and understanding.

The Wiley Finance series contains books written specifically for finance and investment professionals as well as sophisticated individual investors and their financial advisors. Book topics range from portfolio management to e-commerce, risk management, financial engineering, valuation and financial instrument analysis, as well as much more.

For a list of available titles, visit our website at www.WileyFinance.com.

Private Equity Compliance

Analyzing Conflicts, Fees, and Risks

JASON A. SCHARFMAN

WILEY

Library of Congress Cataloging-in-Publication Data is Available:

ISBN 9781119479628 (Hardcover)
ISBN 9781119479635 (ePDF)
ISBN 9781119479642 (ePub)

Cover Design: Wiley
Cover Images: © Myimagine/Shutterstock;
© Phongphan/Shutterstock

Printed in the United States of America

V10002925_080718

For R, Y, Z and T.

Contents

Preface

Historically, private equity general partners (GPs) and their limited partners (LPs) did not pay a great deal of attention to the area of compliance management. This was likely a function of the long-term nature of private equity investing where the focus was on long-term profitability as compared to day-to-day operations of the funds. While notions of emerging investment opportunities and making plans for the next vintage fund were on the forefront, there was the general perception among private equity participants, that as long as a fund was managed in a legal way, compliance was simply an afterthought to be relegated to a GP's lawyers and regulatory agencies.

Today, perspectives on this matter have reversed, and compliance has become one of the fastest growing areas in the private equity space. Mirroring trends from the hedge fund industry, surveys indicate that private equity managers consistently rank compliance as one of the most challenging aspects of their business. Reports also indicate that private equity compliance spending has rapidly outpaced other GP operating costs, with recent estimates indicating that private equity funds increasingly spend large portions of their operating budgets on this area.

Further bringing this issue to the forefront of the industry, private equity regulators such as the US Securities and Exchange Commission (US SEC) and United Kingdom Financial Conduct Authority (UK FCA) have also increasingly stepped up their enforcement of compliance violations on both established and emerging private equity GPs. Additionally, as complex regulations have become more rigorous and complex, GPs have commensurately ramped up hiring of individuals to fill compliance related roles. Further highlighting this trend, private equity fund service providers, including compliance consultants and law firms, are also increasing their compliance-related offerings. LPs have also altered their approaches to private equity fund due diligence to increasingly incorporate detailed evaluations of GP and fund-level compliance considerations.

The scope of private equity compliance has also continually expanded to encompass a wide variety of risk areas. GP compliance programs are now required to regularly engage in areas ranging from traditional fund-level investment compliance, to conflicts of interest, fee management and transparency, and increased oversight of the compliance implications of investment research procedures. Compliance has also become increasingly integrated with the information technology function and in managing cyber-security risks. In order to address these compliance challenges, GPs, LPs, and service providers must make sure they are up to date on the latest developments in this space. This includes ensuring that they not only have a strong foundation in core principles of private equity compliance, but are also engaged in continuing deploying sufficient resources to this critical area. Furthermore, a continuing series of new laws and regulatory guidelines directly affecting the way compliance is implemented in private equity firms facilitates the need for considerable ongoing vigilance in this area. This goal of this book is to equip those involved in the private equity industry to rise to meet these challenges.

To assist in the highlighting of key compliance terminology, as you read through each of the chapters, you will find important terms italicized. This book is also designed to be utilized as an ongoing reference on specific compliance topics. Additionally, to emphasize a focus on the ways compliance challenges present themselves in practice, numerous case studies have been included throughout the book. For ease of navigation in this regard, the chapters of this book have been organized by key compliance topic area.

Specifically, this book is structured to provide an understanding of the core concepts of private equity compliance across three sections. The first section of the book, Chapters 1 through 4, focuses on introductory topics relating to the compliance obligations of private equity firms and funds. Topics covered in this section include an overview of the compliance obligations of GPs, the role of Limited Partner Advisory Committees (LPACs), and valuation compliance.

The second section of the book, Chapters 5 through 8, broadens the analysis of specific topics in GP and fund-level compliance. This section begins by addressing the ways in which GPs, LPs, and regulatory agencies have approached the numerous potential conflicts of interest present in private equity investing. The compliance challenges surrounding the management of fees and expenses are next discussed. The next chapter in this section addresses the increasing importance of information technology in facilitating the implementation of rigorous compliance protocols. Finally, a review of core private equity compliance policies and accompanying documentation is presented.

The third and final section of the book, Chapters 9 through 12, is centered on providing readers with a practical understanding of the application of private equity compliance principles. This section starts with an overview of techniques for compliance training, surveillance, and testing. Next, methods by which LPs can analyze the strengths and weaknesses of GP compliance functions are discussed. To provide direct real-world perspectives, this last section also features interviews with private equity professionals on key issues in private equity compliance in Chapter 11. This is followed by a discussion of emerging topics and trends in the compliance space.

The old attitude of doing just enough to not get in trouble with regulators is no longer acceptable when it comes to private equity compliance. Today, regulators and LPs have increasingly demanded that GPs actively embrace the challenge of implementing and maintaining a rigorous compliance infrastructure. GPs are increasingly viewing compliance not as a stumbling block, but as an opportunity by which they can improve the oversight, governance, and management of their firms and funds. By acknowledging the benefits of thorough compliance management in this way, all constituents in the private equity industry can benefit from continued dialogues in this area and improve the industry as a whole.

Jason Scharfman
July 2018

CHAPTER 1

Introduction to Private Equity Compliance

1.1 INTRODUCTION

At its most basic level the term *compliance* refers to a series of rules and regulations that are applicable to an organization. Most commonly these rules come from laws that are passed by legislative bodies in order to enforce a series of acceptable market practices. The focus of this book is on the practices that a private equity manager and the funds they manage should adhere to in order to implement a program of compliance.

1.2 WHAT EXACTLY IS PRIVATE EQUITY?

The term *private equity* is utilized in many different contexts in the investment world. Traditionally, private equity has referred to an investment strategy that seeks to invest in privately traded securities. This would be compared to strategies that seek to invest in public securities markets. In practice, private equity investments do not necessarily exclude investments in the public markets. An example of this would be what is known as a *PIPE deal*, which represents a private investment in public equity.

1.3 PRIVATE EQUITY TERMINOLOGY

Before proceeding with our discussion of the policies and procedures that constitute a private equity compliance program, it is first helpful to clarify specific terminology to ensure that readers are consistent in their understanding of key terms. The explanation of these terms will also assist with a practical perspective as to how they are commonly utilized among private equity professionals in the marketplace:

- *Private equity firm/Private equity manager/General partner (GP).* A private equity firm, also referred to as a *private equity manager*, is the management entity responsible for managing the private equity company itself. The funds managed by a private equity firm are effectively overseen by an entity known as *GP of the funds.* Although there is often a technical legal distinction in place between the GP and the private equity firm itself, in practice the term *GP* is also utilized synonymously.

  The activities performed at the private equity company level commonly include raising capital for the private equity firm's funds and processing administrative tasks such as employee payroll and benefits administration. Additionally, many firm-wide initiatives such as information technology, fund accounting, and compliance are coordinated across the firm's funds at the GP level. For the purposes of this text, unless otherwise specified, the terms *private equity firm* and *private equity manager* will also include reference to the underlying private equity funds managed by the firm.

- *Private equity fund/Investment vehicle.* Private investors allocate capital to what are known as *private equity funds.* Private equity funds are also referred to as *investment vehicles.*

- *Pooled versus separate account structures.* Private equity funds are typically structured as *pooled investment vehicles* that manage capital for a variety of different investors. To clarify, the term *vehicle* is utilized to mean a specific private equity fund. Another type of private equity fund structure is the *separate account*, which is also known as a *separately managed account.* In this structure, a stand-alone private equity fund is established for a single investor. This is typically done in the case of large institutional investors that merit the extra operational expenses associated with the creation and management of a separate account.

- *Limited partner (LP)/Investors.* Private equity funds are typically established under a legal structure known as a *limited partnership.* Limited partnerships are commonly utilized for US-based funds that are domiciled in jurisdictions such as the state of Delaware. From the perspective of a US-based investor, this would be referred to as a *domestic fund.* Another common fund structure for non-US-based funds would be the *limited liability company (Ltd.)* structure. These funds are commonly domiciled outside of the US in jurisdictions such as the Cayman Islands and would be referred to as an *offshore fund* from the perspective of a US investor. Under both the LP and Ltd. structures the underlying investors in the fund are commonly referred to as *LPs*. In practice, LPs are also referred to simply as investors.

- *Portfolio company/Underlying company/Underlying business.* Private equity funds traditionally allocate capital to companies. These allocations can be made in a variety of different formats, including equity and debt in the company. Due to the fact that the investments in these companies are part of a larger private equity fund's portfolio consisting of multiple investments in different companies, these business entities are commonly referred to as portfolio companies. They may also be called an *underlying portfolio company, underlying company,* or *underlying business.*

1.4 MANDATORY COMPLIANCE

In order to understand the way in which compliance policies and procedures are implemented in at the GP and fund level we must first introduce the concepts of mandatory and voluntary compliance.

There are certain compliance rules and regulations that a private equity manager must follow. This is known as *mandatory compliance*. The penalty for violating these rules can range from financial penalties to sanctions on participating in certain markets and even forcing the complete closure of the organization. Mandatory compliance rules come from two primary sources:

1. *Legislation.* Laws affecting private equity managers may be promulgated by legislative bodies such as the US Congress and the UK Parliament.
2. *Regulatory implementation.* Financial regulators use a process known as *rulemaking* to create and amend rules that implement legislation. These rules are required to be followed by regulated firms and persons. Due to the heavy influence of regulators on mandatory compliance obligations of private equity managers, mandatory compliance is also sometimes referred to as *regulatory compliance.*

In a private equity context mandatory compliance can refer to:

- Applicable laws in the country or countries in which a private equity manager and their funds operate
- Required rules promulgated by regulatory agencies that have jurisdiction over private equity funds' activities

1.5 VOLUNTARY COMPLIANCE

Voluntary compliance refers to the rules and regulations that a private equity manager and their associated funds are not required by any law or regulator to adhere to, but that they voluntarily choose to follow. Voluntary compliance for private equity managers can fall into one of two primary categories:

1. *Self-imposed obligations.* Voluntary compliance obligations may be self-imposed by private equity managers. These self-imposed obligations can be created in two primary ways:

   a. One way these self-imposed obligations can arise would be when a private equity manager makes a decision to create a compliance policy that goes beyond the minimum mandatory requirements. The reasons a private equity manager would go beyond these minimum requirements can include a desire to adhere to industry best practices, increase the oversight of compliance-related risks, and to broaden the scope of compliance oversight beyond minimum mandatory requirements.

   b. Private equity managers may also self-impose voluntary compliance obligations upon themselves when the private equity firm agrees to adhere to principles of a third-party group such as an industry-wide organization. An example of this type of compliance obligation would be a private equity manager that voluntarily outlines in its compliance policies that it will adhere to the Institutional Limited Partner Association's (ILPAs) Quarterly Reporting Standards (QSR).[1]

2. *Regulatory recommended voluntary compliance obligations.* Another type of self-imposed obligation is when a private equity fund manager decides to voluntarily follow what is known as *regulatory guidance.* This type of guidance refers to what effectively amounts to recommendations by regulators with regard to the practice a GP could employ to institute a certain practice. While not typically mandatory this guidance is often recommended by regulators and precedes future rules before they are made mandatory; therefore adherence to these guidelines in GPs is often encouraged. Regulatory guidance is often communicated by financial regulators through avenues such as:

   - Government testimony by regulators
   - Policy speeches at universities or other industry associations events
   - Position papers and commentary on market development

---

[1]More information is available on the ILPA QSR at: https://ilpa.org/wp-content/uploads/2017/03/ILPA-Best-Practices-Quarterly-Reporting-Standards_Version-1.1_optimized.pdf.

- Responses to specific inquiries for legislative bodies or firms registered with regulators
- Regulatory educational events such as webinars and podcasts

For example, the US Securities and Exchange Commission (US SEC) details a list of upcoming US SEC meetings, public appearances of senior Securities and Exchange Commission (SEC) officials, and other events at which regulatory guidance is typically provided on their website at https:// www.sec.gov/news/upcoming-events. The US SEC also issues so-called *Interpretive Releases* that provide guidance on topics in which they publish their views and interpret the federal securities laws and SEC regulations at https:// www.sec.gov/rules/interp.shtml.

The bulk of official websites from financial regulators that have jurisdiction over private equity funds contain links to different regulatory guidance, including agency news, comment letters, and speeches. A representative example of the Internet links to the locations of this information on regulator websites is included in Exhibit 1.1.

The recommendations outlined in regulatory guidance are generally not binding upon GPs. Instead they express an opinion by a regulator that the laws and regulatory rules relating to a certain compliance policy could be

Regulatory Agency	News and Notices
National Futures Association (NFA)	www.nfa.futures.org/news/ indexNews.asp
Commodity Futures Trading Commission (CFTC)	www.cftc.gov/PressRoom/index.htm
United Kingdom Financial Conduct Authority (UK FCA)	www.fca.org.uk/news
Cayman Islands Monetary Authority	www.cimoney.com.ky/about_cima/ current_news_releases.aspx
Hong Kong Securities and Futures Commission (HK SFC)	http://www.sfc.hk/edistributionWeb/ gateway/EN/news-and-announcements/news/
Monetary Authority of Singapore (MAS)	http://www.mas.gov.sg/News-and-Publications.aspx
Swiss Financial Market Supervisory Authority (FINMA)	https://www.finma.ch/en/news

Exhibit 1.1 Representative list of links to information containing regulatory guidance directly on private equity regulatory websites.

implemented in a particular way, or variety of ways, that they recommend. To be clear, this does not mean that if a GP decides to pursue a different practice from the one recommended in the regulatory guidance they would be in violation of any laws or rules. On the contrary, in some instances too-strict adherence to regulatory guidance may be viewed as taking an overly conservative approach to compliance. After all, the regulator is effectively explaining how they feel a certain regulatory rule should be enacted in practice, but these recommendations are not necessarily appropriate for every GP's situation and a lack of strict adherence to regulatory guidance by a GP does not necessarily correlate directly to an overall weak compliance framework.

1.6 DISTINGUISHING INVESTMENT AND OPERATIONAL COMPLIANCE

Now that we have an understanding of the concepts of mandatory and voluntary compliance, another related aspect that will be helpful for our discussion of private equity compliance practices is the distinction between investment and operational compliance.

A key component of the compliance obligations of an investment manager, be they a private equity fund or some other type of fund, are largely determined by the nature of their fund's portfolio holdings. For example, a hedge fund that does not trade in commodities markets would not be subject to the relevant commodity trading regulations. The same is applicable for private equity. In certain instances, a private equity fund may transact in certain types of securities, which may subject it to different compliance obligations. These are known as *investment compliance obligations*. Another factor that may influence investment compliance relates to the jurisdictions in which a private equity fund's transactions occur. For example, a private equity firm that purchases an equity stake in an aerospace manufacturer based in Spain would likely be subject to some degree to the Spanish regulatory regime.

Investment compliance can be distinguished from those compliance obligations that do not directly relate to the investment holdings of a private equity fund. This other group of compliance obligations instead relate to the operational aspects of managing a private equity firm and can be referred to as *operational compliance obligations*. One example of an operational compliance obligation would be the general requirement that a private equity manager registered with the US SEC archive must maintain records of communications which support performance claims for at least five years under Rule 204-2 of the Investment Advisers Act of 1940. This recordkeeping requirement applies regardless of the particular holdings of a covered private equity fund.

The bulk of investment compliance obligations typically reside at the level of the private equity fund while operational compliance obligations generally reside at the GP level. In certain instances, investment compliance obligations may not only impose obligations of private equity funds directly but also impose compliance obligations on the overlying GP as well. This would be an example of what is known as *reach-through compliance*, when the compliance obligations of an underlying entity trigger obligations on an entity above it.

1.7   HISTORICAL GENERAL PARTNER COMPLIANCE EFFORTS

As compared to today, in the early days of the private equity industry there were scant mandatory compliance requirements. Indeed, many GPs may not have even had a stand-alone compliance function. A key reason for this was because there was a lack of legislative and regulatory oversight of private equity activities. The historical thinking at the time was that GPs were raising capital from sophisticated institutions and wealthy individuals, and there was no need for additional material external oversight of these types of groups. It was simply an investment arrangement between knowledgeable parties, both of which could be responsible enough to understand and bear the risks they were signing up for.

Any items which may have been thought of as being somewhat compliance related were likely considered to be thought of as *legal risks* and would have been dealt with by a GP's *General Counsel* or third-party law firm. For reference, historically the title of General Counsel was typically assigned to an individual, likely trained as an attorney, who was responsible for overseeing both the legal and compliance-related functions within a private equity firm. Related compliance matters may also have been outsourced to a third-party law firm as well.

1.8   TRANSITION TO INCREASED REGULATION
OF PRIVATE EQUITY

In recent years private equity investing has become increasingly subject to a whole plethora of complex compliance rules and regulations. This mirrors a broader overall shift toward increased regulation across the global investment landscape in asset classes outside of private equity, including hedge funds and long-only funds. On a market-wide basis, motivations for these increased regulations have included:

- Events such as the 2008 financial crisis
- A series of non-private-equity fund manager frauds, including the Madoff and Galleon cases that subjected the entire investment industry to enhanced regulatory scrutiny
- Increased focus on the tax-avoidance practices of alternative investments managers
- A global effort toward increased transparency from fund managers to both investors and regulators

Looking at private equity specifically, recent drivers of regulatory initiatives have been spurred by compliance concerns focused on the oversight of fees, conflicts of interest, and valuations.

1.9   WHAT IS PRIVATE EQUITY COMPLIANCE?

The area of compliance has become an essential element of the modern private equity investing environment. Broadly our discussion of private equity compliance focuses on three distinct, but related, areas of the private equity landscape:

1. GP-level compliance
2. Fund-level compliance
3. Portfolio company compliance as it relates to the GP and fund

In this list, GP- and fund-level compliance can be thought of as the core aspects of private equity compliance. The focus of our discussion in this book will be on the first two categories in the previous section (i.e. GP-level compliance and fund-level compliance). The third category on the list is certainly important but is more focused instead on aspects related to the underlying management of the portfolio company itself as opposed to the private equity GP or fund. While in Chapter 2 we will address these levels in more detail, here we will examine how portfolio company compliance is in a distinct category.

1.9.1   Portfolio Company Compliance Considerations

The best way to demonstrate this distinction is through an example. A portfolio company is a business that likely has employees. There are a number of laws and rules related to aspects of this employment relationship, including prohibitions on workplace harassment and considerations for the safety of employees. At the portfolio company level, the managers of the underlying company would be responsible for complying with these rules. The private equity fund itself, and by association the GP, would not be responsible for actually implementing these employee-facing procedures. Of course, it would be in the best interest of the private equity fund investors that allocated to the portfolio company if it was operating in adherence to all rules. This would prevent negative action at the underlying portfolio company level, such as penalties from governmental oversight agencies and potential employee lawsuits, which would likely have a direct financial impact on the performance of the company. However, the point is this level of compliance resides at the underlying portfolio level and is in a distinct category from GP- and fund-level compliance.

1.9.1.1 General Partner Board Seat Oversight Considerations In many instances representatives of the private equity fund, and by association the GP, will take a seat on the board of directors of the portfolio company. In these cases, the GP/fund representative sitting on the board may have a more direct oversight role in the implementation of portfolio-company-level compliance (i.e. the employee-facing compliance procedures in our example). However, this type of oversight is rooted more in the compliance considerations of managing different underlying enterprises as opposed to analyzing the compliance considerations involved with investing in private equity firms. As such, our discussion will be focused on portfolio company compliance as it relates back to the GP and private equity fund.

1.9.2 Compliance Similarities Between Private Equity and All Other Investment Managers

In order to understand private equity compliance, we will first examine the similarities between private equity managers and all other types of investment fund managers. Viewed under the framework of investment and operational compliance obligations outlined above, private equity and other investment managers share certain similar operational compliance obligations.

For example, let us consider a long-only mutual fund and a private equity fund, both of which, for the purposes of this example, are US SEC *Registered Investment Advisers (RIAs)*. For reference, the term *RIA* is a special technical designation that applies to certain firms. As an RIA in this example, both the private equity and long-only firms would be subject to a variety of rules and US SEC regulations. Continuing our example, under *US SEC Rule 206(4)-7 of the Investment Advisers Act of 1940* RIAs must adopt written compliance procedures, review the adequacy of those procedures annually, and designate a *chief compliance officer* responsible for their administration. This operational compliance requirement applies regardless of whether the RIA's funds invest in liquid equities or private securities. For reference, the role of chief compliance officer is discussed in more detail in Chapter 2.

1.9.3 Compliance Similarities Between Private Equity and Hedge Funds

If we seek to further narrow down the universe of all investment managers, from a regulatory perspective often the closest corollary entity to private equity managers is hedge fund managers. There are a number of similarities from a compliance perspective between hedge funds and private equity managers.

1.9.3.1 Enhanced Regulatory Scrutiny One key similarity between these two types of managers is that both hedge funds and private equity managers in particular have been subjected to enhanced regulatory scrutiny as compared to other types of fund managers, such as long-only mutual funds. This has caused them both to have similar compliance objectives and requirements among the different global regulatory regimes.

1.9.3.2 Liquidity and Valuation Compliance Similarities Another similarity in the compliance obligations of both hedge funds and private equity managers relates to the nature of the liquidity of their investment holdings. Before explaining how liquidity impacts compliance, we must first provide a brief overview of key liquidity terminology and market practices.

Liquidity refers to how easy it is to execute a transaction in an investment (i.e. its purchase or sale). Private equity funds hold what are known as *private investments* in either equity or debt. These private investments often exhibit a low degree of liquidity. Investments with *low liquidity* often have a very limited set of parties interested in purchasing or selling the security. Based on this low liquidity there can be a great deal of effort involved in locating interested parties and negotiating the terms of a purchase or sale. Additionally, investments with low liquidity typically also have what is known as a large *bid–ask spread*.[2] This is the difference between what a

---

[2] *See* A. Damodaran, "Marketability and Value: Measuring the Illiquidity Discount," New York University Stern School of Business, July 2005.

buyer is willing to pay and a seller is willing to sell. In some cases, a security may be deemed to be effectively *illiquid*, and have no interested purchasers or sellers, or the opportunity costs to engage in such a transaction would be prohibitive. Another expression commonly used to describe this situation is that there is *no market for the securities.*

The liquidity of securities can directly influence the methods in which their prices are determined. Highly liquid securities, such as public equities, have deep markets with large numbers of buyers and sellers. These securities trade freely in the public markets and are easily *marked-to-market* (i.e. priced) in virtual real-time from a wide variety of sources. Lower-liquidity securities might not be priced from market data feeds but instead values for those securities may be available from a smaller set of interested parties typically referred to as brokers. When securities are priced in this way they are known as *broker-quoted securities.*

Other securities with typically even lower liquidity than broker-quoted securities, but still not illiquid, are those for which no broker quotes are readily available. This does not mean that these securities are completely illiquid, but rather that there is not an immediate or easily available price that can be obtained for them. For reference, under the Financial Accounting Standards Board Accounting Standards Codification (ASC) 820 framework (formerly known as the Statement of Financial Accounting Standards 157: Fair Value Measurements), these types of holdings would be classified as Level 3–type assets. The most liquid assets would be Level 1, and medium-term liquidity assets would be Level 2 assets. These Level 3, low-liquidity securities would typically be the type held by a private equity fund. Hedge funds, depending on the strategy they employ, may hold both liquid and low-liquidity positions. Based on the holding of both liquid and low-liquidity position some hedge funds may even go so far as to categorize themselves as *hedge fund/private equity hybrid funds.*

Now that we have outlined the concept of liquidity, we can begin to understand how it impacts the compliance practices of hedge funds and private equity managers. There are a number of compliance obligations, both mandatory and voluntary, that both private equity and hedge fund managers have with regard to the valuation of positions. This applies whether they are highly liquid or of low liquidity. In particular, the obligations are more complex for lower-liquidity positions. To demonstrate this, we can consider the common private equity situations where positions have low liquidity such that they cannot be priced readily through broker quotes. In those situations, a manager has two primary options. The first would be for the GP to price the positions. This is known as a *manager-marked position.* Alternatively, a GP could seek to hire a *third-party valuation consultant* to price the position.

In either case, there are a number of compliance obligations to both hedge fund and private equity managers with regard to valuations, including the ways in which these positions are valued, the frequency of valuations, and the documentation that a fund manager must prepare in order to document the valuation methodologies employed. Based on the fact that increasingly hedge funds may hold less liquid private-equity-like positions, the issue of valuation compliance is one way in which the two types of funds are similar from a regulatory and compliance perspective. Chapter 4 specifically address private equity valuation compliance in more detail.

1.9.3.3 Reliance on Similar Regulatory Exemptions Another way in which hedge funds and private equity funds are similar from a compliance perspective relates to their regulatory status. Historically, both hedge funds and private equity funds were exempt from registration with financial regulators. In the context of regulatory terminology, it is not uncommon for hedge funds and private equity funds to be grouped together under the term *private funds*.

To avoid registration these private funds relied on what are known as *regulatory exemptions*. Certain regulatory rules only apply to private fund managers that meet certain minimum criteria. If a hedge fund or private equity fund did not meet this minimum eligibility requirement, then it would be exempt from the rule. In the United States, an example of this would be the US SEC's *private adviser exemption*, which excludes certain private funds under the definitions of an investment company under sections 3(c)(1) or 3(c)(7) of the Investment Company Act of 1940.[3]

Prior to the enactment of the Dodd-Frank Act, a hedge fund or private equity fund was not generally required to register with the US SEC under the private adviser exemptions if they effectively did not promote themselves or act as an investment adviser and had fewer than 15 clients. After the passage of Dodd-Frank, the private adviser exemption was significantly narrowed to two primary categories of exemptions. The first is a *venture capital exemption*, which provided a carve-out from registration requirements for most venture capital funds. The other exemption, subject to certain exceptions, is for private funds that managed less than $150 million in what are known as *Regulatory Assets Under Management* (RAUM).

To be clear, even if a fund is not required to be US SEC registered as an RIA, it may still be subject to a number of reporting requirements. As such, these private fund managers are referred to as *Exempt Reporting*

---

[3]*See* "Private Fund Adviser Resources," US Securities and Exchange Commission, available at: https://www.sec.gov/divisions/investment/guidance/private-fund-adviser-resources.htm.

Advisers (ERAs). Examples of the types of filings ERAs must file include Form *ADV Part(1)(A)* and subsequent annual amendments. ERAs are also still subject to certain rules that RIAs are covered by the *2010 Rule 206(4)-5* of the Investment Advisers Act of 1940, the so-called *pay-to-play rule.* This rule places restrictions around solicitations and contributions from investment managers to certain elected officials with the goal of securing government business.[4]

Indeed, the enforcement of pay-to-play violations by private equity managers in particular has been on the rise in recent years, particularly as more managers have transitioned from ERAs to RIAs.

Additionally, these rules also prevent advisers from soliciting or coordinating contributions to certain elected officials or candidates as well as prohibitions on payments to political parties where the adviser is providing or seeking government business. There are also guidelines that prescribe that advisers maintain certain records of the political contributions made by the adviser or its executives and employees.

Regardless of whether a private fund is a hedge fund or a private equity fund, from the perspective of regulators such as the US SEC, once the $150 million RAUM threshold is crossed, then both funds are subject to the same registration requirements to become RIAs. Additionally, reporting requirements are generally the same as well for both types of funds once they surpass $150 million, including the requirement to file what is known as *Form PF* on typically at least an annual basis. For reference, Form PF is a non-public form that RIAs that manage over $150 million in private funds file that provides information on fund size, leverage, liquidity, and types of investors among other data.

Despite the common differences in the investment strategies and holdings of both hedge funds and private equity funds, from a regulatory perspective both funds had historically relied on the same registration exemptions. The use of these exemptions impacted the rigor, or lack thereof, of compliance efforts. Today with increasingly narrower registration requirements more hedge funds and private equity funds are no longer able to rely on exemptions and have become forced to register with regulators. In much the same way that there were similarities among the two hedge funds and private fund managers prior to registration, this current grouping of the two types of funds into a single regulatory bucket (i.e. private funds) has logically driven a number of similarities in the initial design and ongoing implementation of their compliance programs.

---

[4]*See* "17 CFR Part 275 Release No. IA-3043; File No. S7-18-09 RIN 3235-AK39 Political Contributions by Certain Investment Advisers," Securities and Exchange Commission, updated August 18, 2017.

1.10 SUMMARY

This chapter provided an introduction to the subject of private equity compliance. We defined what is meant by the term *private equity* and outlined key private equity terminology including the GP, investment vehicles, limited partnership, limited liability company, and underlying portfolio companies. Next, we distinguished the concepts of both mandatory and voluntary compliance, and investment and operational compliance as they relate to private equity. An overview of historical GP compliance efforts and reasons for the increased regulation of private equity managers in recent years was next addressed. The three levels of the private equity compliance landscape were next introduced as well as certain portfolio-specific compliance considerations. Finally, the chapter concluded with a discussion of the compliance similarities between private equity funds and both long-only and hedge funds. With this fundamental understanding of private equity compliance now in place, in the next chapter we can delve deeper into the specific compliance obligations of GPs.

CHAPTER 2

Compliance Obligations of General Partners

2.1 UNDERSTANDING THE DISTINCTIONS BETWEEN GP-, FUND-LEVEL, AND PORTFOLIO COMPLIANCE

In Chapter 1 we introduced a three-tiered framework across important levels at which different aspects of compliance can be implemented within the private equity investing landscape. For reference they are:

1. General partner (GP)–level compliance
2. Fund-level compliance
3. Portfolio company compliance as it relates to the GP and funds

From a compliance perspective, drawing distinctions across the compliance activities in each level is important so that we can assess the appropriate compliance obligations at each level. This will then facilitate our understanding of how compliance policies applicable to each entity are subsequently drafted, implemented, and monitored. It should also be noted that subgroups of these three categories may come into play depending on the specific compliance focus employed.

An example of the use of these subgroups would be compliance as it relates to limited partners (LPs) invested in a fund. If we wanted to, we could break out another additional category, in addition to the three levels above, called LP compliance. However, for the purposes of our discussion here these LP obligations would be included at the GP and fund-level compliance categories outlined above. It is simply a matter of preference in classification systems and a focus on which entities are being analyzed. For our discussion, therefore, we will utilize the three categories referenced above; however, it should be kept in mind that it would also be acceptable to employ alternative methods of more focused subcategorization of compliance obligations focused on specific entities (i.e. LPs).

2.2 GENERAL PARTNER COMPLIANCE

A *GP*, which we will also refer to as the *private equity manager* or *private equity firm*, is the management entity responsible for managing the private equity company itself. The GP can be thought of as the top level of the three-tiered compliance funnel. All compliance decisions made at this level trickle down in some manner to the subsequent two levels. This relationship is summarized in Exhibit 2.1.

At the GP level, the compliance policies and procedures include the following key items:

- Designing the initial compliance framework
- Drafting initial compliance policies
- Ensuring ongoing implementation of compliance policies and procedures
- Revising compliance policies to comply with regulatory requirements and market best practices

To be clear, while the compliance activities at the GP level influence the activities of associated funds and their underlying portfolio companies, for the purposes of our framework here, the above-referenced activities take place solely at the GP level. This distinction will become clearer as we proceed through our discussion.

Exhibit 2.1   Distinguishing GP-, fund-level, and portfolio company compliance.

2.2.1 Fund-Level Compliance

A private equity fund is the entity to which investors allocate capital, and where the actual investments are typically made and held. Compliance policies at the fund level may fall into one of two categories: *fund specific* and *GP related*. Fund-specific policies would be those compliance requirements that are not obligations of the GP itself, but solely of the fund. This area can become a bit muddled because the GP is often the entity responsible for overseeing the implementation of fund-specific policies; however, what we are addressing here is where the compliance obligation lies as compared to which entity is responsible for implementing it.

A good way to illustrate this distinction is through an example. Consider a fund-level obligation to not invest more than 25% of committed capital into a single portfolio position. If we tried to apply this restriction to the GP, it wouldn't make sense because the GP does not invest directly in underlying portfolio positions – that is the job of the fund. In this case, it is clear that this is a fund-specific obligation. A fund is simply a vehicle that manages investments. It does not have any employees. Instead the GP, through its employees, such as portfolio managers, would be the entity actually implementing this 25 percent limit.

Let us contrast this fund-specific compliance policy to a GP-related policy. Consider a GP-level compliance policy requiring all employees to report to the compliance department the receipt of all gifts and entertainment received in excess of US$100 in value. Since a private equity fund has no employees and the fund itself doesn't receive gifts, there is no way such a policy could be applicable to the fund itself. Therefore, it should be clear that this could only be a GP-level policy. In this case, the GP would also be the one responsible for implementing and monitoring this policy.

2.2.2 Portfolio Company Compliance

The final level of compliance obligations we will address relate to compliance obligations that reside at the portfolio companies. These portfolio companies are also referred to as *underlying portfolio companies*, or simply *portfolio companies*, because they are underlying components into which a private equity fund is invested. We can categorize the obligations of underlying portfolio companies into two groups: *fund-related investment compliance* and *portfolio-company-specific compliance obligations*.

Fund investment compliance obligations are those compliance policies that govern the investments in place between the private equity fund and the underlying portfolio company. This type of compliance focuses on the actions of the portfolio company as they relate back to the private equity fund that invested in it. These obligations could include items such as requirements that the portfolio company adhere to certain specific compliance policies of the private equity fund, and by association the fund's GP, as well as compliance-related restrictions on activities of the portfolio company.

One example of this would be if a private equity fund required a certain frequency and type of financial reporting from the underlying portfolio company as part of its fund-level valuation procedures. If the portfolio company was unable or refused to provide the required information, it would cause a fund-related investment compliance violation. Another example of a fund-related investment compliance obligation would be if there was a fund-level restriction on investing in an underlying portfolio company that was related to certain industries such as alcohol or tobacco. If a portfolio company unexpectedly ventured into one of these lines of business, it would cause it to be out of compliance with the private equity fund's investment restrictions.

The second category, portfolio-company-specific compliance obligations, refers to those compliance obligations that are in place as they relate to the day-to-day management of the actual underlying portfolio company. An example of portfolio-company-specific compliance obligations would be the compliance obligations related to a portfolio company's employees.

There are a number of laws and rules related to aspects of employment relationships, including prohibitions on workplace harassment and considerations for the safety of employees. At the portfolio company level, the managers of the underlying company would be responsible for complying with these rules. The private equity fund itself, and by association the GP, would not be responsible for actually implementing these employee-facing procedures. Of course, it would be in the best interest of the private equity fund investors that allocated to the portfolio company if it was operating in adherence to all rules so as not to face penalties from governmental oversight agencies and potential employee lawsuits, which would likely have a direct financial impact on the performance of the portfolio company.

2.2.3 Distinguishing Between GP-, Fund-Level, and Portfolio Company Compliance

To further illustrate the distinction between the three tiers in our compliance framework we can consider the example of a core compliance document known as a *compliance manual*. A compliance manual is the central document that outlines all of the essential policies and requirements of a private equity firm's compliance program. The vast majority of regulatory agencies that oversee GPs require them to maintain some form of compliance manual, either as a stand-alone document, combined with other related compliance documentation such as a *code of ethics*, or as part of a larger *operations manual*. For reference, more details on the contents of key compliance documents, including the compliance manual, are provided in Chapter 8.

Within the context of our three-tiered compliance framework a compliance manual is created and implemented at the GP level. Private equity funds themselves do not maintain compliance manuals. Underlying portfolio companies in which private equity funds are invested may maintain different compliance manuals that outline the relevant compliance practices in their respective businesses; however, this is both a completely different document and relates to a completely different set of compliance considerations for the underlying portfolio company and not to the GP. This relationship is summarized in Exhibit 2.2.

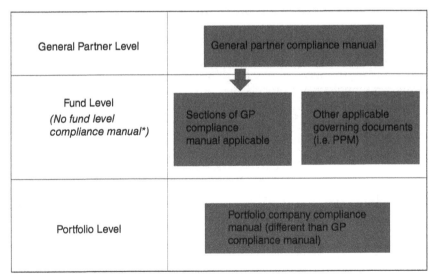

*While there is no compliance manual at the fund level:
- The GP compliance manual may contain provisions which govern or influence compliance related aspects of the fund.

- Other documents governing fund activities, including fund specific compliance related obligations, are present such as the private equity fund's private placement memorandum.

Exhibit 2.2   Example of compliance manual applicability among the GP-, fund-level, and portfolio company.

2.3 GENERAL PARTNER BOARD SEAT OVERSIGHT CONSIDERATIONS

Representatives of the private equity fund, and by association the GP, will in many instances take a seat on the board of directors of the portfolio company. In these cases, the GP/fund representative sitting on the board may have a more direct oversight role in the implementation of portfolio-company-level compliance (i.e. the employee-facing compliance procedures in our example). However, this type of oversight is rooted more in the compliance considerations of managing different enterprises as opposed to analyzing the compliance considerations involved with investing in private equity firms. As we alluded to in Chapter 1, our discussion will be focused on portfolio company compliance as it relates back to the GP and private equity fund.

2.4 FUND-LEVEL COMPLIANCE

As we outlined above, the three-tiered framework did not include a distinct category for compliance focused around LPs. The reason for this is because the three categories above encompass the majority of compliance considerations for LPs that are relevant to the focus of this text. Depending on the specifics of each different LP organization there may be additional compliance protocols that are applicable, such as maintaining appropriate documentation relating to any fiduciary obligations that an LP that manages capital on behalf of others may be subject to. A discussion of the LP evaluation of private equity compliance functions is included in Chapter 10.

2.5 GP COMPLIANCE STRUCTURES

Now that we have an understanding of the relationship between GP-, fund-level, and underlying portfolio-level compliance we can turn our attention the actual structure of the GP compliance function. To begin with, in order to implement a successful compliance program, the GP must decide how to allocate resources toward implementing the compliance function. These key elements fall into three broad categories:

1. *Documentation.* Private equity firms create and maintain a wide variety of compliance-related documentation. Some of these documents deal

solely with compliance policies and procedures. Other documents are not focused entirely on compliance itself, but instead may reference or impact compliance-related guidelines while primarily focusing on other aspects of a GP's investment or operational activity.

2. *Personnel.* GPs will often designate employees and third parties to participate in the design, implementation, and updating of compliance policies.

3. *Additional resources.* Personnel and documentation are often not enough to effectively implement compliance oversight in the modern world. As such, this category refers to additional resources that may be employed by GPs to facilitate the compliance function. Examples of these resources would be software and systems, either in-house or from third parties, that facilitate adherence to the firm's compliance obligations.

When designing a compliance function a GP must consider what resources are required in each of the three categories referenced above. In the increasingly complex compliance and regulatory environment facing GPs, making these determinations is not always a straightforward decision. The good news is that as an initial starting point to this process, often financial regulators will provide minimum basic requirements that a private equity firm must follow. We will continue our conversation with one of the most common minimum regulatory requirements for private equity firms – the appointment of a chief compliance officer (CCO).

2.6 PRIVATE EQUITY CHIEF COMPLIANCE OFFICERS

As the central figure in the compliance framework of a private equity fund, the CCO maintains a number of different responsibilities, ranging from basic compliance oversight and design to ongoing monitoring responsibilities.

2.6.1 Private Equity Chief Compliance Officers Are Required by Regulators in Most Instances

A common core element of the vast majority of regulatory mandated compliance functions across all major jurisdictions in which private equity firms operate globally is for private equity firms to designate what is known as a CCO. As examples, in the United States this requirement comes from *US SEC Rule 206(4)-7 of the Investment Advisers Act of 1940.* In the United Kingdom the Financial Conduct Authority (FCA) maintains a requirement for covered private equity firms to designate a CCO in compliance with the CF *10 Compliance oversight function* designation.[1]

2.6.2 Mandatory versus Voluntary CCO Duties

Some of these CCO obligations are non-negotiable and are required by regulators while the specifics of other CCO duties vary from fund to fund as summarized below:

- *Mandatory CCO compliance duties.* The most basic role of the CCO is to ensure that a private equity firm adheres to mandatory compliance requirements, such as those outlined in legislation or required by regulators.
- *Voluntary CCO compliance duties.* The other primary role of CCOs is to ensure that the voluntary compliance aspects of a GP are implemented and maintained. Examples of these types of items may be any self-imposed obligations a GP may have implemented, such as restrictions on personal account dealing or limitations of the dollar amounts surrounding the receipt of gifts by employees that surpass minimum regulatory guidelines in their rigor.

2.6.3 CCO Implementation of a Culture of Compliance

Related to the notion of implementing voluntary compliance would be the general goal of CCOs to also implement what is known as a *culture of compliance.* This term is not a technical legal or regulatory term. Furthermore, there is not a single uniform definition of a culture of compliance. There is a general consensus, however, that an essential component of establishing a culture of compliance is that the CCO implements a compliance structure and framework that ensures that a private equity manager not only complies with all regulatory rules and guidelines, but also exceeds these guidelines in the pursuit of industry best practice.

A culture of compliance also commonly refers to a private equity CCO seeking to implement what can be referred to as a *culture of ethics* throughout the firm. One common example of the types of activities that would fall under the notion of culture of ethics would include implementing what is known as an *open-door compliance policy.* This refers to the concept that the door to the CCO's physical office is always open to employees with questions

---

[1] *See* Financial Conduct Authority, "Controlled functions," available at: https://www .fca.org.uk/firms/approved-persons/controlled-functions.

relating to the items, including the implementation of the firm's compliance policies. Similarly, should employees wish to speak to the CCO to report any concerns related to potential violations of compliance policies that they may have observed, the door would always be open.

The critical element of an open-door compliance policy is not whether there is an actual physical door that is open in the CCO's officer but rather that employees are empowered to feel that they have access to openly discuss compliance policies and concerns. Furthermore, depending on the size of the private equity firm the CCO may be supported by additional compliance personnel. In those instances, under an open-door framework, employees may not speak directly with the CCO herself, but rather with a representative of the compliance department. Finally, some private equity firms may work with third-party vendors to provide phone numbers employees could call to anonymously report compliance concerns, which would then be forwarded to the GP's compliance department. These are sometimes known as *compliance hotlines* or *ethics hotlines*. The theory behind these arrangements is that employees of a private equity firm would be more willing to report compliance concerns anonymously rather than being forced to be identified as a whistleblower.

2.6.4 Three Types of Private Equity CCO Frameworks

As noted above, all compliance departments typically maintain an individual that holds the title of CCO. The CCO is the leader of the compliance function and the nature of the position can come in many different forms, depending on the particular structure employed at the private equity firm. CCO models can be broadly distinguished into two primary categories:

1. *In-house CCO models.* These models employ utilize a CCO that comes from within the private equity firm. The two most common types of CCO models are:
   a. *Dedicated CCO model.* Under this structure a GP's CCO is focused solely on the compliance function.
   b. *Shared CCO model.* As the name implies, under a shared structure the CCO is not dedicated solely to the compliance function but instead shares his time among other responsibilities outside of compliance.
2. *Outsourced CCO model.* A private equity firm may have a compliance structure whereby the CCO is not actually an in-house employee but a third-party individual who may work for herself or as part of a larger firm.

2.6.4.1 Use of Third Parties to Augment CCO Models Regardless of whether a CCO is dedicated, shared, or outsourced, some of the compliance work of the CCO is generally augmented by third parties. The common reasons for this include:

- Cost efficiencies
- Operational efficiencies
- A requirement for specialized knowledge regarding compliance practices in particular jurisdictions or with regard to certain laws

Common third parties that provide this support include external law firms and *compliance consultants*. A compliance consultant is a third-party individual or firm that provides external compliance support to private equity firms.

2.6.4.2 Is a Particular CCO Model Preferred? In a perfect world every private equity firm would maintain a dedicated CCO with additional support from third parties as appropriate. To begin with there is often not a regulatory requirement that a CCO be dedicated, rather merely that one is appointed. Therefore, referring solely to the technical legal requirements of most compliance regimes, there is no prescribed preference that a CCO be in-house as compared to outsourced. It is important to note that regulatory bodies such as the US SEC have expressed a preferred approach toward in-house CCOs over fully outsourced models.

2.7 SUMMARY

This chapter introduced the compliance obligations of GPs. We began with an examination of the three-tiered private equity compliance framework: GP-level compliance, fund-level compliance, and portfolio company compliance as it relates to the GP and the funds. We then discussed GP board seat oversight considerations and GP compliance structures. Finally, we focused on the various CCO models that are employed by GPs. The next chapter focuses on the way that limited partner advisory committees provide oversight of GP- and fund-level compliance activities.

CHAPTER 3

Limited Partner Advisory Committees and Other Boards

3.1 INTRODUCTION TO LIMITED PARTNER ADVISORY COMMITTEES

As a reminder of the terminology we introduced in Chapter 1, a private equity fund is typically established under a legal structure known as a *limited partnership* and the investors in the fund are commonly referred to as *limited partners (LPs)*, which can also be referred to simply as a private equity fund's investors. As with most investments, at its most basic level LPs in a fund provide money to a private equity fund, and by association the funds, with the hope of capital appreciation.

Throughout the course of their investing relationship LPs and general partners (GPs) interact in a number of ways. For example, the GP may send information regarding the performance of a particular LP account to the LP on a quarterly basis. On a practical basis this information may come directly from an LP herself or a third party known as an *administrator*. An administrator is a third-party firm that is responsible for performing a number of services for a fund, including fund accounting, calculating the net-asset-value (NAV) of a fund, and assisting in the oversight of shareholder services–related activities. Additionally, the LP may engage with the GP regarding questions she may have relating to the performance of a fund in which she is invested or relating to ongoing fund operational due diligence.

In some cases, a select group of investors in a private equity fund may participate in what is known as a *limited partner advisory committee (LPAC),* which is also sometimes simply referred to as an advisory committee. An LPAC is a committee of fund investors that typically maintain the right to be notified of certain fund-level activities as well as the power of approval over certain proposed actions of a fund. The responsibilities and roles played by LPACs can directly influence fund-level compliance, a topic that was discussed in the previous two chapters. This chapter will explore the role of Lpacs as well as other fund boards.

3.2 SOURCE OF LPAC RESPONSIBILITIES: THE PPM AND LPA

As part of the compliance and legal obligations of a private equity fund investing relationship both Lps and the GP have certain rights and responsibilities. The bulk of these are governed by two key related documents. The first document is what is known as a *private placement memorandum (PPM)*. A PPM may sometimes be referred to as an *offering memorandum*. The other key document is a *limited partnership agreement (LPA)*. The PPM and LPA provide an overview of the key terms of the fund offering. Terms covered in a PPM and LPA typically include a wide variety of items such as the fees to be charged by the fund, the permitted expenses of the fund, and the fund's investment mandate. The PPM and LPA also outline the assignment of the responsibilities of the GP and related service providers.

Due to the fact that both documents outline essential fund terms the pair of documents is often referred to as the *fund formation documents*. In practice PPMs and LPAs are often thought of as two separate documents that are linked together. As evidence of this, both documents often reference each other. Therefore, when analyzing the rights of the GP and Lps, both documents are typically reviewed in conjunction with one another and may in practice reference each other.

The bulk of LP rights and responsibilities are typically outlined primarily in the LPA; however, the PPM may also contain information relevant to the LPAC. For the purposes of our discussion here, we will not delineate the source of the language outlining these rights but rather the substance of the LPAC's role.

3.3 THERE IS TYPICALLY NO REQUIREMENT FOR AN LPAC TO EXIST

Before proceeding any further with our discussion of Lpacs, it is important to highlight that there is typically no regulatory requirement for an LPAC to exist. The decision by the GP to form one is often voluntary and not required by law or financial regulators. Why, then, would a GP go through the extra effort to install an LPAC?

Different Lps will often commit different amounts of capital to a private equity fund. Those who pledge to commit more capital, which can be ultimately called down by the GP, often expect to have more oversight and rights as compared to other, smaller LPs who contribute less capital. In order to keep these investors happy, GPs therefore have obliged larger LPs' desires for more input and oversight into the management of the fund in which they are invested.

That being said, the GP wants to maintain the flexibility to manage the fund in their own discretion, subject to a predetermined investment mandate without too much interference from LPs. LPACs are the modern evolution of the governance and compliance mechanism that is the result of this compromise.

Historically, when an LPAC may not have been in place, the roles performed by the LPAC were typically performed directly by the GP. In practice so as not to surprise large LPs with significant fund changes, the private equity fund manager would likely have reached out to these larger fund holders to solicit feedback prior to implementing any changes. However, technically, according to the PPM and LPA the right to make changes or approve transactions that an LPAC would have typically performed would have instead likely resided primarily in the realm of all LPs, and be subject to mechanisms such as a consent vote (i.e. majority or 2/3rd majority) from all LPs.

3.4 COMMON LPAC DUTIES

LPACs serve as an oversight and governance mechanism on the operations of a fund. They are meant to represent the interest of LPs and provide them with a voice in the management of the fund. While the specific duties of LPAC may differ across private equity funds, traditionally the core duties of an LPAC are often centered around the areas that may present the greatest risks to LPs. Specifically, key areas LPACs focus on include:

- *Conflict of interest oversight.* The LPAC may be responsible for overseeing a number of situations in which different conflicts of interest may arise between the actions of the GP, its employees, and the LP. Two of the more common conflicts that LPACs review include:
  1. *Related-party transactions oversight.* These are investments where a fund may seek to enter into transaction with individuals or entities related to the GP. Two common related-party transactions for which LPACs provide oversight are:
     a. *Approval of concurrent investments.* A *concurrent investment* generally refers to a situation in which a fund purchases the securities of a portfolio company concurrently with another fund. In practice, the timing of the investments may not be simultaneous,

and the two purchases could occur at slightly different times. In these situations, inherent conflicts may arise across a variety of areas, including the allocation of securities among the two affiliated funds. Therefore, most funds are structured to submit concurrent investments to the LPAC for review and approval.

     b. *Approval of cross investments.* A *cross investment* refers to a situation where a fund purchases the securities of a company that is a portfolio company of another fund managed by the GP. Due to the dual ownership of both affiliated funds of the investment, the potential for conflicts related to items such as the valuation of the investment may arise either at the time of the initial purchase, throughout the life of the investment, or upon sale. In order to provide additional oversight of such conflicts, LPACs typically are required to grant approval on any cross investments.

2. *LP transaction oversight.* A fund may also seek to enter into a transaction directly with an LP in addition to their capital commitment to the fund. To oversee these conflicts, the LPAC therefore represents LPs in reviewing and ultimately deciding whether to approve or prevent such transactions.

▪ *Valuation oversight.* When disagreements arise between LPs and GPs over the valuation of an asset or group of assets held by a fund, the LPAC typically plays a role in working with the GP, and in some cases third-party appraisers, to determine a valuation. This process is discussed in more detail in Chapter 4, which focuses on valuation compliance.

The duties of LPACs are typically outlined specifically in the fund formation documents. Other common LPAC duties typically include:

▪ *Approving capital calls from investors in certain situations.* Approving the issuing of capital calls by the GP in certain instances where they would not otherwise normally be permitted is one common LPAC role. An example of a situation where this could occur would be if the commitment period for a fund had ended and the GP wanted to issue a special capital call to raise more funds for the purpose of enabling the fund to make additional opportunistic investments in portfolio companies. Typically, since the commitment period had already ended, the fund formation documents would outline that LPAC approval was required to issue these new capital calls.

▪ *Approving tax distributions.* Tax distributions are distributions of capital typically made to LPs in order to offset each individual LP's deemed tax liability with respect to his investment in the fund. To be clear, the purpose of these distributions is to provide the LP with money to pay taxes related to their investment in a fund, not to provide them with any sort of profits related to their investment in the fund. These tax distributions are typically paid by funds within 90 days after the end of the fiscal year of a fund. In some instances, a fund's formation documents may set a ceiling limit on the amount of total aggregate tax distributions the fund can pay out to LPs, such as US$500,000. If the aggregate contributions were to exceed this ceiling amount, then approval from the LPAC would typically be required to pay out a greater amount of tax distributions.

- *Overriding investment limitations.* At the time of formation of a private equity fund, there may be a variety of investment limitations placed on a fund. These are also sometimes referred to as *investment restrictions.* A common example of such a restriction would be a cap on the total investment that may be placed into a single portfolio company. For a variety of reasons, such as shifting market conditions, a GP may wish to override this cap once the fund actually starts investing capital. In order to breach this cap, LPAC approval would typically be required.

- *Approving the advance of GP litigation defense costs.* Under certain circumstances a fund may advance an LP money to fund his defense in litigation related to his duties on the LPAC. Similarly, in some cases a fund may advance the GP capital to fund their defense in a lawsuit brought from other LPs. The advance of capital in these situations typically requires LPAC approval prior to disbursement.

- *Restricting fund principals' activities and new fund launches.* Typically when a private equity fund is in the process of allocating capital, a restriction exists with regards to the principals of the fund (i.e. the portfolio managers) from working on the management of other funds. Similarly, in order to not cannibalize the opportunity set of the current fund, restrictions also exist on the launching and subsequent closing of new funds by the GP. Any decision to violate these restrictions would require approval from either the LPAC or the majority of interest holders of the fund in most instances.

- *Ceasing limited operations mode related to key person events.* A *key person event* refers to a situation that is triggered when a single individual, or multiple persons as the case may be, who are critical to the management of a fund are no longer able to perform their duties. Historically, these provisions were also referred to as *key man events.* An example of such an individual would be a portfolio manager of a fund. Specifically, the common occurrences that trigger a key person clause include the death of a key person, his incapacitation, if he takes bad actions that are determined to constitute items such as fraud or gross negligence, or if he is simply no longer involved in the day-to-day management of the fund for an extended period of time.

While the specifics of key person clauses vary across private equity funds, once a *key person clause* is triggered, many private equity funds formation documents contain a provision that the LPs who hold that majority of the fund's interest can vote to place the fund into what is known as a limited operations mode. In this mode, the fund will not make any new investments and will generally only fulfill the funding of previous investment obligations and make follow-on investments into portfolio companies.

Depending on the circumstances of the key persons involved in the fund, and the specific investment situation of the fund, its LPs may decide to pull the fund out of limited operations mode and continue normal investment activities. An example of such a situation would be if a portfolio manager of a fund suffered an illness that forced the fund into limited operations mode but the portfolio manager had then recovered from the sickness, and the LPs wanted to resume the normal fund operations. Typically, most funds are structured in such a way that in order to resume normal operations of the fund out of limited operations mode, either a majority-in-interest of the LPs of the fund or the LPAC must approve this transition back to normal fund operations.

- *Service provider oversight.* In certain instances the fund formation documents may outline that changes to material service providers relationships, such as the auditor of a fund, would require LPAC approval.

- *Extensions of a fund's term.* The *term* of a private equity fund refers to the entire period of the fund's existence through to the winding-up and liquidation of the fund. The term of a fund is also sometimes referred to as the *life of a fund.* A common fund term would be 10 years from the date of the initial fund closing; however, they may be longer or shorter. Generally, extensions of a fund's term require approval by the LPAC.

- *Other matters the GP deems important.* Many fund formation documents contain a provision such as "The General Partner may consult with, or seek the approval of the LPAC regarding any other matter determined by the GP for any other matter as determined by the GP in its sole and absolute discretion." This means that there may be other situations or potential investments that were not specifically contemplated at the time the original fund formation documents were drafted that have subsequently arisen that the GP feels is a good idea to run past the LPAC.

However, as these clauses are typically written, the other types of items the GP brings to the LPAC are in the GP's complete discretion. So how should a GP, or an LPAC for that matter, determine what other items that should be raised to the LPACs attention? This determination is typically related to a concept known as a *good-faith effort*. The general standard outlined in fund formation documents is that the GP makes what is known as a good-faith effort to bring items to the LPAC's attention and provide them with enough material facts so that they can make an informed determination of the merits of the proposed GP action. This good-faith effort is also related to the issue of GP disclosures, that is discussed in more detail ahead.

3.4.1 GP Disclosures to LPACs

When capital is first committed by LPs to a private equity fund the issue of disclosures by the GP is one that has come under increased scrutiny by private equity regulators. In particular, one of the key areas of focus related to disclosures is their completeness. On one hand, a GP may make disclosures of relevant information that are too limited in nature; on the other hand, a GP might make very broad disclosures that do not specifically address important information material to LPs at the time capital is being committed. Once the initial capital commitments have been made by LPs, similar issues related to GP disclosures to LPs arise in the context of ongoing disclosures that should be made throughout a fund's term.

Disclosures of material information cannot be made by GPs selectively, especially to LPACs that may be tasked with reviewing potential conflicts. Representatives of private equity regulators, including the US Securities and Exchange Commission (US SEC), have highlighted that LPACs' decision making ability has been impaired in many cases by GPs' failure to provide the LPACs with sufficient disclosures to make informed determinations over areas such as conflicts of interest, which are particularly important based on the nature of private equity investing.[1] The incompleteness of these disclosures was particularly noteworthy as it related to the disclosures centered around the potential conflicts surrounding the practice of GP representatives taking board seats on underlying portfolio companies.

3.5 LPAC FORMATION CONSIDERATIONS

Although not a technical requirement, due to the increased input and oversight it affords LPs, today most private equity funds maintain an LPAC. Once a decision has been made to implement an LPAC, there are a number

---

[1] *See* A. Ceresney, "Securities Enforcement Forum West 2016 Keynote Address: Private Equity Enforcement," U.S. Securities and Exchange Commission, May 12, 2016.

of initial questions facing GPs regarding the structure, membership, and duties of the LPAC.

3.5.1 How Many LPs Can Serve on an LPAC?

One of the first questions a GP must determine is how many LP members the LPAC will have. Once again there are no bright-line legislative or regulatory rules with regard to specific minimum or maximum requirements. In practice, many GPs decide to keep the number of LPs to a manageable size. The actual number of LP seats on the committee may vary according to a number of factors, including the magnitude (i.e. assets committed) of the specific fund, and the total number of investors in the fund.

For example, a larger private equity fund would likely have a greater number of large investors and, therefore, the GP may feel obligated to create an LPAC board with more investors represented as compared to a smaller fund. In general, the minimum size for most LPACs is three LPs. The reason for this is that three is an odd number, and from a governance perspective it is considered best practice to have an odd number of members on committees such as an LPAC in order to facilitate the breaking of any ties when votes come up. To be clear, although 1 is an odd number, having a single LP decision maker on an LPAC would not represent best practices, and likely be seen as disadvantaging the other LPs to the benefit of the single LP serving on the LPAC. Larger LPACs may be as big as seven members or more. Ultimately, the decision of how many LPs can serve on an LPAC is often in the sole discretion of the GP when they form the fund. This decision is then memorialized in the fund formation documents.

3.5.2 Determining Which LPs Can Serve on an LPAC

After a determination has been made as to how many seats there will be on the LPAC, often the next question facing a GP is which investors will be invited to sit on the committee. Often to keep their larger investors happy, a GP will invite the larger investors in a fund to serve on an LPAC. These larger investors are sometimes referred to as *seed investors* or *anchor investors*.

It should be noted that certain seed investors may require a seat on the LPAC as part of their own investing process. In these cases, therefore, their committing of capital to the fund is predicated on their receiving a seat on the LPAC. From a legal perspective, this agreement between the GP and LP is often outlined in a supplemental document to the fund formation documents known as a *side letter*. A side letter is a separate agreement applicable to a specific LP as opposed to the entire pool of LPs. Side letters typically outline certain specific rights available to LPs and unique obligations the GP has to a specific LP, such as a requirement to offer them a seat on the LPAC.

Once again, there are no strict rules in this regard. For example, let us consider a new fund that raised capital commitments of US$100 million from 10 different investors. Let us say the top five investors in the fund committed capital as follows:

Investor #	Amount of Capital Committed (millions USD)
1	$35
2	$25
3	$8
4	$7
5	$6

Investors numbers 1 and 2 each contributed 35 and 25 percent of the hundred million respectively. As compared to the other investors in the fund, these amounts represented the largest capital commitments by far. As such, there would likely be little disagreement among the LPs that investors 1 and two 2 should be offered seats on the LPAC, and indeed they would likely demand such seats based on the size of their relative allocations.

Now let us turn to the other investors. Out of the top five list presented in the table there is only a difference of $1 million in the capital committed by investor numbers 3 ($8 million), 4 ($7 million), and 5 ($6 million). If we use the example of a private equity fund that has an LPAC that has only three investor seats available, then how should the GP decide which LPs to invite to the LPAC? Assuming the first two seats go to investors 1 and 2 as outlined above, then really the GP is faced with the question of to whom the third seat should go. Certainly, investor number 3 has the most committed capital but this does not necessarily mean that they will be automatically selected for the LPAC. How should the GP determine which other LP should be invited to the LPAC?

To avoid the issue of selectively choosing which LPs to invite to serve on an LPAC, a GP may instead outline minimum capital requirements for an LP in order to be invited to serve on an LPAC. In this way, the LP takes subjectivity out of the process and may obviate any perceived conflicts of interest that may arise in the selecting of specific LPs to invite for committee membership.

Other items that will likely be considered by the GP in making this decision would typically include:

- *Feedback from other large LPs.* For a variety of reasons other large LPs, regardless of whether they have been offered a seat on the board of the LPAC, may object to a particular LP being extended an invitation to serve on the committee. These reasons may not even be well founded and could be based simply on personal biases or they may be rooted in direct prior business dealings among LPs or a negative reputation of the LP. Regardless, the ultimate decision of which LPs to extend the invitation to serve on the LPAC is in the discretion of the GP; however, the GP understandably would not want to upset other large LPs in their fund.

  Additionally, the GP has to consider how well the LPAC would function if problems that arose among the LPA members prior to the launch of a fund which could cause disruptions in the smooth operating of the committee. On the other hand, large LPs may want a certain smaller investor to serve on the board of the LPAC for reasons including a particular LP's good reputation or the larger investors' relationship with them. In certain instances, a GP may take a formal vote of LPs to decide to eliminate or add a seat on the LPAC or extend membership to another LP in order to gauge formal consent from other LPs in this process. As such, the LP would likely take into consideration feedback from other LPs in making the determination of which LPs to include rather than simply making the decision in a vacuum.

- *Interest of LPs in serving on LPAC.* Despite being offered an invitation by a GP to serve on the board of an LPAC, an LP may not want to make this commitment. Reasons for this could include:
  - An LP is a passive investor and does not want to take an active role in the fund.
  - The LP does not want to make the time commitments necessary to serve on the board.
  - An LP may not want to expose himself to any potential liabilities related to serving as a member of the LPAC.

3.5.3   Importance of Unaffiliated LPAC Members

When discussing the membership of an LPAC it is important to highlight that it is considered best practice for the LPAC to consist of only LPs who are unaffiliated with the GP. You may be thinking that this is a bit of an odd statement since the GP, or entities related to the GP, are not the first thing most investors think about when considering the investor base of a private equity fund. In practice, however, this issue of having GP-affiliated investors can come about in several forms.

One situation would be if a GP decided to provide a baseline amount of initial capital, also called *seed capital* or *proprietary capital*, to the fund. This practice can be referred to as *seeding the fund*. It would not have to be the GP entity directly making this allocation; it could also be other related entities such as an entity known as a *management company*. A management company is simply another legal entity that is controlled by one or more individuals of or affiliated with the GP. In the fund formation documents these entities or individuals may be referred to as *members of the GP*. Putting technical legal definitions aside, the management company can simply be thought of as an entity related to the GP in facilitating certain management and administration responsibilities that are ultimately related to the private equity funds.

An employee of the private equity firm, such as the fund's portfolio manager, would also traditionally be considered to be affiliated with the GP. If a portfolio manager of a fund makes a direct investment into the fund that they manage, this would be a GP-affiliated investment. Such an investment by a portfolio manager would commonly be called *internal capital* or *skin in the game* and is generally viewed as a good thing due to the fact that it aligns the interest of the fund manager more closely with the investors in the fund. Similarly, if another fund managed by the GP allocates capital to a fund, this would be considered an investment by an affiliated entity.

Finally, a situation could occur where a GP maintains an interest in a portfolio company, such as a wealth management firm, that then allocates capital to the fund through its investment activities. Under this scenario the wealth management firm's clients would not be affiliated with the GP per se; however, any direct investment by the wealth management firm itself into the fund managed by the GP could be considered to be affiliated capital.

3.5.4 LPAC Compensation

Investors serving on the LPAC are not typically paid compensation for serving on the committee. Instead, LPACs are reimbursed for any reasonable travel expenses they may have related to attending in-person meetings of the committee. These reimbursements generally come from the fund itself. In general, to keep fund expenses low, LPs do not focus on the issue of compensation for serving on an LPAC, but rather the goal of the LPAC is to provide oversight and an LP voice in the management of the fund.

3.5.5 LPAC Member Indemnification

By taking on membership of an LPAC, an LP is potentially exposing himself to liability. For example, consider a situation where a fund is considering entering into a transaction with an entity affiliated with the GP. Let us further assume that as is common this transaction is subjected to review by the LPAC for the fund. If the LPAC approves the transaction and then the affiliated transaction ultimately turns out to be a financially bad decision for the fund, litigation may ensue from other LPs to seek recoupment of losses. While investors may sue the GP as well, specifically for the purposes of our example, let us assume that LPs who were not serving on the LPAC may choose to sue the LPAC and more particularly those LPs who were on the LPAC that approved the affiliated transaction.

The LPs serving on the LPAC now have a problem. They will be forced to lay out capital for lawyers and related legal fees in order to fund the cost of their defense case. This is particularly troubling because, as we outlined above, LPs serving on an LPAC are not typically compensated other than reimbursement of travel expenses as noted above. To resolve this situation a legal concept known as *indemnification* comes into play. Indemnification can be defined as the duty to make good on any loss, damage, or liability incurred by another.

Typically, LPs serving on the LPAC will be indemnified by the fund for actions taken as part of their role on the LPAC. Practically this means that if there is a threatened or actual claim or litigation, the fund will pay the covered LP's attorney fees and out-of-pocket expenses incurred in investigating, litigating, or settling the claim. There is also traditionally specific conduct of an LP serving on an LPAC that would not be indemnified. While the specific exemptions can vary among different funds, as defined in the formation documents, they typically include exemptions for bad conduct such as gross negligence, willful omission, fraud, and even moral turpitude.

In this way, by providing LPs with this indemnification, it potentially insulates them from the expenses associated with litigation and related claims that may arise from serving on an LPAC. Many LPs will therefore require indemnification provisions to be in place in order to serve on an LPAC.

3.5.6 LPAC Joint Committees

In certain instances, a private equity fund's formation documents may contain a provision for the creation of a related group of funds that are called *parallel funds*. Parallel funds are generally managed in what is known as a *pari-passu manner*. This means that these parallel funds adhere to the same investment strategy of the fund and are managed in the same manner. The reason for the creation of these parallel funds is typically to facilitate certain legal and regulatory matters. A common example would be the creation of a separate parallel fund to exempt the fund from registration as an investment company under Section 3(c)(7) of the US Investment Company Act. Another type of parallel fund would be one created to facilitate advantaged tax treatment.

In the private equity industry, a catchall term that encompasses parallel funds that are created for legal, tax, and regulatory reasons is *special requirements fund*. This can be distinguished from another type of parallel fund known as a *principals fund*. The purpose of these funds is to carve out a separate structure to manage the capital of the GP and related person (i.e. the private equity fund's employees), as well as to facilitate their estate planning.

As part of their membership in the original fund, when these parallel funds are created, the LPAC typically transitions from a single-fund LPAC into what is known as a *joint LPAC*, or simply *joint committee*. This joint committee is responsible for not only the original fund but also the newly formed parallel funds. In practice, the duties of the LPAC are effectively the same as they were before the formation of the new parallel funds with the added complication that the responsibilities are now applicable across both the original and parallel funds. This relationship is summarized in Exhibit 3.1.

3.5.7 Distinguishing Between an LPAC and an Advisory Board

In addition to an LPAC, a GP and its associated private equity fund may employ separately maintain what is known as an *advisory board*. Somewhat

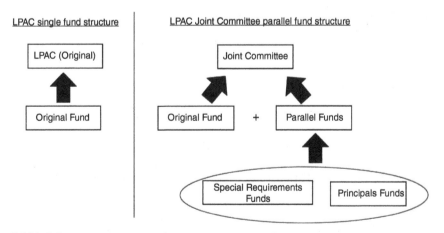

Exhibit 3.1   Limited partner advisory committee and joint committee structure.

confusingly, an LPAC may also be referred to as a *limited partner advisory board (LPAB)* or simply an *advisory board*. For the purposes of our discussion we will use the term *advisory board* to refer to an entity that is different from an LPAC. Advisory boards are typically different from an LPAC in they have no technical prescribed rights and obligations as outlined in the fund formation documents. Rather, the purpose of the advisory board is to serve as a consultative entity that provides guidance to the GP and funds. In this way the advisory board complements the fund-level work of the LPAC.

The members of the advisory board may be different from the LPAC members, although that is not to say that there could be no overlap among the two. In practice, the members of the advisory board are typically high-profile industry experts such as economists, former high-ranking politicians, and seasoned private equity industry executives with well-regarded reputations. Advisory board members may also perform other services for the GP such as utilizing their typically extensive networks to source potential transactions for the GP's funds, as well as introduce other potential investors to the GP. Similar to LPACs, advisory board members are typically indemnified by the fund and reimbursed for reasonable expenses related to their work. Also similar to LPAC members, direct compensation is not typically provided to advisory board members; however, they may be afforded compensation in the form of sharing in a pool of the private equity fund's *carried interest allocation* and through more beneficial investment terms as compared to other non–advisory board LPs. Carried interest, which is also simply referred to as a fund's *carry*, represents the GP's share of the profits for managing the fund, and is linked directly to the fund's performance.

3.6 ARGUMENTS IN FAVOR AND AGAINST LPACS

As outlined above, LPACs can play an important role in providing LP representation in the management of the fund and overseeing the actions of the GP. In summary, the two key arguments in favor of LPACs are:

1. Enhanced oversight of important GP actions by key LPs in areas including valuation and conflicts of interest
2. Facilitation of communication between LPs and GPs

On the other hand, objections can be made as to the structure of LPACs. A primary objection of LPACs is that they give larger investors more of a voice to the exclusion of smaller LPs. The argument could be made that larger investors in a fund are even more incentivized than smaller LPs to ensure actions are taken in the best interest of the fund; however, conversely, situations could arise where the interests of all LPs are not similarly aligned. This could result from differences in the various LP investment requirements and risk tolerances. For example, one LP may have a preference or need for liquidity ahead of other LPs. These types of differences could represent different motivations for investors who may act in their own interests as opposed to the interest of all fund investors.

Let us consider a smaller LP who is not an LPAC member but wants more liquidity, and would want a private equity fund to wind down operations and be paid out rather than extend the fund term. This could be contrasted with a larger investor on the LPAC who could vote to extend the fund term, because the individual larger LPs on this committee do not have immediate liquidity needs; then such a difference could arise. In this example, we do not know which action would be in the best interest of the fund itself, but the point is that conflicts among larger LPs sitting on an LPAC and smaller non-LPAC LPs could arise, leading to calls for enhanced inclusiveness of LPACs.

In much the same vein, differences could arise among the actual members of the LPAC as well. However, if an LPAC has too many members, it may become inefficient and difficulties may arise with regard to making decisions. As such, a compromise is often made between LPs and GPs to limit the size of LPACs to larger LPs, and smaller LPs put their faith in larger LPs to act in the best interests of all fund investors.

3.7 SUMMARY

This chapter provided an overview of the roles of LPACs. We began by defining what an LPAC is. Next, we outlined how the source of LPAC responsibilities can be found primarily in two key fund formation documents, the PPM and the LPA. The lack of a technical requirement for LPACs to exist was then addressed. We then provided an overview of common LPAC duties, including oversight of conflicts of interest of both related-party transactions (i.e. concurrent and cross investments) and direct LP transactions, service provider oversight, as well as key person event oversight. Considerations surrounding the completeness of GP disclosures to LPACs as well as LPAC formation considerations were next discussed. The importance of unaffiliated LPAC members and the role of LPAC advisory boards was also covered. In this chapter we also introduced the fact that LPACs can play an oversight role in determining the value of a private equity fund's positions. With this background in place, in the next chapter we will address the issue of valuation compliance in more detail.

CHAPTER 4

Valuation Compliance

4.1 INTRODUCTION TO PRIVATE EQUITY VALUATION

The majority of investments made by private equity funds are into the securities of underlying portfolio companies. In many instances these securities can be considered to have low levels of liquidity or be considered to be illiquid. As we outlined in Chapter 1, *liquidity* refers to how easy it is to execute a transaction in a particular investment (i.e. its purchase or sale). The result of these low liquidity and illiquid investments is that there are often not readily available prices for these securities. This often results in a situation where a private equity manager must actively pursue third parties (i.e. a broker or valuation consultant) to provide a price, or for the General Partner (GP) to determine the price of the position itself (i.e. manager marked securities).

In either case, the GP typically maintains a great deal of flexibility with regard to the specific valuation of assets held by the fund. Whenever a fund manager maintains such authority over their own funds, a number of inherent potential conflicts of interest are present. In order to provide oversight of these conflicts, there are a number of compliance policies and procedures that are commonly in place.

4.2 INTRODUCTION TO PRIVATE EQUITY VALUATION

The starting point for examining the valuation approach used in determining the value of the fund's holdings is rooted in the fund formation documents, namely the *private placement memorandum* (PPM) and *limited partnership agreement* (LPA).

An example of the valuation approach of the formation documents would typically outline that any assets with high or medium degrees of liquidity would be priced as follows:

- Securities that are listed or quoted on a recognized securities exchange shall be valued at the average closing sales price for that security on a trading day.
- A security that is traded over-the-counter shall be valued at the average closing sales price for that security on a trading day.

An example of the valuation methodology outlined in the formation documents for those assets that are not freely tradeable (i.e. low liquidity or illiquid) is outlined below:

The fair market value of all non-freely tradeable assets of the fund shall be based upon relevant factors as may be deemed so in the sole and absolute discretion of the GP, including:

- Sales prices of recent transactions in the same or similar securities
- Current financial position
- Liquidation terms or other special features of the security
- Operating results of the issuer
- Level of interest rates
- Other general market and economic conditions.
- Significant events that have affected or will influence the underlying portfolio company, including any pending private placement, public offering, merger, or acquisition
- The price paid by the fund in acquiring the asset
- The percentage of the issuer's outstanding securities that is owned by the fund
- All other factors affecting value in accordance with practices customarily employed by the industry

As this example shows, solely based on the formation documents alone the GP maintains significant discretion with regard to the valuation of these types of low liquidity and illiquid assets for which valuations are not readily available. GPs, however, cannot simply make an arbitrary valuation based on what they feel a particular asset may be worth. Instead, GPs often make these determinations through the use of what is known as a valuation committee.

4.3   GP VALUATION COMMITTEES

While often not a technical requirement, to provide additional support for any valuations reached by the GP it is considered best practice for a GP to create a *valuation committee*. This committee typically resides not at the fund level, but instead at the GP level and generally performs valuation work across all funds managed by the GP.

4.3.1   Valuation Committees Membership and Size

The members of the valuation committee typically consist of senior GP personnel, including fund portfolio managers, accounting, compliance, and operations professionals. There is also no prescribed specified size for valuation committees, and the number of members may vary depending on a number of factors, including the size of the private equity firm.

4.3.2   Valuation Committees' Meeting Frequency

Private equity fund valuation committees typically meet on a quarterly basis. They may also meet more frequently as needed to review any valuations issues that arise on an intra-quarter basis.

4.3.3   Valuation Committees' Duties

The primary goal of the valuation committee is to ensure the firm's valuation policies and procedures are being applied consistently across the funds. To be clear, the valuation committee members are not typically the ones calculating the actual values of fund holdings themselves, but are rather reviewing the valuations calculated by others. As part of this oversight, the committee will also typically review prior valuations, financial performance for each portfolio company, recent valuations for comparable companies, and valuation trends of public equity markets.

Due to the relatively small number of holdings in private equity fund portfolios, valuation committees may also have smaller *subcommittees* that specifically focus on the valuations of individual positions. The membership of these subcommittees may overlap with the primary valuation committee. The way these subcommittees typically work is that the investment deal team responsible for a particular portfolio company will meet with a valuation subcommittee to analyze any new developments at a particular portfolio company that have taken place since the most previous valuation. This information would then be used by the subcommittee in determining a valuation to recommend to the larger valuation committee to review. In many cases, the valuation committee would then review their final valuations with the GP's investment committee. In some cases, the investment committee, and not the valuation committee, may maintain final approval of valuations.

4.4 VALUATION POLICIES

In many cases, a private equity firm will develop stand-alone *valuation policies* that describe in more detail the day-to-day practices employed in valuing a fund's holdings. These can be distinguished from the more legally accurate but less practical valuation policy descriptions contained in the fund formation documents as referenced previously.

4.5 VALUATION FREQUENCY

When a position is first purchased a common convention is that it is marked on the books of the private equity fund as being held at cost (i.e. the price paid for the asset). This is fairly straightforward – the asset is worth as much as the fund paid for it. When the asset is eventually sold, the asset is then typically valued at the price that the fund sold the asset for (i.e. it was worth what someone else was willing to pay for it). These two points, the purchase and sale, can be referred to as *transaction-based valuations*. The more complicated situation is determining the value of an asset held by a fund throughout the life of the investment, when a transaction does not occur.

The frequency with which a GP conducts valuation between the time of its purchase and sale may vary. Commonly, a GP may decide to regularly revisit valuations on a predetermined frequency (i.e. quarterly). If they feel that an asset's value has changed, they would likely revalue it accordingly. In other cases, a GP may determine values outside of a predetermined time frame, such as if a material event occurs which they feel would impact the valuation. Regardless of whether a material event occurs or not, it is still considered best practice for a GP to revisit the valuations of the holdings of a fund with at least some predetermined frequency.

4.5.1 Valuation Memorandum and Support

When a GP seeks to value a position in a fund after it has been purchased there are effectively two possible outcomes. The first would be that the GP makes the determination that the value of the asset has not changed since the time of the last valuation (i.e. last quarter). The second option would be that the GP determines that a valuation change has occurred. In either scenario it would be considered best practice for the GP to produce a written summary of their valuation conclusion. This is known as a *valuation memorandum*. To be clear, even if no valuation change has occurred, it is still considered best practice for the GP to write a brief memo to this effect in order to memorialize this determination.

When a valuation change does occur in the asset (i.e. the GP determines that it has either increased or decreased in value), the valuation memorandum should include details of how the new valuation was determined, including:

- An executive summary outlining the new value and the change this represents from the previous value
- A description of the use and application of any models utilized in determining valuations
- Input data and support documentation used in calculating the value
- Recommendations with regard to any concerns that would result in increased monitoring of valuations and valuing the asset more frequently

Due to the often technical nature of the details of the valuation methodology that require extensive familiarity with a fund's holdings, members of the investment team would typically work to produce these valuations for presentation to valuation subcommittees or directly to the primary valuation committee as the case may be.

4.5.2 Use of Third-Party Valuation Consultants

In certain instances, a GP may engage the use of a *third-party valuation consultant*. These are service providers that will provide an independent valuation of a particular asset or group of assets. The use of these third parties is typically at the GP's discretion; however, in certain instances the fund formation documents may mandate that a third-party valuation consultant be engaged in the event a single asset breaches a particular threshold of a portfolio's total size (i.e. greater than 20% of committed capital).

In a private equity context, the use of valuation consultants continues to remain relatively limited as compared to other areas of the asset management industry, including the hedge fund space. The primary reason for this is the considerable expense involved in obtaining these third-party valuations. Additionally, the GP as the manager of the fund is considered to maintain a particular expertise with regard to the valuation of assets in their investment space. To further support this point, even if a fund does utilize a valuation consultant, in most instances it is not bound to accept the work of this consultant as binding; instead whether to use the valuation is in the discretion of the GP. If significant valuation concerns are raised by limited partners (LPs) regarding a GP's valuations, there are typically mechanisms in place by which a limited partner advisory committee (LPAC) or majority in interest LPs can challenge the valuation.

4.8   LPAC VALUATION OVERSIGHT

Private equity funds formation documents typically outline the valuation approach and standards that will be applied in valuing fund investments. The valuation of a fund's investments is critical to LPs as it is a key driver of their overall profitability. As part of this valuation process, LPACs play a critical role in representing LPs in voicing their opinions of the valuations determined by the GP. Fund terms will typically outline that the LPAC has the right to object to the GP's valuation of one or more assets. If they do object, then they may notify the GP of their objection within a pre-specified time period (i.e. within 30 days).

If the LPAC sends this notification to the GP within the required time frame, the fund terms will typically dictate that the GP then has to re-value the asset in question. If the LPAC still disagrees with this revaluation, then the GP may have another opportunity to adjust their valuations again. If no agreement can be made between the GP and LPAC as to the appropriate valuation, then the asset in question would be subjected to an *appraisal procedure*. These procedures may differ among funds; however, in general, within a specific time period (i.e. 21 days) the LPAC would then form a separate *LPAC valuation committee*. In practice the LPAC valuation committee could consist simply of the existing LPAC members or may also contain other LPs.

After the LPAC valuation committee has been formed, the committee and GP would then formally provide each other with the proposed value for the asset. As there would likely still be a disagreement in the two valuations at this point the next step would be for each party to select an *independent appraiser*. Each appraiser must be generally acceptable to the other party. Rather than have each appraiser value the security, these two independent appraisers then select a third appraiser. This third appraiser will then typically not directly value the security themselves, but rather select which proposed value, either the LPAC valuation committee's or the GP's, is closest to the actual fair market value of the asset(s) in question. Once this valuation has been selected, it becomes the new fair market value of the asset.

After the process is complete the LPAC valuation committee would then dissolve. It is also worth noting that throughout the process described earlier,

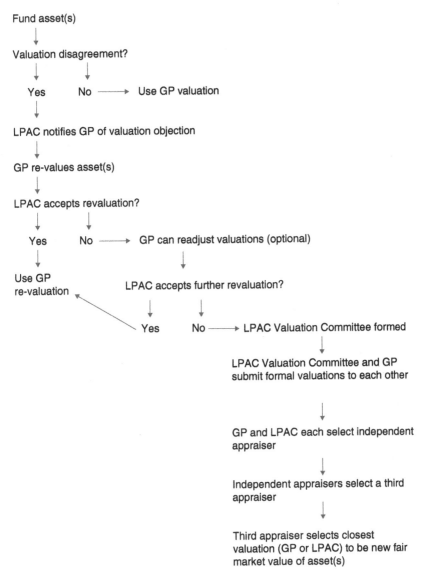

Fund asset(s)

Valuation disagreement?

Yes   No ⟶ Use GP valuation

LPAC notifies GP of valuation objection

GP re-values asset(s)

LPAC accepts revaluation?

Yes   No ⟶ GP can readjust valuations (optional)

Use GP re-valuation   LPAC accepts further revaluation?

Yes   No ⟶ LPAC Valuation Committee formed

LPAC Valuation Committee and GP submit formal valuations to each other

GP and LPAC each select independent appraiser

Independent appraisers select a third appraiser

Third appraiser selects closest valuation (GP or LPAC) to be new fair market value of asset(s)

Exhibit 4.1   LPAC Valuation Oversight Decision Tree Example

if an agreement is made among the parties on the valuation, then the process would just stop at that point. A summary of this entire back-and-forth between the GP, LPAC, LPAC valuation committee, and appraisers is summarized in Exhibit 4.1.

Due to the fact that this is a time-intensive, complicated, and expensive process, unless there is a substantial disagreement among the LPAC and GP with regard to the value of asset, a compromise will generally be reached; or instead the LPs will typically defer to the GP's expertise in valuing assets.

4.6.1 Third-Party Fund Administrators

As we introduced in Chapter 3, a *fund administrator* is a third party that performs two primary services – fund accounting and shareholder services. Within the fund accounting function, the types of services traditionally provided include:[1]

- Logging any new asset purchases and trades made by the private equity fund
- Calculation of profit and loss
- Calculation of fees and accruals
- Calculation of net asset value and preparation of financial statements
- Partnership accounting
- Financial accounting/general ledger maintenance
- Performance measurement
- Reporting for investment managers
- Preparation of interim financial reporting

The primary duties provided by the shareholder services function generally include:

- Overseeing the capital commitment and investor withdrawals process, which includes receiving and processing all the relevant documentation and complying with private equity specific criteria such as required redemption notice periods, lockups, and potential redemption penalties
- Ensuring compliance with the anti-money-laundering and know-your-client requirements in each jurisdiction
- Tax reporting for investors

The majority of private equity firms still follow a *self-administration model*, whereby the GP serves as its own administrator. This is in contrast to the hedge fund industry, which has embraced the third-party administration model. In some cases, certain larger hedge funds have moved

---

[1]Jason Scharfman, "Hedge Fund Operational Due Diligence: Understanding the Risks," Wiley Finance, December 2008.

to a model of utilizing two different third-party administrators to check each other's work. Due to the potential conflict of interest present in this relationship there has been increasing pressure in recent years by LPs to push GPs toward embracing a *third-party administration model* to provide enhanced independence and oversight over the fund processes described earlier.

Although private equity funds are still limited in their use of third-party administrators, the services offered by these administrators have continued to expand over time. One such service that has gained traction is known as asset verification. Under this process the administrator will reach out to a private equity fund's trading counterparties and custodians to independently confirm that the fund is indeed holding the assets that it claims to be holding. This is an example of a way in which fund administrators can provide additional oversight of a fund to LPs.

Typically, due to the highly specialized and illiquid nature of private equity investments the majority of third-party administrators will only be able to provide material valuation support services to any liquid holdings of a private equity fund's portfolio that may be present. This would be assets that are easily priced from third-party exchanges or pricing feeds. However, the bulk of a private equity fund's portfolio typically consists of low liquidity or illiquid assets and, therefore, the role of administrators in providing valuation support is relatively minimal.

4.7 CASE STUDIES IN VALUATION

Regulators have increasingly focused on the valuation compliance practices employed within the private equity industry. The following two cases demonstrate action taken in this area by the US Securities and Exchange Commission (SEC). As you review these matters, keep in mind the inherent potential conflicts of interest present in the private equity valuation process and the compliance oversight measures that can be put in place to monitor these potential conflicts.

4.7.1 Case Study #1: JH Partners, LLC

JH Partners, LLC ("JHP") was a Delaware limited liability company based in San Francisco, CA, that had been registered with the SEC as an investment adviser since March 2012. At the time of the SEC action in this matter, the Firm provided investment advice to three private equity funds, JH Investment Partners, LP, JH Investment Partners II, LP, and JH Evergreen Fund, LP. As of March 31, 2015, JHP's total assets under management were

$465.4 million. The SEC Administrative Proceeding in this mater described the allegations of the case as follows:[2]

From at least 2006 to 2012, JHP and certain of its principals loaned approximately $62 million to the Funds' portfolio companies to provide interim financing for working capital or other urgent cash needs. By doing so, JHP and its principals in certain cases obtained interests in portfolio companies that were senior to the equity interests held by the Funds. JHP also caused more than one Fund to invest in the same portfolio company at differing priority levels and/or valuations, potentially favoring one Fund client over another.

JHP did not adequately disclose to the advisory boards of the affected Funds the potential conflicts of interest created by the undisclosed loans and cross-over investments. Finally, JHP failed to adequately disclose to, or obtain written consent from, its client Funds' advisory boards when certain of their investments exceeded concentration limits in the Funds' organizational documents. Accordingly, JHP violated Sections 206(2) and 206(4) of the Advisers Act and Rule 206(4)-8 thereunder.

JH Partners agreed to a cease-and-desist order and a $225,000 penalty as part of its agreement to settle the case.[3]

4.7.2 Case Study #2: Oppenheimer

The primary entities involved in this matter were:

- Oppenheimer Asset Management Inc. ("OAM")
- Oppenheimer Alternative Investment Management, LLC ("OAIM")
- Oppenheimer Global Resource Private Equity Fund I, LP ("OGR") – a private equity vehicle

As background, at the time of the allegations in this case, the SEC Administrative Proceeding in this matter described that OAM was located in New York City and was registered with the Commission as a Registered Investment Adviser. OAM was a subsidiary of E.A. Viner International Co.,

---

[2]United States Securities and Exchange Commission, Administrative Proceeding File No. 3-16968, "In the Matter of JH PARTNERS, LLC, Respondent., ORDER INSTITUTING ADMINISTRATIVE AND CEASE-AND-DESIST PROCEEDINGS, PURSUANT TO SECTIONS 203(e) AND 203(k) OF THE INVESTMENT ADVISERS ACT OF 1940, MAKING FINDINGS, AND IMPOSING REMEDIAL SANCTIONS AND A CEASE-AND-DESIST ORDER.
[3]A. Ceresny, "Securities Enforcement Forum West 2016 Keynote Address: Private Equity Enforcement," May 12, 2016.

which is a subsidiary of Oppenheimer Holdings, Inc., a publicly held company listed on the New York Stock Exchange. Furthermore, OAIM was wholly owned by OAM, and OAM is the sole member of OAIM. OAIM was the general partner of and, through employees of OAM, provided investment advisory services to several funds, including OGR and other private equity funds. Accordingly, OAM could have been deemed to have served as the investment adviser to OGR. The SEC Administrative Proceeding in this mater described the allegations of the case as follows:[4]

> From October 2009 through 2010, Respondents disseminated marketing materials to prospective investors and quarterly reports to existing investors that contained material misrepresentations and omissions concerning Respondents' valuation policies and OGR's performance. Respondents stated in the marketing materials and quarterly reports to investors that OGR's asset values were "based on the underlying managers' estimated values" when that was not the case with respect to one of the assets in OGR's investment portfolio.
>
> Beginning in October 2009, while OGR was being marketed to new investors, OGR's portfolio manager ("Portfolio Manager") changed the value of OGR's largest holding, Cartesian Investors-A, LLC ("Cartesian"), using a different valuation method than that used by Cartesian's underlying manager. The Portfolio Manager did not inform, and caused Respondents not to inform, investors either of this change or of the fact that the new valuation method resulted in a significant increase in the value of Cartesian over that provided by Cartesian's underlying manager.
>
> Additionally, former employees overseeing OAIM's investments misrepresented and caused Respondents to misrepresent to potential investors that:
>
> (i) the increase in Cartesian's value was due to an increase in Cartesian's performance when, in fact, the increase was attributable to the Portfolio Manager's new valuation method;

---

[4]United States Securities and Exchange Commission, Administrative Proceeding File No. 3-15238, "In the Matter of OPPENHEIMER ASSET MANAGEMENT INC. and OPPENHEIMER ALTERNATIVE INVESTMENT MANAGEMENT, LLC, Respondents., ORDER INSTITUTING ADMINISTRATIVE AND CEASE-AND-DESIST PROCEEDINGS, PURSUANT TO SECTION 8A OF THE SECURITIES ACT OF 1933 AND SECTIONS 203(e) AND 203(k) OF THE INVESTMENT ADVISERS ACT OF 1940, MAKING FINDINGS, AND IMPOSING REMEDIAL SANCTIONS AND A CEASE-AND-DESIST ORDER.

(ii) a third party valuation firm used by Cartesian's underlying manager wrote up the value of Cartesian when that was not true; and

(iii) OGR's underlying funds were audited by independent, third party auditors when, in fact, Cartesian was unaudited.

Former employees overseeing OAIM's investments and the Respondents marketed OGR using the marked-up value of the Cartesian investment from October 2009 through June 2010 and succeeded in raising approximately $61 million in new investments in OGR during that period.

Oppenheimer agreed to pay more than $2.8 million to settle the SEC's charges and the Massachusetts Attorney General's office announced a related action and additional financial penalty against Oppenheimer.[5]

4.8 SUMMARY

This chapter examined various compliance aspects and procedures relating to the valuation of a private equity fund's holdings. We first examined the common language relating to private equity valuation guidance from a fund's formation documents. Next, we addressed the role played by valuation committees in overseeing valuations. This included a discussion of the size of these committees, their specific duties, and meeting frequency. The role of investment personnel in working with valuation committees, as well as the role of valuation subcommittees was also addressed. The production of valuation memorandums and the role of third-party valuation consultants and fund administrators were examined. LPAC valuation oversight and mechanisms for resolving valuation conflicts between the GP and LPs were analyzed. Finally, case studies regarding regulatory actions in the area of valuation oversight were presented. A key consideration in the valuation of private equity fund holdings related to the conflicts of interest inherent in this process. In the next chapter, we will address the subject of conflicts of interest in more detail as they relate not only to valuation, but to the larger private equity fund management process.

---

[5]United States Securities and Exchange Commission, "SEC Charges New York Based Private Equity Fund Advisers with Misleading Investors about Valuation and Performance," March 11, 2013.

CHAPTER 5

Conflicts of Interest

5.1 INTRODUCTION TO CONFLICTS OF INTEREST

Conflicts of interest in various forms are common among all investment management arrangements and private equity presents a number of unique conflicts of interest. As an example, in Chapter 4 we outlined several of the potential conflicts inherent in the private equity valuation process. In this chapter we will expand this discussion to focus on other potential conflicts throughout the private equity fund management process.

5.2 DEFINING A CONFLICT OF INTEREST

In a private equity context, by virtue of their position general partners (GPs) may find themselves in a number of situations that may present a potential *conflict of interest*, or simply *conflicts*. These conflicts are rooted in their obligations to manage funds in the best interest of investors while at the same time pursuing other activities that may conflict with this obligation. For our purposes, we can define a potential conflict of interest for GPs as a situation where a dual obligation exists between their duties to investors and other activities that they, or their employees, are pursuing.

5.3 FUND FORMATION CONFLICT-OF-INTEREST DISCLOSURES

The first place to start when considering a private equity fund's potential conflicts is with the fund's offering documents. In many cases the fund formation documents will disclose that certain conflicts may occur. As we work through each of the common conflict disclosure topics that the fund formation documents reference, keep in mind that simply disclosing that a potential conflict may exist does not mean that it is then permissible for GPs to engage in activities to benefit themselves to the detriment of the limited partners (LPs). Rather disclosure is simply the first step. As you will see, in many cases the GP will be responsible for vetting conflicts through the limited partner advisory committee (LPAC). Furthermore, it is important for the compliance function of the GP to be informed and provide oversight of how the GP may potentially deal with these types of conflicts. The job of compliance function, therefore, is not only to simply document these conflicts but also to provide guidance on how to navigate them.

5.4 PREEXISTING INTERESTS AND THOSE ACQUIRED FROM OTHER FUNDS

A common area of potential conflict relates to a scenario where an investment is being considered for a fund, yet the GP or related persons already maintain a preexisting interest in the underlying potential investment. This could have been purchased directly by the GP, or perhaps acquired from another fund. In this case, the preexisting interest may present a conflict for the GP. An example of the common disclosure language in the fund formation documents addressing this issue would be as follows:

> The Partnership may make investments in underlying portfolio companies that employees, members or affiliates of the General Partner may either have (i) acquired an interest in through other funds; (ii) maintained a pre-existing interest in. Under this scenario the interests held by these employees, members or affiliates may differ in a substantial manner from the interests held by the Partnership.

One reason for the differences in the goals relating to the management of these interests could be due to liquidity preferences. For example, a portfolio manager who maintains a personal investment in an underlying portfolio company may have a shorter investment horizon as compared to the fund she manages, which also holds an investment. This would result in the portfolio manager wanting to exit the position sooner, and perhaps at a lesser value, than the fund may wish to sell its interest. These liquidity preference differences could create a potential conflict of interest. For reference, the logic behind this is similar to the liquidity preference conflict example among LPs and non-LPAC LPs we discussed in Chapter 3.

Another related conflict that may be present would be that the portfolio manager was an earlier investor in a portfolio company and therefore may have been granted equity with superior voting rights compared to the share class invested in by the fund. This disconnect in voting rights may also pose a potential conflict.

Additionally, the terms of the two investments may be different. For example, let us assume that a fund invested a larger amount of money into a portfolio company as compared to the amount invested by the individual portfolio manager. In this case, the fund may have received a discount on the shares in the portfolio company due to their willingness to make a larger upfront capital outlay. Based on the changing value of the portfolio company, and the prices paid by the individual portfolio manager, a theoretical situation could arise whereby the fund is holding the equity at a profit while the portfolio manager's own personal investment is being held at a loss. This could potentially create perverse incentive for the portfolio manager to take riskier activities than might be merited in an attempt to make up the lost value of his own personal investment as compared to protecting or growing the fund's gains. Therefore, while disclosing such conflict is important, it is also important from a compliance perspective to oversee the implementation of such conflicts.

Yet another way that the fund offering documents may address the issue of preexisting GP investments will be through fund formation document disclosures such as this:

> The Partnership shall not invest in any underlying portfolio company in which the GP maintains an existing interest in excess of $75,000 or more than ten percent (10%) of the outstanding capital stock of the underlying portfolio company.

These types of limitations entirely preclude a fund from being investing into an underlying portfolio company in which the GP has too large an investment. A key motivation for these types of limitations is to prevent conflicts that may be present between the GP, or other fund managed by the GP, that maintains this investment in the portfolio company, and the actual fund investment itself.

5.5 GP EMPLOYEE OR AFFILIATE DIRECT INVESTMENTS

In certain instances, a GP may be presented with an investment opportunity in which they, or their employees or affiliates, wish to invest directly themselves. There is nothing inherently wrong with this; however, a GP's first obligation is to the investors in the funds that they manage. It would not be considered equitable, therefore, if the GP were to jump the line and cherry-pick the best opportunities for their direct investment ahead of the funds they manage.

Depending on the formation documents of the fund, the GP may be allowed to utilize their discretion as to whether an investment is appropriate for a fund that they manage. If they determine that it is not, then they could make a direct investment themselves. This is not to say that the GP cannot make an error in judgment and determine that an investment might not be appropriate for a fund when it actually may be. The point is that some funds are structured so that the GP would be the primary entity tasked with making the decision. An example of disclosures a fund formation document may make in regard to these direct investments would be as follows:

> In certain instances, employees, members or other affiliates of the General Partner may make investments that will be made separately or congruently alongside the Partnership. The General Partner will be able to make this investment during the Partnership's time, any of which may compete with the Fund.

> In other cases, to assist in the decision making the LPAC may be consulted prior to direct GP investments.

5.6 FRONT-RUNNING CONSIDERATIONS

Front running refers to the practice where an employee possesses advance knowledge that the GP, through its affiliated funds, is going to be making a particular transaction, and the employee benefits from this information by executing trades for his own personal account in advance of the firm's funds.

Due to the fact that private equity companies typically engage in the purchase of securities that are not publicly traded, many GPs and investors consider the risks surrounding front running to be relatively low for private equity as compared to investment vehicles that trade in more easily available, liquid securities such as hedge funds. In some instances, a private equity fund may purchase publicly traded securities as part of its overall investment strategy. Furthermore, a private equity strategy such as venture capital may own shares in an underlying portfolio company which then undergoes an initial public offering (IPO) that would result in a private equity fund holding public shares. As such, front-running considerations are still relevant for private equity firms.

To illustrate the way front running would work, let us utilize the example of a private equity that is planning to make a large purchase of shares of outstanding stock in a thinly traded company that would likely be significant enough to move the market higher for those shares. To benefit from this knowledge, an investment analyst employed at the GP could rush out in advance of the fund and buy shares of the same stock for her own personal account. After the private equity fund then proceeds with trades for its respective funds, the stock price would likely significantly increase, and the employee would benefit from her advance purchase of the stock. The problem with having employees front run the activities of the fund is that it creates a disadvantage for the investors of the private equity fund to the benefit of the individual GP employees. This is why front running is not only considered a conflict of interest, but many jurisdictions make the practice of front running illegal.

A second potential area of conflict in regard to personal account dealing conflicts relates to the potential for trading in *material nonpublic information (MNPI)*. This is also referred to as insider information and could be applicable to transactions in both public and private securities. To avoid even the appearance of any such conflicts, private equity funds generally prohibit employees from trading private securities for their own account which may be considered for investment by the firm's funds. The relationship between MNPI and other aspects of compliance outside of personal trading, such as expert network use, is discussed in Chapter 8.

A key way that the risks associated with front running and MNPI are mitigated by compliance is through oversight of a private equity fund's policies for the management of personal trading accounts by GP employees and their relatives. These are known as personal account dealing policies and procedures. Key best practices for the compliance oversight of personal account dealing include:

- *Restricted list.* A restricted list is a predetermined list of holdings that the GP's employees are currently prohibited from trading in for their personal accounts. These could include positions that may be currently held by the funds. A restricted list facilitates the trade preclearance process. An example of typical language contained in the fund's offering documents concerning restricted list prohibitions would be as follows:

  > Unless specific approval is granted by the Limited Partners Advisory Committee (LPAC) neither the General Partner nor any Manager shall invest for its own account in any security of any company in which the Fund is actively considering an investment or an existing portfolio company, except for purchases of securities that are traded on a public securities market.

- *Pre-clearance.* This refers to having the GP's employees submit notice to the compliance department prior to executing any trades. The compliance department would then review the details of any potential trades to determine if they would conflict with any current or planned holdings of the fund. If they did, then compliance would not approve the employee's proposed trade.

Related to the granting of pre-clearances is to have the compliance function set a restriction on the time period for which pre-clearances are valid. In general, the shorter the window during which preclearance approvals are valid, the better. The reasoning for this thinking is that the investment activities of the private equity fund as well as the conditions of markets change frequently. Pre-clearances that are valid for a number of days may extend the potential for conflict that may arise that could otherwise have been avoided if the validity of the preapproval window had been shortened.

▪ *Post-clearance.* This is a process where after trades are executed the compliance department would perform checks on the trades executed in an employee's personal brokerage account. In practice, the way a private equity GP's compliance function performs these checks is by collecting brokerage statements from employee accounts and comparing them to preclearance requests. It is considered best practice for the compliance department to collect copies of these brokerage statements directly from the brokers in order to preserve independence of the information.

▪ *Minimum holding periods.* A minimum holding period is a predetermined minimum amount of time that an employee is required to hold purchases made in a personal brokerage account prior to selling out of them. One common exception to this rule is when an employee purchases a security for his personal brokerage account that significantly declines in value soon after the purchase is made. In these cases, the private equity fund permits employees to take advantage of a hardship exemption and sell out of the position. One reason this exemption is allowed is because personal account dealing policies are not intended to penalize employees who trade for their own account but rather to prevent potential conflicts of interest with the funds. When the employee takes a hardship exemption, there is little likelihood that the interest of the private equity fund's investors would be placed behind those of the employee.

▪ *Penalties for policy violations.* Technical violations of a private equity fund's personal account dealing policies can occur for a wide variety of reasons. As a deterrence, it is considered a best practice for a GP to maintain some mechanisms to enforce penalties against employees who continually violate the policies. Common penalties include requiring employees to disgorge any profits from violations and possibly include termination of employment in extreme circumstances.

5.7 RELATED-PARTY TRANSACTIONS

A *related-party transaction* involves a deal in which the two parties are related. A common example of such a transaction would be if one fund managed by a GP (i.e. Fund A) were to directly purchase an asset from a different fund (i.e. Fund B) that was also managed by the same GP. This can be contrasted with what is known as an *arm's-length transaction*, in which neither party is affiliated.

Related-party transactions present a number of inherent conflicts. In addition to trade allocation considerations, discussed in more detail below, conflicts may also be present with regard to the price paid by the parties in such a transaction. Due to the close relationship among the parties, for example, one party, say Fund A in our example above, may decide to sell an asset well below fair market value to Fund B, because the two are managed by the same GP. While such a transaction could be to the ultimate benefit of the GP, it would be to the detriment of the LPs in Fund A since they are selling the asset an at unreasonable discount. Similarly, the transactions would unfairly enrich the investors in Fund B, because they would be purchasing the valuable asset at a significant discount. Neither situation is equitable; as this example demonstrates, such transactions present the need for additional oversight.

An example of typical language contained in the fund's offering documents referencing these related-party transactions would be as follows:

> The Fund may sell to one or more successor funds managed by the General Partner securities of one or more underlying portfolio companies which were warehoused by the Fund at the time of purchase for the express purpose of being transferred to a successor fund. The Fund may also purchase from an affiliate of the General Partner securities of one or more underlying portfolio companies that were warehoused by the affiliate for the purpose of a transfer to the Fund, at a combined amount of the cost and the prime rate plus 3.5% interest per annum.

This example paragraph references two terms that we should clarify. First is the term *successor fund*. This is a fund that is launched after the current fund. It is also sometimes called a *vintage fund*. For example, the first private equity fund may be called the Jason Opportunities Fund I, LP. The second, successor fund would then typically be called the Jason Opportunities Fund II, L.P. Second, the *prime rate* outlined above is the interest rate that is typically charged by banks to customers with very good credit such as larger corporations.

In this example, the fund formation documents clearly spell out the way that the transaction between the two entities should be valued. Of course, this would only apply if, as the example describes, it is a situation where the securities were being warehoused. *Warehousing* refers to a situation where securities are purchased for the purposes of being temporarily held at a particular fund and later being sold to a successor fund. This would not be applicable if a fund purchased the securities without the intent of warehousing them at the time and then later decided to send them to an affiliate or successor fund. In those situations, it would likely be in the discretion of the GP and the LPAC whether to follow this provision or apply the other valuation processes outlined in the formation documents.

Due to the inherent conflicts present in these related-party transactions, as we outlined in Chapter 3, this is why LPACs traditionally are required to review and approve related-party transactions such as co-investments and cross-investments prior to their taking place.

5.8 DEAL ALLOCATION

Deal allocation, sometimes also called trade allocation, refers to the way in which a private equity firm makes a determination as to how to split up shares in a particular asset among the various funds it manages. For simplicity, consider a GP that manages only a single fund. They purchase equity or debt in an underlying company. In this case, they only have one fund in which to place this investment and allocation is not a concern.

Now let us consider a GP that manages a single fund strategy with different versions of the fund that are managed in a *pari-passu* manner. As a reminder, this means that they are managed in substantially the same manner and adhere to the same investment strategy. The reason for different funds is often to facilitate tax efficiency for investors. From the perspective of a US-based investor, common structures would be an *onshore fund* (i.e. one that is domiciled in the United States) and an *offshore fund* (i.e. one registered outside of the United States). Two of the more common jurisdictions where onshore and offshore funds are registered include the state of Delaware in the United States and the Cayman Islands respectively.

Returning to our example, let us say the GP is allotted a certain number of shares in the portfolio company. How should they allocate them among the two *pari-passu* funds? An even 50–50 division of the shares might seem like the most straightforward approach; however, that might not be equitable to the investors in both funds. If the offshore fund has substantially more assets than the onshore fund, and therefore the offshore fund will likely be able to put up more capital for more shares, then perhaps it would be the most equitable approach to award the shares on what is known as a *pro-rata basis*, or proportional basis. If indeed it would be appropriate for both funds to put up an equal amount of capital, then an even split of the shares would be equitable.

The same logic can be applied for a GP that manages multiple fund complexes. A *fund complex* is a group of related funds that adhere to a similar strategy. It is also sometimes referred to as a *fund family*. An onshore–offshore fund pair as described above could be deemed to be a fund complex. Another common fund complex is a *master-feeder structure*. Under this structure a master fund sits above feeder funds, which feed capital up to the master fund. If a GP is allocated a certain fixed number of shares, then first a determination should be made as to how many shares are to be allocated to each fund in the complex. In this instance, the methodology employed would not be a straightforward calculation of the amount of capital available to invest from each fund in the complex, as we employed with the onshore–offshore example above. The reason for this is that the GP must also consider the different investment strategy of each fund complex.

A GP may also manage multiple fund complexes adhering to different strategies. Consider a GP that has been allocated $10 million worth of shares in an underlying portfolio company and they must then allocate the money among the two different fund complexes that they manage. One fund family follows an investment strategy of seeking investments in the healthcare space while the other fund complex is focused around early stage fintech companies. If the shares under consideration were from a portfolio company that was developing cancer treatments, then it would be most suited for the healthcare fund. As such, the GP could correctly decide to allocate all the shares to the healthcare company. Similarly, if the shares were in a company developing a new software platform to facilitate the direct transfer of cryptocurrencies between banks, then all of the shares could go to the fintech fund.

What if the shares were in a portfolio company that facilitated the transfer of electronic payments among healthcare providers? This deals with healthcare, so perhaps it is appropriate for the healthcare fund. Similarly, it also deals with fintech, so perhaps the other fund as well. It is in these types of situations where the GP must make sometimes difficult determinations as to which fund complexes should be given shares and how much. To provide guidance in these situations many of the formation documents for most private equity funds will contain references to the procedures for deal allocation.

5.9   PLACEMENT AGENTS' CONFLICTS OF INTEREST

When raising capital from investors for a new private equity fund, be it a brand-new fund or the next vintage of an existing fund, a GP may work with third parties to assist in the marketing efforts. One reason for this is that the GP may have a limited geographic network of potential investors (i.e. throughout the United States) while a third party may have expertise in dealing with investors in other regions of the world (i.e. Europe and Asia). Additionally, even within the GP's home country or region, there may be certain types of investors that a third party may have more established relationships with that the GP can leverage to assist in fundraising. These third parties are often simply called *third-party marketers.* They may also be referred to as *placement agents* since they place investor capital with the GP. Placement agents are typically compensated by fees paid by the GP based on the amount of funds raised.

The relationship a GP has with a placement agent can present potential conflicts of interest. A key concern relates to the disclosures that should be made to potential investors being solicited by the placement agent. Specifically, when providing an overview of a private equity fund's investment strategy and potential profitability a placement agent should disclose that it is being incentivized to solicit investments into the GP's funds through compensation. Another area of disclosures relates to a practice where in some instances the private equity firm may intend to recover or attribute costs associated with the use of a third-party placement agent to the fund.[1] This practice of effectively charging the LPs of a fund a fee for having been solicited by a placement agent is sometimes referred to as a *sales charge, placement fee,* or *sales rebate.* Any such intentions to pass placement fees onto the fund would present a potential conflict that should be disclosed to all investors that have come to the GP through this placement agent.

5.10   CASE STUDIES IN CONFLICTS OF INTEREST

In the private equity space, regulators have increasingly focused on compliance related to conflicts of interest. The following two cases demonstrate actions taken in this area by the US Securities and Exchange Commission (SEC). As you review these matters, keep in mind the roles played by conflicts of interest throughout the entire private equity investment process and

---

[1] "Final Report on Private Equity Conflicts of Interest," Technical Committee of the International Organization of Securities Commissions (November 10, 2010).

the ways in which compliance policies and procedures may be designed to mitigate and oversee these potential conflicts.

5.10.1 Case Study #1: Fenway Partners, LLC

The primary entities involved in this matter were:

- Fenway Partners, LLC ("Fenway Partners") – a private equity fund adviser that was owned and controlled by:
  - Peter Lamm ("Lamm") and William Gregory Smart ("Smart") between January 1, 2011 and December 31, 2013 ("Relevant Period"), and
  - Timothy Mayhew, Jr. ("Mayhew") between January 1, 2011 and May 31, 2012.
- Walter Wiacek, CPA ("Wiacek") – the firm's vice president, chief financial officer, and chief compliance officer during the Relevant Period

The SEC Administrative Proceeding in this matter described the allegations of the case as follows:[2]

2. Fenway Partners served as the investment adviser to Fenway Partners Capital Fund III, LP ("Fund III"), a private equity fund, during the Relevant Period. Fund III's portfolio was comprised primarily of investments in branded consumer products and transportation/logistics industry companies (each, a "Portfolio Company").

3. Fenway Partners entered into Management Services Agreements (each, an "MSA") with certain Portfolio Companies pursuant to which Fenway Partners received periodic fees for providing management and other services to the Portfolio Company ("monitoring fees"). In accordance with the terms of Fund III's organizational documents, the monitoring fees were offset against the advisory fee paid by Fund III to Fenway Partners.

4. Beginning in December 2011, Fenway Partners, Lamm, Smart, Mayhew, and Wiacek (collectively, "Respondents") caused

---

[2]United States Securities and Exchange Commission, Administrative Proceeding File No. 3-16968, In the Matter of JH PARTNERS, LLC, Respondent., ORDER INSTITUTING ADMINISTRATIVE AND CEASE-AND-DESIST PROCEEDINGS, PURSUANT TO SECTIONS 203(e) AND 203(k) OF THE INVESTMENT ADVISERS ACT OF 1940, MAKING FINDINGS, AND IMPOSING REMEDIAL SANCTIONS AND A CEASE-AND-DESIST ORDER.

certain Portfolio Companies to terminate their payment obligations to Fenway Partners under their MSAs and enter into agreements (each, a "Consulting Agreement") with Fenway Consulting Partners, LLC ("Fenway Consulting"), an entity affiliated with Fenway Partners and principally owned and operated by Lamm, Smart, and Mayhew. Under the Consulting Agreements, Fenway Consulting provided similar services to the Portfolio Companies, often through the same employees as Fenway Partners had under the MSAs. Mayhew was involved solely with respect to one Portfolio Company.

5. Fenway Consulting ultimately received an aggregate of $5.74 million from the Portfolio Companies during the Relevant Period. However, in contrast to the monitoring fees paid pursuant to the MSAs, the $5.74 million in Portfolio Company fees paid to Fenway Consulting were not offset against the Fund III advisory fee, resulting in a larger advisory fee to Fenway Partners. The Respondents did not disclose the conflict of interest presented by the termination of monitoring fees pursuant to the MSAs and collection of fees pursuant to the Consulting Agreements. Respondents Fenway Partners, Lamm, and Smart also made, and Wiacek caused to be made, material omissions to fund investors concerning the Consulting Agreements.

6. In addition, in January 2012, Fenway Partners, Lamm, and Smart asked Fund III investors to provide $4 million in connection with a potential investment in the equity securities of a Portfolio Company ("Portfolio Company A"), without disclosing that $1 million of the requested amount would be used to pay an affiliate, Fenway Consulting. Wiacek signed and sent the letter to investors making this request.

7. In June 2012, Fund III sold its equity interest in a second Portfolio Company ("Portfolio Company B"). As part of the transaction, Mayhew, and two former Fenway Partners employees were included in Portfolio Company B's cash incentive plan ("CIP") and ultimately received an aggregate of $15 million from the proceeds of the sale, thereby reducing Fund III's return on its investment in Portfolio Company B. Mayhew and the two former Fenway Partners employees (collectively, the "Fenway CIP Participants") were employees of Fenway Consulting, an affiliated entity, at the time the payments were made, and received the payments as compensation for services almost entirely performed while they were Fenway Partners employees. The Respondents did not disclose the conflict of interest

presented by the payments to the Fenway CIP Participants. Respondents Fenway Partners, Lamm, and Smart also made, and Wiacek made or caused to be made, material omissions to investors concerning the CIP payments.

To settle the SEC's charges without admitting or denying the order's findings, Fenway Partners, Lamm, Smart, and Mayhew agreed to jointly and severally pay disgorgement of $7.892 million and prejudgment interest of $824,471.10. They and Wiacek also agreed to pay penalties totaling $1.525 million.[3]

5.11 CASE STUDY #2: CENTRE PARTNERS MANAGEMENT, LLC

Potential conflicts of interest may also be present between a private equity firm, its principals, and third-party service providers. One case of note which highlights the increased regulatory focus relating to the duty of a general partner to sufficiently disclose potential conflicts relating to service providers was an administrative proceeding brought by the U.S. Securities and Exchange Commission (US SEC) against Centre Partners Management, LLC (CPM). Interestingly in this case although neither the GP nor its principals financially profited from their relationships with the third-party service provider, the SEC still found that "CPM breached its fiduciary duty to its fund clients and made materially misleading statements to the funds' investors by failing to disclose these potential conflicts of interest."[4]

The following is an excerpt of the allegations as outlined in the SEC administrative proceeding in this matter which provides background on the facts of the case, including a focus on the nature and sufficiency of

---

[3]United States of America Before the Securities and Exchange Commission, Investment Advisors Act of 1940, Release No. 4253/November 3, 2015, In the Matter of Fenway Partners, LLC, Peter Lamm, William Gregory Smart, Timothy Mayhew Jr., and Walter Wiacek, CPA, Respondents., ORDER INSTITUTING ADMINISTRATIVE AND CEASE-AND-DESIST PROCEEDINGS, PURSUANT TO SECTIONS 203(e), 203(f) AND 203(k) OF THE INVESTMENT ADVISERS ACT OF 1940, MAKING FINDINGS, AND IMPOSING REMEDIAL SANCTIONS AND A CEASE-AND-DESIST ORDER.

[4]United States Securities and Exchange Commission, Administrative Proceeding File No. 3-17764, "Private Equity Fund Adviser Settles with SEC for Failing to Disclose Potential Conflicts of Interest," January 10, 2017.

conflict-of-interest disclosures related to the use of a third-party service provider.[5]

1. These proceedings arise out of the failure by a registered investment adviser and its principals to disclose potential conflicts of interest to its private equity fund clients and the adviser's material misleading statements to the funds' investors. CPM is a private equity firm that provides investment advisory services to four funds and their related parallel entities. From 2001 through 2014, CPM failed to disclose relationships between certain of its principals and a third-party information technology ("IT") service provider (the "Service Provider"), and the potential conflicts of interest resulting from those relationships. During the same period, CPM engaged the Service Provider to perform due diligence services for portfolio company investments on behalf of and paid for by its fund clients, and several of the fund clients' portfolio companies separately retained the Service Provider for assorted technology services.

2. Three of CPM's principals (collectively, the "CPM Principals") have personal investments in the Service Provider that were made approximately 15 years ago, two of CPM's principals occupy two of the three seats on its board of directors, and the wife of one of the principals is a relative of the Service Provider's co-founder and Chief Executive Officer ("CEO"). These potential conflicts were not disclosed, as required by the funds' governing documents, to the advisory committees responsible for reviewing such conflicts. In addition, while CPM provided extensive disclosure of its use of the Service Provider in the investment due diligence process and presented its business relationship with this Service Provider as a competitive advantage to investors, absent from these disclosures was any mention of the relationships between the CPM

---

[5]United States of America Before the Securities and Exchange Commission, Investment Advisors Act of 1940, Release No. 4604/January 10, 2017, Administrative Proceeding File No. 3-17764, In the Matter of CENTRE PARTNERS MANAGEMENT, LLC Respondent., ORDER INSTITUTING ADMINISTRATIVE AND CEASE-AND-DESIST PROCEEDINGS, PURSUANT TO SECTIONS 203(e) AND 203(k) OF THE INVESTMENT ADVISERS ACT OF 1940, MAKING FINDINGS, AND IMPOSING REMEDIAL SANCTIONS AND A CEASE-AND-DESIST ORDER.

Principals and the Service Provider until, while Centre Capital Investors VI, L.P. was being marketed, its Private Placement Memorandum ("PPM") was revised.

3. Although neither CPM nor the CPM Principals financially profited from their relationships with the Service Provider, CPM breached its fiduciary duty to its fund clients and made material misleading statements to the funds' investors by failing to disclose these potential conflicts of interest. CPM violated Section 206(2) of the Advisers Act by failing to make timely disclosure of the potential conflicts of interest. CPM also violated Sections 206(4) of the Advisers Act, and Rule 206(4)-8 promulgated thereunder, by virtue of omissions of material facts from its disclosures to investors concerning the relationships of the CPM Principals with the Service Provider.

Respondent

4. *CPM* is a Delaware limited liability company with its principal place of business in New York, New York and an additional office in Los Angeles, California. It is an investment adviser registered with the Commission since November 9, 1999, with total assets under management of approximately $880 million as of March 31, 2016.

Other Relevant Entities

5. Centre Capital Investors III, L.P. ("Fund III"), Centre Capital Investors IV, L.P. ("Fund IV"), Centre Capital Investors V, L.P. ("Fund V"), and Centre Capital Investors VI, L.P. ("Fund VI") (collectively, the "Funds") are Delaware limited partnerships that commenced operations in 1999, 2003, 2007, and 2014, respectively. CPM serves as investment adviser to the Funds.

The Service Provider

6. In 2002, CPM began utilizing the Service Provider. Pursuant to the services engagement agreement between the parties (the "Agreement"), the Service Provider provides IT due diligence services with respect to potential portfolio investments for the Funds at a flat fee capped at $25,000 per engagement. The due diligence fees are paid by the Funds. The Agreement also

provides for, among other things, exclusivity that prevents the Service Provider from performing similar due diligence services for other investment advisers and private equity firms. The CPM Principals have stated that the terms of the Agreement were negotiated for the benefit of the Funds and their LPs. The Agreement expired on January 15, 2007, and, although the Agreement was not formally renewed, the parties still operate under its terms.

7. The Service Provider also provides back office support services directly to CPM, such as computer network and hardware support, the terms of which are not covered by the Agreement. These back office support services are paid for directly by CPM.

8. The Service Provider is available for direct engagement by the portfolio companies. CPM, however, does not require or promote the retention of the Service Provider by the portfolio companies for any services.

9. CPM and the portfolio companies have not been large consumers of the Service Provider's services. From January 2008 through January 2016, approximately 2% of the Service Provider's total sales revenues came from CPM and approximately 9.5% were from portfolio companies. During the same period, approximately 21% of portfolio companies retained the Service Provider directly. At the time CPM engaged the Service Provider for its first transaction in 2002, the Service Provider had been in business for approximately 18 months.

The Service Provider Is Showcased

10. The PPM's for Funds IV and V provide extensive descriptions of the Service Provider and the services it offers, as well as the advantages of their relationship (the PPM for Fund III predated CPM's relationship with the Service Provider). For example, the PPM for Fund V describes the Service Provider as follows:

> [The Service Provider] ... For many middle market companies, the development of information systems can present a strategic opportunity for (or challenge to) continued future growth. IT is an area where most private equity investors must rely heavily on third-party consultants. Having learned from experience that this traditional approach does not present the optimal solution to a potentially material issue, we have taken a novel route. Since 2001, we have partnered with [the Service

Provider], a seasoned and result oriented group of business technology experts, in an exclusive arrangement for private equity to add a powerful systems expertise skill set to the Centre Resource Model. [The Service Provider] has a staff of 50 consultants, many of whom have spent more than 20 years delivering tailored software applications and systems integration services. Throughout their careers, members of this team have designed, developed, deployed, supported and managed innovative and practical IT solutions for an array of clients, including businesses similar to those we target in the middle market. [The Service Provider] has broad experience in difficult industrial and commercial situations and state-of-the-art technical qualifications, driven by the needs of both its commercial and government clients. [The Service Provider] assists Centre Partners with due diligence and business systems assessment of our investments pre-closing and with implementation, if necessary, and systems monitoring post-closing. By teaming with [the Service Provider], we have a differentiated ability to help avoid IT pitfalls in our [due] diligence and during the life of our investments.

11. In addition to the above disclosure, the Service Provider is mentioned or described in at least six other instances in the PPM for Fund V. However, omitted from the detailed descriptions was any discussion of the relationships between the CPM Principals and the Service Provider and the potential conflicts of interest they presented. The Potential Conflicts

12. The CPM Principals – Principals A, B, and C – made and continue to hold personal investments in the Service Provider. Principal A, prior to joining CPM, personally invested $100,000 in the Service Provider at the time of its formation approximately 15 years ago, and solicited other investors from colleagues and friends (Principal A invested another $25,000 in the Service provider approximately a year later). Two of the investors solicited by Principal A are the other two CPM Principals, who each invested $25,000 at or about the same time. Principal B's investment was made, also prior to joining CPM, through a partially-owned corporation (the "Corporation") in which he is a minority shareholder that provided him with a personal share of approximately $8,000 at the time of the investment. Collectively, Principals A, B, and C own approximately 9.6% of the outstanding shares of the Service Provider.

13. Principals A and B hold two of the three seats on the Service Provider's board of directors.

14. The Service Provider's co-founder, majority shareholder, President and CEO is the brother of Principal A's wife. The importance of the Service Provider's CEO is evinced by a "Key Man" provision in the Agreement. According to the provision, if the Service Provider's CEO ceased "to be actively involved in, or responsible for, the activities of [the Service Provider] for any reason," CPM had the right to terminate the Agreement, "upon written notice delivered to [the Service Provider] within 30 days after having been notified by [the Service Provider] of such event."

15. Neither CPM nor the CPM Principals have financially profited from the relationships with the Service Provider. The Potential Conflicts Are Flagged.

16. In connection with raising capital for its new Fund VI, in May 2012 CPM retained a global private equity placement agent ("Placement Agent"). During the course of the engagement, the Placement Agent was informed by CPM about the Service Provider and, specifically, about Principal A and Principal C's investments. The Placement Agent was also informed that the Service Provider's CEO is the brother of Principal A's wife.

17. During meetings with the Placement Agent, investors inquired about the ownership of the Service Provider, and at least one potential investor also inquired about payments to the Service Provider.

18. The Placement Agent discussed with the CPM Principals their ownership interests in the Service Provider since it had the appearance of a conflict of interest and could raise questions with potential investors. At least one CPM Principal stated his belief that potential investors were aware of the relationship because, among other things, the Service Provider had a similar name to CPM. Also, Principal A informed the Placement Agent that the portfolio companies were not required to retain the Service Provider.

Potential Conflicts Remain Undisclosed

19. Despite the assertions to the Placement Agent that potential investors were aware of CPM's relationship to the Service Provider, there was at the time, in fact, no disclosure of any of the CPM Principals' investments, the two Principals' seats

on the Service Provider's board of directors, or of the family relationship between the wife of Principal A and the Service Provider's CEO. No disclosure of these relationships appeared in the PPMs or LPAs for Funds IV and V, in the audited financial statements distributed to investors, or in CPM's Forms ADV.

20. Although the LPAs set forth the means to address potential conflicts, they provided no disclosure of any potential conflicts of interest related to the Service Provider. As set forth in their respective LPAs, Funds III and IV have an "Advisory Board" and Fund V has an "LP Advisory Committee" ("LPAC") to which material potential conflicts of interest were to be brought for review and approval or disapproval. The potential conflicts posed by the CPM Principals' investments in the Service Provider, certain CPM Principals' membership on the Service Provider's board of directors, and the relationship between the wife of Principal A and the Service Provider's CEO were not presented to the Advisory Boards or to the LPACs.

21. The audited financial statements for Funds III, IV, and V each had a footnote discussing related party transactions, but no mention of the Service Provider or the potential conflicts of interest.

22. CPM's Forms ADV filed in March 2011 through March 2013 made no mention of the potential conflicts of interest.

Without admitting or denying the SEC's findings, CPM agreed to a censure, a cease-and-desist order, and to pay a $50,000 penalty.[6]

5.12 SUMMARY

This chapter provided an overview of the many potential conflicts of interest present in private equity investing and fund management. We began by defining a potential conflict of interest. Next we examined conflict-of-interest disclosures commonly contained in fund formation documentation. We then proceeded to discuss potential conflicts relating to preexisting interests and to multiple funds managed by the same GP. Conflicts related to affiliated and direct investments were next addressed. Potential conflicts

---

[6]C. Witkowsky, "SEC Settles with Centre Partners over Disclosure Issue," PE HUB, *Buyouts*, January 12, 2017.

surrounding issues of front running and MNPI as well as related compliance controls for oversight of personal account dealing were next discussed. We then proceeded to examine related-party transaction and deal allocation considerations among multiple funds. Finally, we examined conflicts relating to placement agents as well as case studies in regulatory activity in this area. Now that we have established potential conflicts of interest are inherent in private equity valuations and discussed the broader aspects related to the management of private equity funds, in the next chapter we will address another area of private equity investing filled with potential conflicts of interest: fees and expenses.

CHAPTER 6

Fees and Expenses – Compliance Considerations

6.1 INTRODUCTION TO PRIVATE EQUITY EXPENSES AND FEES

In a private equity context, a *fee* can be defined as money paid to the general partner (GP) for a service performed. Fees are collected by private equity managers from investors as part of their management of a fund. Fees are also collected by GPs as part of their activity with underlying portfolio companies. Fees can be distinguished from expenses. An *expense* can be defined as the cost charged for a service. In addition to fees, private equity funds often charge a wide variety of expenses as part of their investment in a fund. For the purposes of our discussion we will classify a *fee* and an *expense* as described above; however, as you read this material note that in practice the two terms are sometimes used interchangeably.

6.2 WHY ARE FEES AND EXPENSES IMPORTANT TO COMPLIANCE?

Expenses are charged by private equity managers to investors in their funds. From an investment perspective the fees collected by a GP and the expenses charged are key considerations in the overall profitability of a fund. Understanding the scope of fees and expenses charged by a GP and related funds as well as ensuring that appropriate disclosures are made surrounding these charges is not always a straightforward exercise.

Properly accounting for fees and expenses is an essential part of not only ensuring fund profitability, but also maintaining compliance with regulatory and fund-level compliance obligations to limited partners (LPs). In a similar vein to our discussion of conflicts of interest, from a compliance perspective a key issue relating to fees is ensuring that fees and expenses are properly and fully disclosed. Other issues relate to overall fee and expense related policies and the ways in which fees may be charged, including their timing. Fees and expenses have also increasingly come under scrutiny from not only private equity investors but regulators as well. The results of more than 150 examinations of private equity advisers noted that in regard to the handling of fees and expenses the US Securities and Exchange Commission (US SEC) identified what they believed to be material weaknesses or direct violation of the law in controls over 50 percent of the time.[1]

The results of these types of examinations has caused the regulatory enforcement landscape in recent years to demonstrate shifting attitudes toward formerly commonly held fee practices that both investors and GPs should be conscious of in interpreting acceptable practices in this area going forward.

6.3 TRANSACTION FEES VS. FUND-LEVEL FEES

We can bifurcate the broad category of fees into two smaller categories. The first group of fees are known as transaction fees. A *transaction fee* is a broad term that refers to a variety of fees that a private equity firm would charge to a fund portfolio company for work that the GP performed in order to complete a fund-related transaction. Two examples of transaction fees are *underwriting fees* and *arrangement fees*. Transaction fees can be distinguished from *fund-level fees*. These are the other types of fees earned by the portfolio manager related to their fund-level activities (as opposed to related to underlying portfolio companies).

6.4 TYPES OF FUND-LEVEL FEES

The two most common fund-level fees charged to investors are management fees and carried interest.

6.4.1 Management Fees

A *management fee* is the fee charged to limited partners invested in a fund for managing their assets. In the vast majority of instances, a management fee is collected regardless of whether a fund generates a profit. A common

---

[1]G. Tan and M. Wutsthorn, "SEC Finds High Rate of Fee, Expense Violations at Private-Equity Firms," *Wall Street Journal*, May 6, 2014.

private equity fund management fee would be in the range of 1–2 percent of LP capital commitments. For private equity funds, it is not uncommon for management fees to typically be set at one level during the initial commitment period and then reduced during the investment period. An example of this would be a reduction of certain fixed percentage each year after the commitment period ends up until some floor amount.

6.4.2 Carried Interest

A management fee can be contrasted with a fee known as *carried interest*, a term we introduced in Chapter 3. Carried interest is a performance fee earned by the GP based on the performance of the fund. Carried interest may also be referred to as a *performance fee, incentive fee*, or *incentive allocation*. Carried interest provisions are typically paid out according to what is known as a *distribution waterfall*, or simply a *waterfall*. How this waterfall is commonly implemented would be for the GP to not earn a carried interest percentage until the limited partners in the fund have first earned a fixed stated percentage.

6.4.3 Management Fee and Fund Size

During the fundraising process another area that may present a conflict of interest relates to an agreement between the LPs and GP regarding the final total amount of capital that will be committed to the fund. This can also be called the *size of the fund* or the *assets under management* (AUM) of the fund. While the GP may earn a wide variety of fees, some of those fees (such as a management fee) are tied directly to the amount of AUM. The larger this figure the greater the fees earned by the GP. Additionally, with more capital to invest the GP may also gain access to larger deals once the fund is up and running, which could increase the overall fund performance and generate higher additional GP fees (i.e. incentive allocation).

With regard to the management fee in particular, as we noted earlier, this fee typically starts at a high figure, such as 2 percent, during the investment period and typically being charged after the fund has had its first closing. As noted, the fee is then reduced by a predetermined percentage each year after the commitment period ends up until some floor amount. Due to the fact that management fees continue to be charged throughout the life of the fund there is a potential for a conflict to arise with regard to the incentives of the GP and fund investors. Specifically, a GP may be incentivized to raise more capital than they could sensibly invest simply because they know they will be earning management fees from this capital.

In order to mitigate these potential conflicts, LPs often insist that GPs commit to invest a significant enough amount of capital in order to align the interests of the GP with investors. This is commonly referred to as the GP having enough *skin in the game*. Typically, the GP will commit to make a matching investment of a specific percentage of LP committed capital into the funds alongside the LPs up to a certain dollar amount. One issue with this is that the GP does not necessarily need to invest direct capital into a fund to meet these commitments and instead can satisfy these skin-in-the-game obligations through management fee offsets, thereby deferring fees owed to it as counting against these contribution amounts. Under this arrangement, while the GP is indeed still contributing money owed to it (i.e. the management fee) into the fund, the issue is that the GP could earn this management fee without first having the LPs invest any actual capital in the fund. In acknowledgment of this, many GPs will limit the amount of management fee offset that can be contributed, either in aggregate or on a yearly basis, and indeed contribute some actual capital to the fund as well, rather than simply relying entirely on offsets to fulfill this skin-in-the-game requirement.

Another way that LPs may seek to limit potential conflicts related to the GP raising too much capital for a particular fund would be to negotiate for reduced management fees as well as specific caps on the total amount of capital the GP can raise. These caps are sometimes called *hard caps* and would represent the total amount of capital a GP could raise form all investors as of the time of the final close, when the last of all LP capital has been committed.

6.4.4   Side Letters – Fee and Expense Considerations

As introduced in Chapter 3, a *side letter* can be defined as an agreement entered into directly between a GP and an LP whose terms are applicable only to that particular LP. This is as opposed to the more general fund terms outlined in the fund offering documents that would be applicable to all LPs invested in a particular fund. Some LPs may not negotiate any side letters with LPs and instead would be bound by the terms of the fund formation documents alone.

For a variety of reasons other LPs may wish to negotiate certain specific terms. This can be a modification of an existing fund feature. An example of this would be negotiating for a reduced management fee in exchange for committing a large amount of capital to a fund. Side letters could also be negotiated by investors seeking an additional new feature that they require such as an assertation from a GP that they will provide reporting on fund performance in a specific format required by an LP.

6.5 FEES AND PORTFOLIO COMPANY DIRECTORSHIP CONFLICTS

When a private equity fund makes investments in underlying portfolio companies, it is not uncommon for investment personnel of the GP such as portfolio managers to serve in some formal advisory capacity for the underlying portfolio company. One of the most common ways this is carried out is by having a GP employee, such as a portfolio manager or other relevant investment professional, serve on the board or as a director of the portfolio company. This is considered to be beneficial to the investment of the private equity fund because it allows the GP to have more direct control and insight into the management of the portfolio company. Such a relationship, however, can present conflicts of interest with regard to how those investments are managed on behalf of a particular fund or multiple funds managed by the GP.

When an individual, be it a portfolio manager or employee of the GP, serves in an advisory capacity or as a director, or on the board of a portfolio company, he typically receives compensation. When this fee is earned exclusively for directorship services, it can be referred to as a *director's fee*. For services that encompass either solely advisory or both advisory and directorship services, the broader term, *monitoring fees*, is often utilized.

Related conflicts may arise with regard to this compensation. The fund formation documents typically contemplate conflicts surrounding the fees earned and contain disclosure language on this matter. An example of these disclosures is as follows:

> The Partnership will be subject to various potential conflicts of interest. As an example, employees and members of the General Partner may receive director's fees or other types of compensation from portfolio companies in which the fund invests.

Related conflicts may also arise with regard to the relationship of the fees earned and something called a *management fee offset*, a term we referenced earlier in this chapter. As noted, a management fee is one of the many fees that LPs are charged for investing in a fund. It is typically paid to the GP in two stages. The first is during the so-called *commitment period* for a fund. This is the stage during which capital is being raised for the fund and LPs are agreeing to capital commitments. The second stage of the management fee typically comes about after the commitment period ends.

When we first raised the point that a representative of the GP serving on the board of a company was going to be paid compensation, did it raise any concerns? After all, isn't the GP already being compensated by LPs through the various fees, such as the management fee, being charged? Also, aren't the employees of the GP both potentially sharing in the fund's profits directly and being paid a salary by the GP? Doesn't this type of additional compensation represent double-dipping by the GP? Should the compensation go back into the pool of fund capital? As these questions demonstrate, there are a number of potential concerns LPs could raise with regard to the accounting for this underlying portfolio company directorship compensation.

To address these concerns, we can now return to the concept of a management fee offset. This is a common private equity fund provision that outlines that if the GP or a certain set of related or affiliated individuals or parties receive compensation from a portfolio company, then the future management fees that the fund would owe to the GP are reduced by that amount. Therefore, the fees earned serve as a credit to reduce the management fees and are not double-counted to enrich the GP to the detriment of the LPs.

This does not completely resolve the issue, however, because not all employees or related members of the GP are always covered by this offset provision, such as consultants, advisers, or other operating parties. In these cases, the compensation may be retained by these parties or the GP as the case may be. An example of the disclosure language in the fund offering documents relating to management fee offsets and non-covered persons would continue as follows:

> Although such fees may result in the triggering of a management fee offset provision there can be no assurances given that the Partnership will benefit in an economic manner from the fees paid by any particular portfolio company to the General Partner or its employees or members. Furthermore, it should be clarified that the management fee offset provision will not be generally applicable with regard to fees received by certain individuals or advisors to the General Partner.

6.5.1 Monitoring Fee Extension

When the GP earns fees by having employees advise or sit on the board of underlying portfolio companies, the GP will often require a portfolio company to enter into a contract outlining the terms of the advisory services, including the details of compensation to be paid to the GP. While there is nothing inherently wrong with such contracts, in many instances they often outline that the agreement will run for a specified time period. One issue that regulatory agencies in particular have raised is the length of these contracts. Some may surpass the life of the typically anticipated holding period of the private equity fund's investment in the underlying portfolio company, or in some cases these contracts may even have an indefinite term.[2] This practice of extending such agreement is known as *fee extension*.

Unreasonable fee extension practices can place unnecessary costs on the underlying portfolio companies and therefore hurt the overall performance of the funds all at the expense of the limited partners and to the benefit of the GP. Furthermore, the specific details of the agreements between GP and underlying portfolio companies may not be disclosed to a fund's limited partners, or such disclosures may be too vague to be useful, particularly in the eyes of regulatory agencies.

6.5.2 Monitoring Fee Acceleration

Another common clause contained in contracts between underlying portfolio companies and GP relates to situations where an event occurs which causes the GP to realize monitoring fees earlier than they normally would have under the terms of their contract. This typically occurs when the contract is terminated by *acceleration triggering events* which influence the ownership of the portfolio company. Examples of these would be as an initial public offering (IPO) or merger-and-acquisition activity at the underlying portfolio company. This is a practice known as *fee acceleration*.

There is nothing inherently wrong with the practice of fee acceleration; however, from a compliance perspective a key issue relates to the sufficiency of the disclosures surrounding this practice by the GP. This is particularly important, because as noted earlier the benefit of these fees accrues directly to the GP and not to the fund and limited partners. Depending on the terms of the original contract in place between the GP and the portfolio company, an acceleration triggering event could cause a large financial outflow from the portfolio company that normally would have taken place over several years. This is not to say that the GP should not be compensated for providing advisory and directorship services to the portfolio company, or that it is inherently inequitable for such services to be accelerated; however, regulators have continually reinforced the concept that limited partners need to be made aware of such agreements. This includes not only disclosing the potential that acceleration triggering events could occur, but actually making disclosures to limited partners when they occur.

---

[2]A. Bowden, "Spreading Sunshine in Private Equity," speech given at Private Fund Compliance Forum 2014, May 6, 2014.

6.6 OPERATING PARTNER FEES

A private equity fund may sometimes utilize the services of a third-party consultant known as an *operating partner*. In practice, they may be referred to under a number of different names, including *entrepreneur-in-residence, executive-in-residence, strategic advisor*, or simply *advisor*. Also due to the common use of operating partners in the venture capital space, in that context they may also be referred to as a *venture partner*. For simplicity we will use the term *operating partner*, but these other terms may be used interchangeably in the private equity industry.

6.6.1 Operating Partner Background and Roles

Operating partners are typically seasoned generalist executives, such as the former chief executive officer (CEO) of a well-known company, with track records of success. An example of this type of operating partner would be the role played by the former CEO of General Electric Co., Jack Welch, when he joined the private equity firm Clayton, Dubilier & Rice, Inc.[3] They may also be individuals with specific expertise, such as the law or technology, in certain industries. Operating partners may work with underlying portfolio companies in a variety of ways. For example, they could utilize their often extensive networks to facilitate useful introductions for portfolio companies. They could also be available to underlying portfolio companies on an as-needed consulting basis or serve as hands-on onsite consultants and coaches to further assist the underlying portfolio companies invested by the GP's funds in achieving operational goals, including realizing or improving profitability. The use of an operating partner is not required, and some have questioned whether their hands-on role adds any actual value over the existing work of the private equity fund managers themselves, particular because many of them may be self-described generalists.[4]

6.6.2 Compliance Challenges of Operating Partner Compensation

A key compliance issue surrounding operating partners relates to the ways they are compensated.

---

[3]K. Scannell and M. Murray, "Not-So-Retiring Welch Joins Clayton Dubilier as 'Special Partner' after Month on Sidelines," *Wall Street Journal*, October 3, 2001. Mr. Welch was technically a "special partner" of the firm advising on both management and leadership issues; however, his role also encompassed traditionally operating partner type roles.

[4]*See* R. Caldbeck, "Private Equity's Dirty Little Secret: Why Operating Partners Don't Make Sense," PE HUB Network, July 7, 2015.

Many operating partners are paid not by the GP but by portfolio companies or a private equity firm's funds. For clarification, if they are paid by a portfolio company, it is an expense which is ultimately passed on to the fund either entirely or in some form through the decreased profitability of the portfolio company.

These compensation arrangements can create a number of compliance challenges for GPs as well as potential conflicts of interest. While a fund's offering documents usually disclose this arrangement, the issue has been raised, especially by certain regulatory agencies, that the disclosures to limited partners regarding these arrangements are not sufficiently clear or equitable to investors.[5]

6.6.3   Operating Partners and Management Fee Offsets

To begin with, in many instances operating partners effectively look like a GP's other employees. One reasons for this is that just like the other employees of a firm, operating partners are often bound by exclusivity to a particular private equity firm. Operating partners also typically have access to and utilize the offices provided by the manager. They can also typically invest in the GP's private equity funds alongside the same terms as other employees, may be referred to as partners of the firm, may share in the overall profitability of the firm and particular funds, and may be listed in the GP's marketing materials and websites as full-time members of the firm's team.

As we outlined earlier, in a situation where an employee of a private equity firm receives fees from a portfolio company there is often a management fee offset applied. However, since the operating partners are not technically employees of the GP, no such offset in fees is applied to their services. Effectively therefore, a fund's limited partners and not the GP are paying for the services of the operating partner. While the details of such arrangements may be disclosed in some form in a fund's offering documents, limited partners may not realize that no offset is being applied and this fact may not be highlighted by GPs. Alternatively the disclosures in this area may be vague and not sufficiently thorough. Furthermore, even if LPs do realize this fact, there may be little that they can do about it in practice.

Let us consider the following representative series of events which could demonstrate potential inequalities in this relationship. First let us assume a GP selects an operating partner to work with at a particular portfolio company. Next, assume that the operating partner is successful in generating positive performance at the portfolio company. The operating partner is then

---

[5]A. Bowden, "Spreading Sunshine in Private Equity," speech given at Private Fund Compliance Forum 2014, May 6, 2014.

paid a fee of $100 for their services by the private equity fund managed by the GP into which an investment in the portfolio company has been made.

This positive portfolio company performance subsequently enhances the performance of the fund and generates a net $10,000 gain. Let us further assume that at this point in the distribution waterfall the GP earns a full 20 percent carried interest allocation of this $10,000, or $2,000. While there are of course other GP expenses involved, and the performance of the portfolio company could have been attributable to multiple factors aside from the contribution of the operating partner, for the purposes of demonstration this example shows how the limited partners of the fund paid the operating partner $100 for a gain to the GP of $2,000, and of course the fund would earn the remaining $8,000 less any management fees and other expenses. Even from a legal perspective if such arrangements are disclosed to meet the technicalities of the law, the argument can be raised that such relationships inordinately benefit the GP at the expense of the LPs. As noted before, many regulators have increasingly found that GPs' disclosures in this area were historically either nonexistent or insufficient.

Another factor to consider is that operating partners may frequently be held out by GPs to serve as differentiators from a marketing perspective of the quality of one private equity firm as compared to others. This is particularly true for high-profile executive operating partners. In this way, the role of the operating partners as marketing tools effectively assists the GP in raising the profile of a firm.

6.7   CASE STUDIES IN FEE AND EXPENSE MANAGEMENT

There have been a number of instances in which regulators have focused on the management and allocation of fees and expenses at private equity firms. Reviewing case studies in regulatory activity in this area can provide insights into activities that have presented compliance challenges in this area as well as recommended best practices.

6.7.1   Due Diligence Fees and Broken-Deal Expenses

In some instances, a GP may incur expenses related to a potential investment in an underlying portfolio company. These *due diligence fees* can relate to the analysis that the GP performs as part of its evaluation of the target portfolio company. Examples of these fees could include items ranging from broad research into geographic regions or industries to expenses related to specific deals, including the sourcing of a deal, deal-specific travel expenses for onsite visits with the portfolio company, and related professional fees and other research costs. To clarify, these due diligence fees are often expended at the GP level and then allocated among the relevant funds. This arrangement is often practical from a cost perspective since the research efforts of the GP may be beneficial to multiple funds. Furthermore, the individuals performing this research work for the GP and not individual funds, which have no employees. The alternative would be an arrangement where the individual funds each were responsible for performing their own research, which is not feasible in practice, and therefore an expense allocation approach is preferred.

Ultimately the GP may be seeking to make an investment in a company or in some instances, such as the strategy pursued by certain buyout funds, acquire the entire company. In some cases these deals are not completed. There could be a variety of reasons for this, including disputes over valuation, better investment alternatives located by the GP, and other GPs chosen by the portfolio company. When these are not completed the due diligence fees that were spent by the GP are commonly then referred to as *broken-deal expenses*. Other terms for this include *dead-deal expenses* or *aborted costs*.[6]

From a compliance perspective, GPs face a number of considerations relating to the transparency and methods surrounding the ways in which broken-deal expenses are allocated.

6.7.1.1 Case Study #1: Kohlberg Kravis Roberts & Co., LP One case of note in this area was brought by the US SEC in June 2015 against private equity firm Kohlberg Kravis Roberts & Co., LP (KKR). What follows is an excerpt of the allegations as outlined in the Securities and Exchange Commission (SEC) Administrative Proceeding in this matter, which provides background on the facts of the case, including a focus on the broken-deal expense allocation considerations:[7]

KKR's Private Equity Funds

5. KKR primarily advises and sources potential investments for its Flagship PE Funds and other advisory clients that invest capital for long-term appreciation through controlling ownership of portfolio companies or strategic minority positions in them.

---

[6]C. Demaria, "Private Equity: Don't Overlook the Hidden Costs," IP&E, May 2010.
[7]United States of America Before the Securities and Exchange Commission, Investment Advisors Act of 1940, Release No. 4131 / June 29, 2015, Administrative Proceeding File No. 3–16 656, In the Matter of Kohlberg Kravis Roberts & Co. L.P., Respondent, ORDER INSTITUTING CEASE-AND-DESIST PROCEEDINGS PURSUANT TO SECTION 203(k) OF THE INVESTMENT ADVISERS ACT OF 1940, MAKING FINDINGS, AND IMPOSING A CEASE-AND-DESIST ORDER.

As of December 31, 2014, KKR had over $51 billion in AUM in its private equity line of business.

6. KKR's Flagship PE Funds pursue investment strategies that are focused on investing in buyout and other opportunities primarily in one of three designated regions: North America, Europe, or Asia. The 2006 Fund was KKR's largest and most active flagship fund during the period 2006–2011. The 2006 Fund has to date invested over $17 billion in a total of 42 portfolio companies.

7. The limited partners in KKR's private equity funds include many large pension funds, university endowments and other large institutional investors, and high net worth individuals. As limited partners, these investors commit and subsequently contribute a specified amount of capital to a fund for its use to make qualifying investments during a specified period, which is usually six years.

8. KKR provides investment management and administrative services to its private equity funds. KKR charges its funds a management fee, which generally ranges from 1% to 2% of committed capital during the fund's investment period. As a GP in its private equity funds, KKR also receives a profits interest or carried interest of up to 20% of the net profits realized by the limited partners in the funds.

9. KKR enters into management or monitoring agreements with certain of its portfolio companies pursuant to which it receives periodic fees for providing management, consulting, and other services to the companies. KKR also receives transaction fees for providing financial, advisory, and other services in connection with specific transactions. KKR typically shares a portion of these fees with its Flagship PE Funds based on their proportional ownership of the underlying portfolio companies. KKR shares a portion of the fees with its Flagship PE Funds as a credit against the management fee that KKR charges them. Similarly, KKR shares with its Flagship PE Funds any break-up fees that it may receive from the termination of potential transactions based on the intended amount of a fund's proposed investment.

10. KKR's Flagship PE Funds are entitled to invest at least a minimum amount in every portfolio investment within its investment strategy under the applicable limited partnership agreements (LPAs). The 2006 Fund had a specified minimum portfolio investment level of $600 million at its inception before the threshold was lowered to $250 million in 2009.

KKR Co-Investors

11. Beyond capital from its Flagship PE Funds, KKR raises capital from coinvestors for its private equity transactions. For all KKR transactions regardless of size, the Flagship PE Fund LPAs reserve a percentage of fund portfolio investments for its executives, certain consultants, and others. KKR establishes dedicated co-investment vehicles for its executives, certain consultants, and others to make co-investments (the "KKR Partner Vehicles"). The 2006 Fund's LPA reserved up to 5% of every portfolio investment for KKR executives and up to 2.5% for certain consultants and others. These vehicles invested on a deal-by-deal basis with no specified committed capital. During the relevant period, these vehicles did not receive a share of monitoring, transaction, or break-up fees.

12. When the size of a private equity transaction exceeds a Flagship PE Fund's specified minimum investment level and any additional amounts determined to be appropriate for that fund's investment objectives, the LPAs contemplate that KKR may obtain additional capital necessary to complete the transaction from co-investors. For certain co-investors, KKR has established and manages separate co-investment vehicles or similar investment account arrangements independent of any specific transactions ("KKR Co-Investment Vehicles"). The KKR Co-Investment Vehicles invest in private equity transactions alongside the Flagship PE Funds either on a committed or noncommitted capital basis. The committed capital vehicles generally invest with KKR's Flagship PE Funds in all eligible co-investment opportunities consistent with the vehicles' investment mandates. The non-committed capital vehicles invest on a discretionary basis in eligible co-investment opportunities.

13. Additionally, KKR sponsored a publicly traded partnership that it established and managed independently of any specific private equity transactions. KKR offered co-investment opportunities to this publicly traded partnership from 2006 to 2008, as well as co-invested capital from its own balance sheet in one transaction in 2011 (collectively, with "KKR Partner Vehicles" and "KKR Co-Investment Vehicles," the "KKR Co-Investors").

14. When KKR requires more capital to complete a private equity transaction beyond what is available from its Flagship PE Funds and the KKR Co-Investors, KKR syndicates additional capital with respect to specific transactions to third-party

investors, limited partners in its funds, and participants in KKR Co-Investment Vehicles (collectively, the "Syndicated Co-Investors"). As Syndicated Co-Investors, these limited partners in KKR's funds, and other participants in KKR Co-Investment Vehicles are interested in making additional investments beyond what they are allocated in the ordinary course of KKR's general sourcing of transactions. Syndicated Co-Investors are therefore not included within the term "KKR Co-Investors."

15. From 2006 to 2011, KKR Co-Investors invested $4.6 billion alongside the $30.2 billion invested by KKR's Flagship PE Funds. KKR Partner Vehicles invested $750 million of the $4.6 billion, while the other KKR Co-Investors invested the remaining $3.9 billion. KKR Partner Vehicles invested in almost every transaction during the period, while the other KKR Co-Investors collectively invested in many of the transactions that exceeded the applicable flagship fund's minimum investment level.

Broken-Deal Expenses

16. KKR incurs significant expenses to source hundreds of potential investment opportunities for its Flagship PE Funds and KKR Co-Investors but consummates only a few of them each year. KKR is reimbursed directly from portfolio companies for the expenses incurred in connection with successful transactions. KKR is reimbursed for broken-deal expenses through a different mechanism described below.

17. Broken-deal expenses include research costs, travel costs and professional fees, and other expenses incurred in deal sourcing activities related to specific "dead deals" that never materialize. Broken-deal expenses also include expenses incurred by KKR to evaluate particular industries or geographic regions for buyout opportunities as opposed to specific potential investments, as well as other similar types of expenses.

18. Consistent with other LPAs during the relevant period, the 2006 Fund LPA requires the fund to pay "all" broken-deal expenses "incurred by or on behalf of" the fund "in developing, negotiating, and structuring prospective or potential [i]nvestments that are not ultimately made."

19. KKR is reimbursed for broken-deal expenses through fee sharing arrangements with its funds. Consistent with other

LPAs during the relevant period, pursuant to the 2006 Fund LPA, and the accompanying Management Agreement between KKR and the 2006 Fund, KKR shared a portion of its monitoring, transaction, and breakup fees with the 2006 Fund. More specifically, KKR reduced its management fee by 80% of the 2006 Fund's proportional share of those fees after deducting broken-deal expenses. Accordingly, KKR received 20% of those fees, and economically bore 20% of broken-deal expenses. The 2006 Fund in turn received 80% of those fees, and economically bore 80% of the broken -deal expenses.

20. While KKR bore 20% of broken-deal expenses pursuant to the 2006 Fund LPA fee sharing arrangement during the period, neither the 2006 Fund's LPA nor any other offering materials related to the 2006 Fund included any express disclosure that KKR did not allocate broken-deal expenses to KKR Co-Investors even though those vehicles participated in and benefited from KKR's general sourcing of transactions.

KKR's Historical Broken-Deal Expense Allocations

21. From 2006 to 2011, KKR incurred approximately $338 million in broken-deal expenses. KKR allocated broken-deal expenses based on the geographic region where the potential deal was sourced. For example, KKR allocated broken-deal expenses related to potential North American investments to the 2006 Fund. However, prior to 2011, KKR did not allocate or attribute any broken-deal expenses to KKR Co-Investors.

22. In June 2011, KKR recognized during an internal review that it lacked a written policy governing its broken-deal expense allocations. From July to October 2011, KKR drafted a policy to memorialize its expense allocation methodology at the time. Before 2011, KKR had not considered whether to allocate or attribute broken-deal expenses to KKR Co-Investors because in its view the Flagship PE Funds bore all broken-deal expenses less the portion of those expenses that KKR bore pursuant to its fee sharing provisions with the applicable funds.

23. While drafting its fund expense allocation policy, KKR considered whether to allocate or attribute broken-deal expenses to KKR Co-Investors. KKR decided at the time to allocate some share of broken-deal expenses to several committed capital co-investment vehicles. For its fiscal year ending December 31,

2011, KKR allocated $333 500 of broken-deal expenses to those co-investment vehicles.

24. In October 2011, KKR engaged a third-party consultant to review the firm's fund expense allocation practices. At the time, there was public awareness of heightened regulatory scrutiny on the private equity industry.

25. Effective January 1, 2012, KKR revised its broken-deal expense allocation methodology in the wake of the third-party consultant's review of KKR's fund expense allocation practices. In addition to committed capital co-investment vehicles, KKR's new allocation methodology began in 2012 to allocate or attribute a share of broken-deal expenses to KKR Partner Vehicles and other KKR Co-Investors. KKR's new methodology considered a number of factors, including the amount of committed capital, the amount of invested capital, and the percentage of transactions in which KKR Co-Investors were eligible to participate given the Flagship PE Funds' minimum investment rights. The new allocation methodology is not a subject of this Order.

OCIE Compliance Examination

26. In 2013, staff from the Commission's Office of Compliance Inspections and Examinations ("OCIEs") conducted an examination of KKR. One area of the examination concerned KKR's fund expense allocation practices. During the examination, KKR refunded its Flagship PE Funds, including the 2006 Fund, a total of $3.26 million in certain broken-deal expenses that KKR had allocated to them from 2009 to 2011. The $3.26 million represents a total of $4.07 million in broken-deal expenses less the portion of those expenses borne by KKR pursuant to its fee sharing arrangements with the applicable funds. KKR refunded the $3.26 million to the Flagship PE Funds in the first quarter of 2014.

Misallocation of Broken-Deal Expenses to Flagship PE Funds

27. Prior to the adoption by KKR of its new allocation methodology and except for partial allocations to certain committed capital co-investors in 2011, KKR did not allocate any share of broken-deal expenses to KKR Co-Investors, whether paid

by the KKR Co-Investors or KKR, for the relevant period even though KKR Co-Investors participated in and benefited from KKR's general sourcing of transactions. Nor did KKR expressly disclose in the LPAs or related offering materials that it did not allocate or attribute any broken-deal expenses to KKR Co-Investors. As a result of the absence of such disclosure, KKR misallocated $17.4 million in broken-deal expenses between its Flagship PE Funds and KKR Co-Investors during the relevant period, and, thus, breached its fiduciary duty as an investment adviser. The $17.4 million represents the sum total of $22.5 million in broken-deal expenses for the relevant period as calculated based on a methodology consistent with KKR's post-2012 allocation methodology less the portion of those expenses borne by KKR pursuant to its fee sharing arrangements with the applicable funds.

Deficient Compliance Policies and Procedures

28. In October 2008, KKR registered with the Commission as an investment adviser and became subject to the applicable Advisers Act rules governing registered investment advisers, including Section 206(4) of the Advisers Act and Rule 206(4)-7 thereunder, which requires registered investment advisers to adopt and implement written policies and procedures reasonably designed to prevent violations of the Advisers Act and its rules. KKR did not adopt and implement a written compliance policy or procedure governing its broken-deal expense allocation practices until 2011.

Ultimately KKR agreed to pay nearly $30 million to settle the charges, including a $10 million penalty.[8]

6.7.1.2 Case Study #2: Platinum Equity Advisors, LLC Another subsequent case involving allegations brought by the US SEC involving the allocation of broken-deal expenses, among other allegations, were the charges brought against Platinum Partners, and various related individuals, including the firm's founder Mark Nordlicht.[9] At the time of the filing of the case Platinum Management had its headquarters in New York, New York,

---

[8] Securities and Exchange Commission, "SEC Charges KKR with Misallocating Broken Deal Expenses," June 29, 2015.
[9] Securities and Exchange Commission, "SEC Charges Platinum Funds and Founder with Defrauding Investors," December 19, 2016.

and had reported on the firm's March 30, 2016, Form ADV that it had approximately $1 billion in AUM.[10] The following is a summary of the facts and outcome of the case from the SEC Administrative Proceeding in this matter:[11]

> According to the SEC's order, from 2004 to 2015, the three private equity funds invested in 85 companies, in which co-investors connected with Platinum also invested. During this time, Platinum incurred expenses related to potential fund investments that were not ultimately made, known as "broken-deal expenses." While the co-investors participated in Platinum's successful transactions and benefited from Platinum's sourcing of private equity transactions, Platinum did not allocate any of the broken-deal expenses to the co-investors. Instead, it allocated all broken-deal expenses to the private equity funds even though the agreements governing the funds did not disclose that the funds would be responsible for anything other than their own expenses. The Commission found that from Q2 2012 to 2015 (the applicable limitations period for disgorgement in this matter), the private equity funds were allocated $1,811,501 in broken-deal expenses that were not disclosed in the fund agreements. In addition, Platinum did not adopt and implement a written compliance policy or procedure governing its broken-deal expense allocation practices. The SEC's order finds that Platinum violated Sections 206(2) and 206(4) of the Advisers Act, and Rule 206(4)-7 thereunder. Without admitting or denying the findings in the SEC's order, Platinum consented to the entry of a cease-and-desist order and agreed to pay a total of $1,902,132 in disgorgement and prejudgment interest and a $1.5 million civil penalty.

In December 2016, US federal agents arrested Mr. Nordlicht and six others on charges related to a $1 billion fraud that led the firm to be operated like an alleged Ponzi scheme.[12]

---

[10]*Securities and Exchange Commission v. Platinum Management (NY) LLC et al.*, available at: https://www.sec.gov/litigation/complaints/2016/comp-pr2016-267.pdf.

[11]Securities and Exchange Commission, Administrative Proceeding File No. 3–18194, "SEC Charges Investment Adviser for Allocating All Broken Deal Expenses to Private Equity Funds without Disclosure," September 21, 2017.

[12]A. Stevenson, "Platinum Hedge Fund Executives Charged with $1 Billion Fraud," *DealBook*, December 19, 2016.

6.7.2 Other Fees and Expenses – Case Study #3: Potomac Asset Management Co.

The key entities in this matter were Potomac Asset Management Company, Inc. ("PAMCO") and Goodloe E. Byron, Jr. ("Byron") (collectively, "Respondents"). The SEC brought a case against PAMCO, a registered investment adviser, and Byron, its principal, relating to the improper allocation of fees and expenses to two private equity fund clients, Potomac Energy Fund, LP ("Fund I"), and Potomac Energy Fund II, LP ("Fund II") (collectively, "the Funds").

The following summary outlines key facts from the SEC Administrative Proceeding in this matter:[13]

11. The Funds' LPAs provided terms for, among other things, the calculation, and payment of capital contributions by the partners. Generally, partners of the Funds committed a specific amount of capital to either Fund I or Fund II pursuant to periodic capital calls by the GP, and a percentage of their commitment was invested in Fund portfolio companies. The LPAs required all partners to make their capital contribution payments by the due date in the capital call notice made by the GP.

12. The LPAs also set forth the amount and manner of management fees paid by the Funds to PAMCO, as well as the Funds' responsibility to pay organizational and partnership expenses. According to the LPAs, PAMCO was entitled to receive an annual management fee equal to 2% of committed capital, which was to be offset by a percentage of PAMCO's other income, including consulting, and other fees received by PAMCO or its affiliates from portfolio companies. PAMCO bore responsibility for paying manager expenses, which were the costs and expenses of PAMCO for normal operating overhead of the adviser, including the compensation of PAMCO's employees, the cost of office rent related to PAMCO's business, and PAMCO's own regulatory expenses.

---

[13]United States of America Before the Securities and Exchange Commission, Investment Advisors Act of 1940, Release No. 4131 / June 29, 2015, Administrative Proceeding File No. 3–16656, In the Matter of Kohlberg Kravis Roberts & Co. L.P., Respondent., ORDER INSTITUTING CEASE-AND DESIST PROCEEDINGS PURSUANT TO SECTION 203(k) OF THE INVESTMENT ADVISERS ACT OF 1940, MAKING FINDINGS, AND IMPOSING A CEASE-AND-DESIST ORDER.

B. PAMCO's Improper Use of Fund Assets to Pay Portfolio Company Fees

13. The LPAs contemplated that PAMCO may provide services to portfolio companies held by the Funds in exchange for fees or other remuneration. Between 2012 and 2013, PAMCO provided services to a portfolio company of Fund I that generated $2.2 million in charges ("the Portfolio Company Fees"). Instead of charging the portfolio company directly, PAMCO, at Byron's direction, allocated to Fund I, and caused Fund I to pay, the Portfolio Company Fees.

14. Neither the LPA nor the Private Placement Memorandum (PPM) authorized PAMCO to charge the Portfolio Company Fees to Fund I. Moreover, Respondents did not disclose to Fund I's limited partners the misuse of fund assets, and Respondents could not effectively consent to this use of fund assets on behalf of Fund I because they were conflicted as the recipients of the Portfolio Company Fees. The portfolio company ultimately reimbursed the cost of the Portfolio Company Fees.

C. Failure to Offset Advisory Fees

15. Pursuant to the LPA, PAMCO was required to reduce the Fund I management fees by 50% of portfolio company remuneration, after adjusting for taxes, and other costs. However, PAMCO did not offset its receipt of $2.2 million in Portfolio Company Fees against Fund I's management fee. As a result, PAMCO collected $726 000 more in management fees from Fund I than it was entitled to receive.

D. Improper Use of the Funds' Assets to Pay Adviser-Related Expenses

16. PAMCO, at Byron's direction, used the Funds' assets to pay various adviser-related expenses, including the following: (i) compensation to a member of PAMCO's investment team; (ii) office rent and other operational expenses; and (iii) certain costs Respondents incurred arising from an examination by the OCIEs and an investigation by the staff of the Commission's Division of Enforcement ("Commission Enforcement staff"). The use of the Funds' assets to pay for these expenses was not

authorized by the Funds' governing documents or disclosed to the Funds' limited partners. Respondents could not effectively consent to this use of fund assets on behalf of the Funds because they were conflicted as the beneficiaries of the Funds' payments for adviser-related expenses.

17. The use of the Funds' assets to pay adviser-related expenses was contrary to Fund I's PPM dated May 2010 and later, and Fund II's PPM dated February 2013, which PAMCO provided to the limited partners and contained the following disclosure: In general, PAMCO shall bear compensation and expenses of its employees and fees and expenses for administrative, clerical, and related support services, maintenance of books and records for the Fund, office space and facilities, utilities, and telephone insofar as they relate to the investment activities of the Fund. All other expenses will be borne by the Fund.

18. Compensation to Member of PAMCO Investment Team 18. In April 2011, PAMCO confirmed its arrangement with an individual ("Individual A") who had been working alongside other members of the PAMCO management team since January 1, 2011. Specifically, PAMCO provided Individual A with a letter confirming his "employment" with PAMCO, his title of "Principal" and the requirement that he perform a minimum of 35 hours of "consulting" per week to PAMCO. Internally, PAMCO did not record or otherwise identify Individual A as a salaried employee of PAMCO. Instead, PAMCO treated him as a third-party consultant. From 2012 to 2015, Individual A submitted fees and expenses to PAMCO on a monthly basis totaling $489 121, which PAMCO, at Byron's direction, in turn, allocated to the Funds, and caused the Funds to pay.

19. The vast majority of services Individual A provided, and the manner in which he provided them, were typical of the services advisory employees provide to private equity funds in exchange for a management fee. In various communications with the limited partners and others, including those contained in Fund II's February 2013 PPM, PAMCO not only represented Individual A to be a "Principal" of the adviser, but also a member of the adviser's "Investment Team." The investment team played a comprehensive role in creating and implementing PAMCO's investment strategy. Indeed, Individual A engaged in typical adviser activities, including attending investor meetings, communicating with investors, selecting investments, and working

with the Funds' auditor and third-party administrator to prepare audited financial statements.

20. Moreover, Individual A's association with PAMCO did not have the characteristics of a third-party consultant relationship. He worked full-time in PAMCO's Frederick, Maryland office, was required to work a minimum of 35 hours per week, received health and other benefits from PAMCO, and performed the same or similar job functions as other members of PAMCO's investment team, including those who held the same title, and whose compensation was not charged to the Funds.

21. PAMCO was not authorized to charge Individual A's compensation and expenses to the Funds. Individual A was effectively an employee of PAMCO and provided the same advisory services as other employees whose compensation PAMCO paid out of the management fee. ii. PAMCO's Rent and Other Operational Expenses

22. Between 2013 and 2014, PAMCO, at Byron's direction, allocated to the Funds, and caused the Funds to pay for, PAMCO's office rent and other operational expenses, totaling $212 252, despite language in the Funds' PPMs and LPAs that PAMCO was to bear these expenses. iii. PAMCO's Regulatory Costs

23. The Funds' LPAs provided that the Funds would be responsible for the cost of legal and other professional services provided to the Funds in connection with the administration or operation of the Funds. In 2013, the Commission Exam staff conducted an examination of PAMCO and, in January 2015, PAMCO received notice that the Commission Enforcement staff was conducting an investigation of, among other things, PAMCO's allocation of expenses to the Funds. PAMCO incurred expenses in connection with responding to the exam review and the enforcement investigation. PAMCO, at Byron's direction, allocated to the Funds, and caused the Funds to pay for, certain of these expenses, totaling $2482.

24. Allocating these expenses to the Funds was improper since they arose from regulatory expenses incurred by PAMCO, the investment adviser (and not the Funds) and the Funds' governing documents did not otherwise authorize PAMCO to charge the Funds for its own regulatory costs.

25. Altogether, between 2012 and 2015, PAMCO improperly used the Funds' assets to pay $703 855 in adviser-related expenses.

E. Material Omissions in Forms ADV Concerning PAMCO's Compensation

26. PAMCO's Forms ADV Parts 1 and 2 for 2012 through 2014 did not disclose that PAMCO charged the Funds for the adviser-related expenses discussed above.

27. Item 5.E of Part 1 of Form ADV for 2012, 2013 and 2014 required that an investment adviser identify the ways it is compensated for providing advisory services. In response, PAMCO indicated only that it received a percentage of AUM and performance-based fees. PAMCO did not disclose that, in addition to such amounts, the Funds paid a portion of PAMCO's operating expenses, which constituted compensation to the adviser, even though Item 5.E required an investment adviser to indicate whether it received "other" forms of compensation, and to specify the nature of that compensation.

28. Item 5.A of Part 2A of Form ADV for 2012, 2013, and 2014 required that an investment adviser describe in its brochure how the adviser is compensated for advisory services. With respect to the Funds, PAMCO indicated that it would receive "an annual fee equal to 2.0% of the total capital commitments of the partners." PAMCO did not disclose that, in addition to such amounts, the Funds paid a portion of PAMCO's operating expenses, which constituted compensation to the adviser.

29. Byron reviewed and ultimately approved PAMCO's Forms ADV and amendments thereto for years 2012, 2013, and 2014, which he caused to be filed with the Commission in order to maintain PAMCO's registration as an investment adviser.

F. Violation of the Custody Rule by Failing to Disclose Related Party Transactions in the Funds' Audited Financial Statements in Violation of GAAP

30. As a registered investment adviser with custody of client assets, PAMCO was required to comply with custody rule. PAMCO, as part of its reliance on the exception to the custody rule for an adviser to a pooled investment vehicle found in Advisers Act Rule 206(4)-2(b)(4), engaged a PCAOB registered auditor as the Funds' independent public accountant to audit their

financial statements for the fiscal years ended December 31, 2011, 2012, 2013, and 2014. To comply with the custody rule, PAMCO needed to provide the Funds' limited partners with GAAP-compliant financial statements within 120 days of the end of the fiscal year pursuant to the custody rule exception found in Advisers Act Rule 206(4)-2(b)(4).

31. GAAP provides disclosure requirements for related party relationships and transactions in financial statements. (See, generally, Financial Accounting Standards Board (FASB) Accounting Standards Codification (ASC) 850-10-50). PAMCO and the Funds were related parties because, for purposes of GAAP, Byron had common control over each entity since Byron formed and directed all investment activities and operating policies of each entity. Individual A was a related party of PAMCO and the Funds because he, too, was directly or indirectly under Byron's common control. (See ASC 850-10-20, et seq.) This common control allowed Byron to (i) pay PAMCO $2.2 million for the Portfolio Company Fees with Fund I's assets; and (ii) pay PAMCO $703 855 for adviser-related expenses, including Individual A's compensation, PAMCO's office rent and other operational costs, and PAMCO's own regulatory expenses. Fund I's payments to PAMCO for the Portfolio Company Fees and the Funds' payment of PAMCO's adviser-related expenses were material, related party transactions in fiscal years 2011 through 2014.

32. Fund I's audited financial statements for 2011 through 2014 and Fund II's audited financial statements for 2013 and 2014 were not in compliance with GAAP. The Funds' audited financial statements did not disclose (i) the nature of the related party relationship with Individual A, and (ii) the material related party transactions concerning PAMCO's receipt of $2.2 million in Portfolio Company Fees from Fund I and the Funds' payment of certain adviser-related operating expenses. In addition, the Funds' 2013 and 2014 audited financial statements violated the custody rule because they were significantly delayed and not distributed to the Funds' limited partners within 120 days of the end of the respective fiscal years as required under Rule 206(4)-2(b)(4).

33. Byron reviewed and ultimately approved the Funds' audited financial statements for 2011 through 2014. Byron signed the

Funds' management representation letters to the Funds' auditor, which inaccurately stated that related party relationships and transactions had been properly recorded and disclosed in the financial statements.

34. The audit reports from the PCAOB-registered auditor attached to the financial statements for Fund I's fiscal year-ends 2011 through 2014 and Fund II's fiscal year-ends for 2013 and 2014 stated that the auditor had audited each financial statement in accordance with generally accepted auditing standards, and included unqualified opinions, in each year, that the financial statements were presented fairly in conformity with GAAP. This was inaccurate, as the audited financial statements were not GAAP compliant since they failed to disclose related party relationships and material related party transactions.

35. Because the audited financial statements were not GAAP compliant and, in certain instances, not distributed to the Funds' limited partners within 120 days of the end of the fiscal year, PAMCO, with substantial assistance from Byron, failed to meet the requirements for the exception to the custody rule found in Advisers Act Rule 206(4)-2(b)(4), for fiscal years 2011 through 2014.

G. Byron's Failure to Make Timely Capital Contributions to the Funds

36. As the owner and controlling person of the GPs of both Funds, Byron was obligated under the LPAs to make capital contributions on a timely basis to the Funds as follows: The GP or its Affiliate shall contribute in cash to the capital of the Partnership an amount equal to not less than 1% of the total amount contributed to the Partnership by all Partners (including the GP). Such amount shall be contributed at such times as the Capital Commitments of the Limited Partners are called for.

37. Byron failed to cause the GPs to timely contribute actual cash to the Funds, as required, in response to each capital call. Instead, Byron caused the Funds to record receivables for certain unpaid capital contributions.

38. Byron's failure to cause the GPs to contribute actual cash to the Funds on a timely basis was not adequately disclosed to the Funds' limited partners.

H. Failure to Adopt and Implement Reasonably Designed Compliance Policies and Procedures

39. From 2012 through 2014, PAMCO's compliance manual did not include policies and procedures to address allocations of expenses between PAMCO and the Funds, Byron's control of related parties, and how that control might affect related party transactions and required disclosures. In particular, the manual lacked specific provisions reasonably designed to prevent violations of the Advisers Act arising from failures to disclose material conflicts of interest or to act in the best interest of clients in connection with expense allocation and related party transactions involving PAMCO's private fund clients.

Without admitting or denying the SEC's allegations, Potomac agreed to pay a $300,000 civil penalty, for which it is jointly and severally liable with its principal.

6.7.3 Other Fees and Expenses – Case Study #4: Lincolnshire Management

The case involves a firm named Lincolnshire Management, Inc. ("LMI"). During the relevant time period, LMI served as the investment adviser for Lincolnshire Equity Fund, LP ("LEF") and Lincolnshire Equity Fund II, LP ("LEF II"). The funds were formed to make private equity investments in middle-market companies. The SEC charged the firm with misallocation of portfolio company expenses as described in the following summary from the SEC Administrative Proceeding in this matter:

7. During the relevant time period, LMI advised multiple private equity funds, including LEF, and LEF II. LEF and LEF II had separate LPAs and distinct sets of limited partner investors. The LPA for each fund governs the rights and obligations of its limited partners, including their obligations to pay advisory and other fees and expenses to LMI pursuant to a separate management agreement between each fund and LMI.

8. In April 1997, LMI caused LEF to acquire PCS through a $5 million equity investment. PCS was a California-based company that primarily serviced and repaired computer hard disk drives.

9. In September 2001, LMI caused LEF II to acquire CTS through an $8.5 million equity investment. CTS was a Texas-based

company that primarily serviced and repaired laptop computers and handheld devices.

10. The investment opportunity in CTS was brought to LMI's attention by PCS management. The LMI investment committee believed PCS and CTS would have valuable synergies and that each company would complement the other. However, by 2001, LEF's commitment period was closed and it could not call capital to make a new acquisition. Therefore, LMI caused LEF II to acquire CTS with the intention of integrating PCS and CTS where possible and ultimately marketing the two companies for a combined sale. In connection with the 2001 acquisition of CTS, LMI disclosed to LEF's and LEF II's limited partners its intention to integrate and jointly sell the two portfolio companies. In quarterly fund disclosures thereafter, LMI provided regular updates to LEF's and LEF II's limited partners on the operations of the respective portfolio companies, together with additional information regarding the progress toward integration and plans to sell the two companies together.

11. From at least July 2009 to January 2013, PCS was the only portfolio company held by LEF.

12. LMI entered into consulting agreements with each portfolio company that was owned by an LMI-advised fund. Pursuant to the terms of the consulting agreements, LMI charged each portfolio company an annual fee in exchange for rendering consulting and advisory services concerning the portfolio company's financial and business affairs, its relationships with lenders, and the operation and expansion of its business. With regard to LEF II, a percentage of any consulting fees paid to LMI, as well as certain other fees charged by LMI, were used to offset the limited partners' share of the management fees owed to LMI under the LPA.

13. LMI entered into consulting agreements with PCS and CTS in April 1997 and September 2001, respectively. CTS paid LMI $250 000 annually under its consulting agreement; $125 000 of the $250 000 was used to offset management fees owed to LMI. PCS also paid LMI $250 000 annually during the relevant period, but was unable to pay its consulting fee from 2001 through 2004 based on its financial condition. No portion of PCS's $250 000 annual consulting fee was used to offset management fees.

B. The Integration of PCS and CTS

14. Although LEF could not purchase CTS because its commitment period had closed, LMI believed that owning both PCS and CTS together would create value for each set of limited partners in LEF and LEF II. Accordingly, in September 2001, LMI caused LEF II to purchase CTS.

15. At the time LEF II purchased CTS, in 2001, LMI disclosed to the limited partners of both LEF and LEF II that it believed there were synergies between PCS and CTS that would provide customers with a single venue to support their personal computing and mobile device support needs. LMI believed that these synergies would allow the companies to compete more effectively in the industry and would add value to both companies. LMI further disclosed its intention to exit the PCS and CTS investments by combining both companies and selling them together. As contemplated, the management of PCS and CTS – at LMI's direction – took various steps to integrate certain operations of the two companies.

16. By 2005, PCS and CTS had integrated their financial accounting systems, and a number of business and operational functions, including all payroll and 401(k) administration, and substantial portions of their respective human resources, marketing, and technology.

17. PCS and CTS also integrated their financing needs. For example, the two companies entered into a line of credit on a joint and several basis.

18. The integration of PCS and CTS operations extended to subsidiaries outside the United States. For example, a wholly owned subsidiary of PCS in Singapore supplied various parts and labor to CTS at cost. Likewise, CTS sold parts to various PCS subsidiaries at cost.

19. By March 2009, to further streamline operations and costs, LMI helped recruit a joint management team for PCS and CTS, including a joint chief executive officer and chief financial officer. Additionally, PCS and CTS shared a joint head of sales and controller.

20. From at least March 2009 to January 2013, the two separately owned companies had a joint "PCS CTS" logo that was used in marketing, advertising, and on employees' business cards.

21. From at least 2005 to January 2013, PCS and CTS were integrated and, in certain respects, operating as one company, although they remained two separate legal entities with separate audited financial statements.

22. During the relevant period, LMI made three separate efforts to sell the two companies jointly. In 2003 and later in 2007, LMI retained investment banks who developed marketing materials aimed at selling the two companies as a single entity under the joint "PCS CTS" marketing logo. While these two efforts were unsuccessful, in January 2013, PCS and CTS were sold together to a single buyer.

C. Expense Allocation Policy

23. Although certain operations of PCS and CTS were integrated, they were owned by separately advised LMI funds – LEF and LEF II, respectively – and LMI owed a fiduciary duty to each fund.
24. From at least 2005 until January 2013, PCS and CTS generally allocated expenses that benefitted both companies based on the proportion of each company's revenue to the combined revenue of PCS and CTS. For example, in 2011, the combined revenue of PCS and CTS was approximately $120 million, with approximately $22 million (or 18%) attributable to PCS. Under the expense allocation policy, PCS was required to pay 18% of any relevant shared expense.
25. There was no written guidance or detail that accompanied this expense allocation policy. While the expense allocations were documented in the CTS and PCS financial records and subject to review during the respective annual audits, neither CTS nor PCS had any written agreements relating to sharing or allocating expenses. There were no documents setting forth the parties' respective rights and obligations toward each other.
26. The shared expenses of PCS and CTS related to administrative fees associated with: payroll and 401(k) benefits; information technology; sales and marketing; and corporate management.

D. Misallocated Expenses

27. From at least 2005 to January 2013, PCS and CTS shared numerous annual expenses. While generally the shared expenses were properly allocated and documented in certain instances, a portion of the shared expenses was misallocated and went undocumented, which resulted in one portfolio company paying more than its share of expenses that benefitted both companies.
28. Prior to the integration of PCS and CTS, PCS utilized administrator services to assist with payroll and 401(k) benefits.

PCS paid these administrators a fee for the services they provided.

29. After PCS and CTS were integrated, management decided to use PCS's third-party administrators to provide payroll services, and to administer the 401(k) programs for both PCS's and CTS's employees. Notwithstanding the fact that the related administrative expenses covered CTS employees, PCS paid all of the administrative expenses for at least eight years and did not receive any reimbursement from CTS. During this eight-year period, the estimated administrative expenses paid by PCS averaged approximately $25 000 annually.

30. In addition to these administrative expenses, there were several employees who performed work that benefitted both PCS and CTS, but their salaries were not allocated between the two companies, as required under the policy.

31. PCS's wholly owned Singapore subsidiary performed services for, and sold supplies and parts to, CTS at cost. For example, in 2011 PCS Singapore sold approximately $150 000 in supplies and parts to CTS at cost. However, CTS did not contribute to the general overhead costs of running the Singapore subsidiary. Notably, there were PCS Singapore employees devoted solely to performing work for CTS. CTS reimbursed PCS for the salaries of those specific employees but did not pay any of the costs associated with their office space, their computers, or the local business licenses that PCS had to maintain in order to do business in Singapore.

32. When PCS and CTS were sold in January 2013, PCS's and CTS's then-existing executives were paid transaction bonuses. LEF, which owned PCS, paid 10% of the transaction bonuses of two executives who were solely CTS employees.

E. LMI Failed to Adopt and Implement Policies and Procedures to Prevent Violations Arising from Integrating PCS and CTS

33. On March 28, 2012, LMI registered with the Commission as an investment adviser and became subject to the Advisers Act rules relating to registered advisers, including the requirement to adopt and implement written policies and procedures reasonably designed to prevent violations of the Advisers Act and its rules.

34. At the time LMI registered as an investment adviser certain operations of PCS and CTS were integrated. Although PCS and

CTS were integrated, they were owned by separately managed LMI funds and LMI owed a fiduciary duty to each fund.

35. Despite LMI's integration of PCS and CTS, LMI did not adopt or implement any written policies or procedures designed to prevent violations of the Advisers Act arising from such integration.

Without admitting or denying the findings, Lincolnshire agreed to cease and desist from committing or causing future violations of these provisions and to pay $1.5 million in disgorgement plus $358,112 in prejudgment interest and a $450,000 penalty.[14]

6.7.4   Other Fees and Expenses – Case Study #5: Apollo

In August 2016, the SEC announced that four private equity fund advisers affiliated with Apollo Global Management agreed to a $52.7 million settlement for misleading fund investors about fees and a loan agreement and failing to supervise a senior partner who charged personal expenses to the funds. The SEC press release relating to this case summarized the matter as follows:[15]

An SEC investigation found that the Apollo advisers failed to adequately disclose the benefits they received to the detriment of fund investors by accelerating the payment of future monitoring fees owed by the funds' portfolio companies upon the sale or IPO of those companies. The lump sum payments received by the Apollo advisers essentially reduced the portfolio companies' value prior to their sale or IPO and reduced amounts available for distribution to fund investors.

The SEC also found that one of the Apollo advisers failed to disclose certain information about interest payments made on a loan between the adviser's affiliated general partner and five funds. The purpose of the loan was to defer taxes on carried interest due the general partner. The loan agreement obligated the general partner to pay interest to the funds during the course of the loan, and the funds' financial statements disclosed that interest was accruing as an asset of the funds. But that interest was instead

---

[14]Securities and Exchange Commission, "SEC Charges New York Based Private Equity Fund Adviser with Misallocation of Portfolio Company Expenses," September 22, 2014.

[15]Securities and Exchange Commission, "Apollo Charged with Disclosure and Supervisory Failures," August 23, 2016.

ultimately allocated solely to the general partner, which made the disclosures in the financial statements misleading. . . . According to the SEC's order instituting the settled administrative proceeding, Apollo's supervisory failures pertain to a then-senior partner at the firm who was twice caught improperly charging personal items and services to Apollo-advised funds and their portfolio companies. Other than verbally reprimanding the partner and requiring repayment of improperly submitted expenses, Apollo took no further remedial or disciplinary steps on either occasion. A firm-wide expense review eventually revealed even more personal expenses the partner improperly charged to fund clients, and this led to the partner's separation from the firm.

Apollo agreed to cease and desist from further violations without admitting or denying the findings, and must pay $37,527 million in disgorgement, $2,727,552 in interest, and a $12.5 million penalty.

6.7.5   Improper Fee Withdrawals — Case Study #6: SLRA

Another area related to fees and expenses that has come under regulatory scrutiny relates to the withdrawal of funds for related-party transactions. A February 2017 US SEC order involving an individual named Scott M. Landress and his investment advisory firm SLRA, Inc. deals with this issue. Mr. Landress was a principal of a group of affiliated entities doing business under the name Liquid Realty Partners ("Liquid Realty"), which formed the Liquid Realty Partners III, LP and Liquid Realty Partners III-A, LP in 2006 for the purpose of investing in securities in the form of real estate private equity secondary transactions. In 2012, the *Wall Street Journal* reported that Liquid Realty laid off the firm's entire investment staff after determining it couldn't raise new funds.[16] The firm's investors included pension funds and university endowments, including Harvard University and Duke University.

The SEC Press Release dated February 7, 2017, described the SEC findings as follows:[17]

The SEC's order finds that Scott M. Landress formed the funds to invest in real estate trusts with underlying investments in

---

[16]C. Karmin, "Short of New Funds, Firm Takes a 'Pause,'" *Wall Street Journal*, April 3, 2012.

[17]U.S. Securities and Exchange Commission Press Release, "Private Equity Adviser Barred from Industry for Improper Withdrawal from Funds," February 7, 2017.

properties throughout the UK. His investment advisory firm SLRA Inc. earned management fees based on the net asset value of the underlying investments. SLRA's fees shrank and its management costs increased as real estate property values fell during the financial crisis, and the funds' limited partners declined several requests by Landress for additional compensation to cover the shortfalls.

According to the SEC's order, Landress directed SLRA to withdraw 16.25 million pounds from the funds in early 2014, purportedly as payment for several years of services provided by an affiliate. He subsequently transferred the money to his personal account. SLRA and Landress did not disclose the related-party transaction and the resulting conflicts of interest until after the money had been withdrawn.

Furthermore, the SEC in an Administrative Proceeding outlined that approximately one month after directing the transfer of the 16.25 million pounds, Mr. Landress for the first time asserted that he had earned the fees.[18] The SEC also outlined that:

Landress asserted that these services were allowed by the Funds' Limited Partnership Agreements and performed pursuant to an oral agreement entered into in 2006 with Landress acting both on behalf of the Funds (through their general partner) and on behalf of the Liquid Realty affiliate that performed the services.

The administrative order also clarifies,

Prior to this time, the Funds and the Limited Partners were not aware of the existence of these claimed fees or the retention of the Liquid Realty affiliate to perform any such services for additional compensation. Indeed, it was only during the early fall of 2013, as Landress began to prepare to withdraw these fees, that Liquid Realty's Finance Director and the Funds' auditors first learned of these fees.[19]

---

[18]P. Brush, "SEC Bars Real Estate Investor over His $20 M Fee," *Law360*, February 7, 2017.

[19]*See* United States of America Before the Securities and Exchange Commission, Investment Advisers Act of 1940 Release No. 4641 / February 7, 2017; Investment Company Act of 1940 Release No. 32740 / February 7, 2017; Administrative Proceeding File No. 3–17 826, In the Matter of SLRA Inc. as Successor Entity to LIQUID REALTY ADVISORS III, LLC and SCOTT M. LANDRESS.

Further aggravating the issue is that the SEC administrative order outlines that:

- From 2006 to 2014 in addition to not disclosing the existence of the service fees in any communications with the Funds or Limited Partners he also did not disclose them to Advisory Committee which was supposed to consist of representatives of the Limited Partners and possessing the authority to review and approve of certain actions of the GP.
- From 2006 to 2012 the audited financial statements of the Funds did not account for or disclose these Service Fees.

With such a lack of communication, limited partners and auditors would not have been afforded a chance to properly vet this relationship. The SEC outlines as much in their administrative order in this case by stating, "Even if Landress had in fact hired a Liquid Realty affiliate in 2006 to perform services for the Funds, the retention of an affiliate of the General Partner and LRA III was a related-party transaction and created a conflict of interest."

The SEC permanently barred Mr. Landress from the securities industry and that he must pay a $1.25 million penalty to settle charges.

6.8 SUMMARY

We began this chapter with an introduction to the compliance considerations surrounding private equity fees and expenses. Our discussion began with an overview of the distinction between fees and expenses and why they are important from a compliance perspective. We next discussed the differences between transaction and fund-level fees and reviewed different types of fund-level fees. An examination of other related fee considerations, including side letters, portfolio directorship conflicts, and fee accelerations and extensions was conducted. We then analyzed management fee offsets, fee extensions, and accelerations as well as operating partner fees. The chapter concluded with regulatory case studies in fee and expense management. In the next chapter, we switch topics from conflicts of interest to the compliance-related aspects of private equity technology, business continuity, and cybersecurity, which have become increasingly important in the management of modern private equity firms.

CHAPTER 7

Private Equity Compliance Technology, Business Continuity, and Cybersecurity

7.1 INTRODUCTION TO THE ROLE OF TECHNOLOGY IN PRIVATE EQUITY COMPLIANCE

Technology has played an increasingly important role in the management and operations of private equity firms. This is true across all aspects of a private equity firm's business, ranging from investment management through to operations. As technology has evolved it has also played an important role in influencing compliance management at both the general partner (GP) and fund level.

Increasingly GPs have devoted more of their compliance budgets toward technology-related initiatives. Similarly, the resources of a private equity firm's information technology function and associated budgets are increasingly focused on compliance-related tasks. There are a number of reasons for this. First, as noted earlier, with technology come a number of process efficiencies that GPs and their investors can benefit from.

Second, limited partners (LPs) who invest in private equity do not typically focus exclusively on this asset class and also typically allocate to other types of alternatives investments such as hedge funds and real estate funds as well as traditional fund managers. This is particularly true of large institutional investors such as pension funds and endowments and foundations. Other areas of the asset management industry have been strong adopters of information technology–related compliance initiatives. This has been particularly true of heavy users of technology to facilitate compliance oversight of funds that execute large volumes of trades, such as high-frequency-trading hedge fund strategies. As investors have seen the ways in which these other asset managers have embraced technology in all areas of their firms, including compliance, they have increasingly pressured private equity managers make similar technological improvements in their firms.

7.2   REGULATORY FOCUS ON TECHNOLOGY COMPLIANCE

Regulatory agencies that oversee private equity funds have increasingly focused on the role technology plays. This includes providing guidance on the ways technology should be utilized and a focus on technology-related expense management.

7.3   CYBERSECURITY COMPLIANCE IMPLICATIONS

While technology has afforded GPs and their investors a number of benefits and efficiencies, it has also brought with it a number of new and increasingly complex challenges. One area rife with the greatest potential risks is cybersecurity. *Cybersecurity* is a broad term without a single universally recognized definition. Practically, it can encompass a wide variety of considerations and risks, depending on the context.[1] For the purposes of our discussion, we will define cybersecurity as the risks associated with maintaining the integrity of a private equity firm's information and architecture, with a focus on protecting data and intellectual property from unauthorized access or theft. Cybersecurity-associated risks include unauthorized penetration into a fund's computer systems and theft of data by the firm's own employees. In this chapter we will focus on the compliance implications of cybersecurity risks as they relate to private equity investing.

7.3.1   Penetration Testing

Penetration testing is a series of testing procedures which simulates the attempt by a bad actor, such as a hacker, to breach the integrity of a GP's data security architecture. Once inside the network of a GP, a hacker could perform a number of different malicious acts, ranging from the outright

---

[1]J. Scharfman, "Hedge Fund Compliance: Risks, Regulation and Management" (Hoboken: Wiley Finance, December 2016).

theft of proprietary GP data and secrets to installing malware to cause damage to a firm. Penetration testing may be performed:

- Through the use of in-house information technology personnel
- By third-party vendors
- By a combination of in-house and third-party resources

Each of these approaches has different benefits and drawbacks. For example, an in-house-performed penetration test utilizing existing resources is likely more cost effective as compared to engaging a third-party firm. The drawback, however, is that a third-party vendor that specializes in this area would likely have a better understanding of industry-wide best practices with regard to information security and testing in this area. Furthermore, cybersecurity is often a fast evolving area with a need for remaining up to date on current technologies and their weaknesses and updating patches to fight off unwanted attacks.

It is generally considered best practice for a GP to utilize a combined approach whereby the work of third-party specialists is complemented by in-house resources that perform related cybersecurity work, such as ensuring that any software update patches that may repair vulnerabilities are appropriately installed.

In practice such patches themselves are not always entirely effective as in some cases the patches are not released by the manufacturers of software until after they have been exploited by hackers. This was the case with a widespread ransomware attack called *WannaCry* in 2017, launched by North Korea.[2] This attack affected firms in many industries, including financial services, and was a special type of attack called a computer work that exploited weaknesses in the Microsoft Windows operating system.[3] *Ransomware* is a type of criminal cyberattack where the attackers effectively block an organization from accessing their own data and then require a payment in order to provide the user with the ability to re-access their own data.

As it relates to compliance, penetration testing is important not so much because of the actual testing being performed but rather for the potential vulnerabilities that a penetration test can reveal. The best way to illustrate this is through an example. Consider a situation where a GP's network is penetrated by a third-party hacker. This hacker steals sensitive personal information about individual LPs and then sells it on the dark web to other

---

[2] T. Bossert, "It's Official: North Korea Is Behind WannaCry," *Wall Street Journal,* December 18, 2017.
[3] *See* "The WannaCry Attack Is a Wake-Up Call," *The Financial Times,* May 14, 2017.

hackers, who utilize this information to expose financial information about the LPs. In this case, although the GP obviously didn't want this to happen, weaknesses in their network allowed the hacker to cause damage to the LPs. In addition to potential violations of privacy laws and exposure to action from regulatory agencies, the GP may also be financially liable to LPs for all or a portion of the damage done to LPs. A penetration test may not have prevented the hack as described in this example; however, had the GP performed this test they likely would have been much more prepared than if they had not performed this testing.

7.3.2 Vendor Cybersecurity Risks

Traditionally, a private equity fund manager's information security efforts focused primarily on the risks present at the GP. Increasingly there is an acceptance of the realization that cybersecurity risks at service providers to both a GP and their associated funds can also present significant information security vulnerabilities.

One common technique utilized by hackers to exploit cybersecurity vulnerabilities at vendors involves a technique known as *phishing.* Phishing is a type of social engineering cyberattack where a bad actor impersonates a legitimate information source in order to fool someone to act on the attacker's behalf or to try to steal valuable information. Phishing schemes in the fund management industry are commonly executed through email. A specialized form of phishing is known as *spear phishing.* Spear phishing involves an attacker performing significant research in order to specifically target security weaknesses. Based on the amount invested in crafting these spear phishing attacks, they commonly target individuals or companies where highly valuable data or large financial sums can be stolen. This includes fund managers such as hedge funds and private equity funds.

In some instances in spear phishing attacks, hackers utilize misspellings of legitimate domain name extensions in an attempt to fool a GP's employees or vendors into believing that the correspondence is coming for a legitimate party. An example of this allegedly occurred in 2016 in the case of a commodity fund manager named Tillage Commodities, LLC ("Tillage") and its fund administrator, SS&C Technologies ("SS&C"). In that instance Chinese hackers allegedly utilized a practice called *domain spoofing.* Under this practice, legitimate domain names are misspelled, typically in minor ways, in order to appear legitimate. In this case Tillage alleged that the Chinese hackers utilized spoof domains to fool SS&C into initiating fraudulent wire transfers. Specifically, in a lawsuit against SS&C, Tillage alleged that the hackers added an extra *l* to the correct name of Tillage's email domain in order to make it appear as if the hackers were legitimate. Therefore, instead of

"@tillagecapital.com," the fraudulent emails used a domain name with one additional *l* (i.e. "@tilllagecapital.com").[4] The aspect of the Tillage situation regarding considerations for GPs to draft compliance policies to incorporate the role and oversight of service providers such as fund administrators, and potential regulatory liability for not doing so, is addressed in Chapter 10.

7.4 DATA ROOMS

A *data room*, sometimes also referred to as a *virtual data room*, is a common tool utilized by GPs to archive and exchange data. This term does not refer to a physical room where information is stored but instead a software-based repository that is often cloud based and accessed through the Internet.

Data rooms have increasingly risen in popularity as data room technology has continued to become more readily available and affordable. While not every GP may utilize data room technology there are a number of compliance benefits that they may provide. There are three primary uses for data rooms. The first instance relates to situations in which the GP shares data with LPs at various stages of their investing lifecycle. The second instance is where data is shared among the GP and underlying companies that it is invested in or that are being considered for investment. The third way in which data rooms are utilized involves the GP storing and sharing data among its various employees.

In these last two instances it should be noted that data may flow in each direction. That is to say, the GP itself may be the one initiating the data transfer through the data room, or alternatively, data may be uploaded by the other parties (i.e. from the LPs, underlying companies, or GP employees) for review by the GP. These situations are summarized in Exhibit 7.1.

We will address each of these situations in more detail and discuss the compliance considerations and challenges a GP may encounter in each data room usage situation.

7.4.1 GP Sharing Data with Limited Partners

GP's share data with LPs at two primary points in their investment lifecycle. The first is during the GP fundraising process, when a LP has not yet committed capital to a fund. At this stage LPs are referred to as *prospects* or *prospective investors*.

---

[4]See *Tillage Commodities Fund, L.P. v SS&C Tech., Inc.*, 2016 N.Y. Misc. LEXIS 4834 (Dec. 22, 2016) and associated filings.

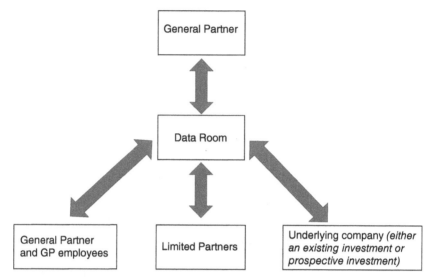

Exhibit 7.1   Three common private equity general partner uses of data rooms.[a]

[a]Double sided arrows indicate that data may flow in either direction.

When dealing with prospects, a key compliance consideration GPs must take into account relates to drawing a distinction among what types of data LPs should be sent. Certain information is required by law to be provided to prospective investors. This is called *required documentation*. A common example of required pre-investment documentation that all LPs must be provided with is the fund's offering memorandum. The second type of data provided to prospects would be what is known as *optional data*. This information is not necessarily required to be provided by GPs, but they may provide it for a number of reasons.

An example of how optional data functions would be if a prospect were evaluating a potential investment in a GP's fund. The prospect would likely request documentation beyond that which is required during a process known as *due diligence*. An example of the type of documentation an LP may request could be a due diligence questionnaire prepared by the GP or the previously audited financial statements of a prior vintage fund operated by the GP. Continuing this example, while the GP may readily provide the due diligence questionnaire requested by the prospect in their discretion, the GP may make the determination that they would not like to share the prior audited financial statements for a different fund. This could be because the GP felt that historical financial statements from previous funds were not relevant to the current fund that they were raising capital for, or they simply did not want to comply with the request. While a deviation from market practices, technically there would be no specific law that would require the GP to provide this information; therefore, under our example this could be classified as optional data.

This is not to say that the offering memorandum of a fund is the only document required to be provided by GPs to prospective investors. Indeed, other documents, including those without as much legal jargon such as due diligence questionnaire or marketing presentations, may be required to comply with other notions, including ensuring appropriate transparency and sufficient disclosures; however, the extent of such required documentation distribution must be evaluated on a case-by-case basis and would not typically be spelled out as a bright-line rule by any law or regulatory guidance.

From a compliance perspective, GPs must generally fulfill a number of requirements relating to tracking the data provided to prospective investors. First, once they have determined what data is required to be provided to LPs, they must indeed ensure that LPs receive this data. As noted, rather than transmit this information to LPs in hardcopy or through other electronic media, data rooms are increasingly utilized in the private equity industry to fulfill this purpose. The way this would work in practice would be for the GP to upload the required documentation, as well as any optional documentation, to the data room. These documents would then remain on the virtual shelf in the data room.

When dealing with a prospective LP, the GP would then invite the prospect to the data room. This is typically done through a password-protected and encrypted system. The LP would then have the ability to access the documents from the data room. To be clear, the LP cannot edit the documents in the data room. As noted above, the GP may limited which documents an LP can access while maintaining a larger set of documents on file in the data room for other purposes, such as to share internally among the GP employees.

The reason data rooms are helpful to GPs is that on the backend of the data room technology, data rooms facilitate compliance recordkeeping requirements. One way they do this is providing a paper trail at each stage of the process. For starters, the GP would have a record of when the LP was invited to access the data room. Then the GP would similarly have a record of not only which documents the LP had access to, but also which documents they accessed online and downloaded as well as when these actions occurred.

Another feature of data rooms that assist with private equity compliance recordkeeping requirements relates to concepts known as *document labeling* and *document numbering*. Document numbering is also called *serialization*. As noted, financial regulators often require GPs to keep detailed records of which documentation was provided to prospective investors. A common practice that has evolved in this area is for GPs to create a number system for different documents. For example, the first offering memorandum distributed to a prospective investor for a new fund could be labeled "Number One" on the front page of this document. Typically, these labels would be inserted electronically into the document. The second offering memorandum distributed to a second prospective investor would be labeled "Number Two." This process would continue with sequentially increasing numbers for all offering memorandums that were distributed. While this may seem fairly straightforward, throughout the fundraising process the initial version of the offering memorandum may undergo a series of updates. One common reason for this could be based on feedback on certain fund terms from investors.

Once the GP decides to make these updates they need to ensure that all prospective LPs are provided with access to these changes. This could involve editing the original offering memorandum or keeping the existing one in its original format and issuing an additional amendment document known as a *supplement*. In either case, a single investor could receive multiple versions and supplements of an offering memorandum throughout the GP's fundraising process.

Prior to the use of data rooms, the records of which LPs received what documents would have been kept either in hardcopy or in a kind of electronic ledger such as Microsoft Excel. Data room technology can automatically place numbers on documents and keep track of which LPs receive what data.

A similar concept to document numbers relates to document labeling. This involves a process whereby a specific LP's name, or other piece of identifying information such as an email address, is placed on the documents she is receiving. This is typically known as a *watermark*, and helps to ensure that LPs receive the documents that were intended for them and not another LP. Watermarking also facilitates document security and tracking. For example, if a GP document were exposed via a hack and uploaded to the Web, or in some other public forum, then the electronic watermark would allow them to track down the source of the documentation.

After an LP decides to allocate capital to a particular fund, the GP typically has an additional series of documentation that is shared with LPs on an ongoing basis throughout the life of the fund. One example of this would be a quarterly update from a GP regarding the performance of the fund's investments and the value of the LP's investments in the fund. This type of document could also be distributed by a GP through a data room; this would be similar to the ways in which information was distributed on a pre-investment basis to the LP. The facilitation of LP tracking of access to documentation as well as document number and labeling are ways in which GPs implement compliance oversight of the document distribution process to both prospective investors and existing investments through data rooms.

7.4.2 GP Sharing Data with Underlying Companies

The GP may also utilize a data room to facilitate the collection of documentation from portfolio companies. When dealing with underlying companies, private equity firms have a number of compliance obligations requiring them to keep appropriate records of their due diligence and ultimate investment activities.

Similar to the two main stages at which the GP works with the LP, the GP deals with underlying companies at the same two stages: pre-investment and post-investment. The difference in this case is that an investment is not being made by the LP into a fund managed by the GP, but instead the GP is considering an investment in an underlying company.

When the GP is conducting due diligence on a portfolio company being considered for investment both the GP and portfolio company may require certain documentation, such as a nondisclosure agreement to be executed prior to the start of the due diligence process. These types of documents may be shared and stored in a data room.

Once these pre–due diligence documents are in place, the GP may then request a series of documents to facilitate their analysis of the underlying portfolio company. Examples of these types of documents may include financial, legal, and various types of investment and operational information. In these cases, one of two scenarios could occur. The first would be for the GP to create a special data room focused around document sharing between itself and the underlying company. This can be referred to as a *deal-specific room*. The second alternative would be for the portfolio company to set up its own data room, similar to the one a GP would set up with an LP. In this case, the data room would be administered by the portfolio company instead of the GP.

Due to the recordkeeping compliance obligations of GPs referenced above, the more common scenario is for the GP to create their own deal-specific room as opposed to the latter alternative.

After a GP has made an investment into a portfolio company there is a series of regular documentation and reporting that the GP will often require from these companies. Examples of this would include cost and profitability information to facilitate managing the investment by a fund managed by the GP into the fund. The collection of this data, as well as the sharing of any data by the GP with the portfolio companies, is also typically performed via a GP-hosted deal-specific room.

7.4.3 GP Sharing Data Among Its Employees

The third common way data rooms are utilized by GPs is to share information among their employees. This may be accomplished via a data room application or through an internal shared drive. In either case, from a compliance perspective the important thing is that the GP must comply with requirements relating to the retention and archiving of records throughout their firm.

7.4.4 Business Continuity Planning and Disaster Recovery

Business continuity planning and disaster recovery (BCP/DR) is an area of increased importance for private equity funds and represents another key area in which the compliance and IT functions overlap. Business disruptions can occur for a wide variety of reasons. These range from the more commonplace disruption in utilities, such as phone service, Internet connectivity, or power outages, to more widespread disaster events, such as terrorism or extreme weather.

While it is a good business practice to ensure that a private equity fund can continue operations in the event of disruption, increasingly regulators are also mandating that private equity funds develop written *business continuity and disaster recovery policy document*s that outline a private equity fund's plans to deal with BCP/DR events. As an example, in the United States, the National Futures Association (NFA) Compliance Rule 2-38 requires funds registered with the NFA to adopt business continuity and disaster recovery plans.

Another example is the guidance provided by the Securities and Exchange Commission (SEC) with regard to Rule 206(4)-7, which outlines in part:

> We believe that an adviser's fiduciary obligation to its clients includes the obligation to take steps to protect the clients' interests from being placed at risk as a result of the adviser's inability to provide advisory services after, for example, a natural disaster or, in the case of some smaller firms, the death of the owner or key personnel. The clients of an adviser that is engaged in the active management of their assets would ordinarily be placed at risk if the adviser ceased operations.

Increasingly the compliance function is providing insight into the design and oversight of a private equity firm's BCP/DR plans. This is not only to comply with regulatory guidance in this area but also to promote the ongoing oversight and integrity of the GP's operations as well as facilitate data sharing and archiving as referenced above. When designing a firm's BCP/DR policy documents key areas typically addressed in a BCP/DR plan include:

- Data backup and recovery.
- Developing communication plans so key employees can communicate in the event of a disaster event, including the use of tools such as a *calling tree*.
- Clarification regarding the process by which employees can continue to work while outside the office. This can include details of remote employee secure access and the ability to continue trading via alternative measures, such as using mobile phones.
- Designating alternative locations from which employees may continue operations. This includes designating a formal location, known as a *disruption gathering location*, where employees would be directed to go in the event of disruptions that render a private equity fund's office inaccessible.
- Details of how communications with investors and fund service providers should continue in the event of a business disruption.
- Does the firm maintain written BCP/DR procedures? If yes, what is the scope of such procedures?
- Has the firm customized its business continuity and disaster recovery plans or is a generic plan in place which may not address the operational aspects of the firm?
- Are any written BCP/DR plans structured around industry certifications or guidelines?
- Do BCP/DR plans cover multiple scenarios, including inaccessibility of the firm's offices?
- Do BCP/DR plans provide for coverage of plans for outages of telephony and Internet loss?
- Who oversees updating the plans?
- Are employees provided with contact information for each employer in a manner that is not linked to the firm's systems functioning properly (i.e. such as a laminated calling tree card)?
- Backup power:
    - Are uninterruptible power supplies (also uninterruptible power sources [UPSs] or battery/flywheel backup) in place? If yes, are UPSs available for desktop PCs and servers?
    - How long do UPSs provide power?
    - Does the firm have backup power-generation facilities? If yes, what type of generator (i.e. diesel, natural gas) is utilized?
    - Who is responsible for maintenance of such devices?

- If backup power-generation capabilities are in place, does the firm own such devices exclusively or are they shared among other firms?
- Data backup and restoring:
  - What are the firm's data backup capabilities?
  - Is data backed up in multiple locations and via multiple media?
  - Is data stored onsite, offsite, or both?
  - Is a separate backup facility maintained for data storage?
  - Has the firm performed test restores from any backups?
  - How long would it take the firm to perform a data restore for system-critical functions in the event of a disaster?
- Does the private equity firm have a disruption gathering location?
- Does the private equity firm maintain a separate facility from which employees may continue operations? If yes, how many seats are in such locations?
- Has the private equity firm ever had to activate its BCP/DR plan? If yes, what happened?
- Who is responsible for activation of the BCP/DR plans? How is plan activation communicated to employees?
- If the private equity firm has multiple offices, how are these offices supposed to coordinate with each other in the event of a business disruption in either location?

Another key component of BCP/DR planning compliance departments now focus on is continued testing of said plans once implemented. While plan testing may be coordinated by departments other than compliance, such as a private equity GP's IT department, the compliance department is often instrumental in ensuring that plans are tested according to a predetermined schedule and that testing is documented appropriately. Key testing considerations that should be addressed by compliance in designing BCP/DR testing and oversight programs include:

- Is the plan tested? If so, how often?
- Are BCP/DR plans tested from a technology perspective solely or are personnel tests employed as well?
- When was the most recent test?
- What were the results of the test? Were any material issues noted? How have these issues been addressed?

7.5   SUMMARY

This chapter began with an overview of the increasingly important role played by information technology in implementing a successful compliance function in a private equity firm. We next discussed the reasons for the increased regulatory focused on the importance of a GP developing a robust compliance infrastructure. The discussion proceeded to a focus on the importance of cybersecurity in the modern private equity compliance risk management. The benefits of penetration testing and various methods by which it can be performed were examined. The risks posed to GPs and LPs through vendor cyber-vulnerabilities were also addressed. Common techniques utilized by hackers, including phishing, spear phishing, and domain spoofing, were introduced. The extensive use of data room by GPs in sharing information with LPs and underlying portfolio companies and among GP employees was also covered. Finally, the critical role of the compliance function in working with the information technology department and vendors in implementing the GP business continuity and disaster recovery program was analyzed. In this chapter we emphasized the importance of private equity compliance documentation related to information technology policies and procedures. In the next chapter we will expand this discussion to private equity compliance–related documentation outside of the information technology function.

CHAPTER 8

Understanding Private Equity Compliance Documentation

8.1 INTRODUCTION TO KEY PRIVATE EQUITY COMPLIANCE DOCUMENTS

The previous chapters outlined a framework for developing and analyzing private equity compliance. This discussion made reference to several different types of compliance-related documentation. In this chapter we focus in more detail on the function and role of private equity documentation. This will include a discussion of both fund-level and general partner (GP)–level compliance documentation. As we have addressed fund-level documentation in previous chapters, the bulk of the discussion will focus on GP-level compliance documentation. Prior to diving into specific compliance documents, it is beneficial to discuss the purposes and benefits of documenting compliance.

8.2 PURPOSES OF DOCUMENTING COMPLIANCE

Both at the fund and GP level, documenting compliance serves two primary purposes. The first is what is known as meeting *minimum regulatory compliance*. For example, US Securities and Exchange Commission (US SEC) Rule 206(4)-7(b), the Investment Advisors Act of 1940 (Advisers Act), outlines that a broad regulatory classification of entities known as *investment advisers*, which would include covered private equity funds, must conduct an annual review of their policies to ensure "the adequacy of the policies and procedures established pursuant to this section and the effectiveness of their implementation." Therefore, if a registered GP did not both document that they would perform the review, and then of course perform it, they would be violating the regulatory guidance in this area.

A second goal of compliance documentation is to outline the actual compliance practices in place, known as *demonstrative documentation*. This documentation goes above minimum regulatory requirements to describe the actual policies employed by a GP. For example, a specific financial regulator may require that the compliance function provide oversight of any gifts and entertainments given and received by a GP's employees. The way that this policy is actually implemented by a private equity firm's compliance function would not necessarily be spelled out in detail by the regulator. Instead, a chief compliance officer (CCO) at one GP may require all employees to fill out a specific form to report these gifts and entertainment. Another GP's compliance program may require that employees input this information into a compliance tracking system which the CCO can then review. Both practices may be completely acceptable and in adherence with the rules of the financial regulator in question. Due to these potential policy implementation differences, the creation of demonstrative documentation by the GP provides a guide for employees to follow in adhering to the policies as well as allowing the GP to demonstrate that they actually have a specific documented policy in place that can then be referenced for both employees and regulatory authorities.

8.3 BENEFITS OF DOCUMENTING COMPLIANCE

Before discussing the different aspects of specific private equity documentation, the question can be posed as to why compliance documentation needs to be developed at all. There are three primary reasons why the documentation of compliance policies and procedures is essential.

8.3.1 Regulatory Required Documentation

In order to comply with the minimum regulatory compliance goal of documenting compliance described earlier, GPs must develop a certain minimum number of specific documents and address certain topics in these documents. This is known as the concept of *regulatory required documentation*. This required documentation may vary across jurisdictions. An example of this would be the requirement by the US SEC to maintain a compliance manual.

8.3.2 Communication of Compliance Policies to GP Employees

Another reason why the documentation of compliance policies and procedures is critical relates to the ability of documentation to effectively communicate policies among the firm's employees. This is related to the goal of demonstrative documentation outlined previously. Beyond regulatory required minimums, different GPs maintain different compliance programs as relevant to their specific firms. Additionally, compliance policies and their implementation at private equity funds are often subject to oversight not only by compliance personnel, such as the CCO, but by other individuals as well. These individuals typically include senior management of the GP that is not necessarily focused directly on the compliance function such as the chief investment officer and chief operating officer. While compliance policies may be verbally communicated to employees and senior management through avenues such as new and ongoing employee training, documenting the policies in writing is another way to enhance communication of the policies and practices in place.

8.3.3 Facilitating Investors' Understanding of Compliance

During the initial pre-investment due diligence process, prospective and existing investors may want more information regarding a GP's compliance practices. Having written documentation of policies and procedures in place that can be shared with investors facilitates limited partner (LP) analysis of compliance functions. Additionally, once a limited partner has allocated capital to a fund, he may seek to monitor changes in a private equity firm's compliance program as part of his ongoing due diligence. Written documentation also facilitates this oversight by providing reference documentation, and is similarly related to the goal of demonstrative documentation.

8.3.4 Service Provider Insights into GP Compliance

Private equity firms work with a variety of third-party consultants. Some of this work is focused directly on compliance matters while other documentation relates only tangentially to compliance. Those service providers that are more focused on compliance may also participate directly in the management and implementation of a GP's and associated fund's compliance policies and procedures. For example, at the GP level, a compliance consultant would need to have a well-developed understanding of a GP's compliance policies and indeed may even be instrumental in initially crafting them.

Another example at the GP level would be the use of a private equity firm of a third-party firm known as an *expert network*. Expert networks are service providers that provide introduction between a GP's investment personnel and a so-called expert in order to facilitate investment research. These experts are typically individuals with expertise in specific industries or at particular companies. Once introduced the expert and the GP's investment personnel typically have a conversation regarding the investment individual's areas of interest. In the vast majority of jurisdictions, when these phone calls occur there is generally a prohibition on the communication of what is known as *material non-public information (MNPI)*, a concept we introduced in Chapter 5. For reference, MNPI is also referred to as *insider information*.

The practice of utilizing MNPI to trade, commonly called insider trading, is illegal in the United States and most other jurisdictions. In recent years there have been a number of inquiries related to fund managers' use of expert networks and trading on insider information. As such, a GP will likely outline a number of policies in their compliance procedures that prohibit employees from acting on MNPI. In many instances, a private equity firm will share these policies with an expert network before utilizing them. While the expert network may have their own policies that prohibit their experts from passing on MNPI, increasingly GPs are asking expert networks to affirmatively acknowledge that they will comply with the GP's specific policies in this area. In this way, the GP benefits from having clearly defined and documented compliance policies that it can share with both its employees as well as expert networks.

Another example of the benefits of documenting compliance when working with service providers for a GP would be a third-party member of the board of directors of a private equity fund. As part of this role, they would likely have some oversight responsibility for overseeing the implementation of fund-level compliance requirements. Having these policies in writing as opposed to in an oral format facilitates oversight in both situations. For clarification, this benefit would apply to both affiliated and unaffiliated (i.e. third-party directors).

8.3.5 Change Management Compliance

Over time a GP may be required to alter their compliance policies and procedures. One reason for this may be that since the time of the initial writing, or last update, of the firm's compliance policies the practices at the firm have changed. For example, a GP may have opened a new office in a different jurisdiction since the initial launch of the firm. The firm may now be under a requirement to perform annual compliance training for employees in both the original and new office and the compliance policies should be revised to reflect this new practice. Stale compliance documentation that describes outdated procedures and does not reflect the current practice at the GP are not useful and may cause confusion among employees and service providers.

Additionally, incorrect or old information contained in compliance documentation may even expose the firm to potential regulatory actions due to their inaccuracy. As such, the GP would need to update their compliance documentation to reflect current practices at the firm. The creation of an initial written record of a private equity firm's compliance program facilitates the updating of records and creates an ongoing archive by which the changes can be monitored.

8.4 DISTINGUISHING LEGAL AND COMPLIANCE TERMS IN FUND OFFERING DOCUMENTS

In Chapter 1 we introduced a three-tiered approach toward categorizing the different aspects of entities across which compliance can be implemented within the private equity landscape. These tiers were GP-level compliance, fund-level compliance, and portfolio compliance as it relates to the GP and funds.

Throughout this book we have also discussed the concept of a fund's offering and formation documents. While the specific nature and volume of offering documentation may vary among private equity funds, the two key offering documents are generally:

- Offering memorandum (OM), also sometimes called a private placement memorandum (PPM)
- Limited partnership agreement (LPA)

These documents contain a variety of information covering a broad range of topics related to a fund's planned investment activities, key fund terms, and relevant fund-level compliance information. The information in these documents can be thought of as serving different functions.

Certain pieces of information in the documents are statements that are effectively required by law, and most of a GP's lawyers will typically advise them to insert a number of relatively standard information disclaimers relating to areas such as conflicts of interest and taxes by default. An example of a standard disclaimer contained in an OM utilized for US-based funds would read as follows:

The investor should make their own decision whether this offering meets their investment objectives and risk tolerance level. No federal or state securities commission has approved, disapproved, or recommended this offering. No independent person has confirmed the accuracy of this disclosure, nor whether it is complete. Any representation to the contrary is illegal.

These of course are typically customized to the applicable activities of the firm's funds.

Some of this information may be classified by parties such as GPs, their lawyers, or LPs as so-called *legal information*. This can be distinguished from what others may deem as *compliance information*. The way these distinctions may be employed in practice is that an LP, for example, may deem a description of fund terms in a fund's OM to be legal as opposed to compliance information. The LP's thinking may be rooted in the fact that if the fund violates its term (i.e. charging a management fee in excess of what is permitted in the OM), then the LP could pursue legal recourse through the judicial system.

On the other hand, an LP may also view a description in the OM regarding prohibitions on the use of MNPI by the GP's employees as compliance information as opposed to legal information. This thinking may be based in the fact that if a fund were to trade on MNPI, the primary initiator of any investigation and subsequent action would likely be a financial regulator. This would be opposed to a more legally rooted action such as a lawsuit brought by an LP if, for example, the fund lost money and it was found that MNPI violations were responsible for these losses.

In practice, in the majority of instances both terms are interchangeable and there is no material distinction between whether a piece of information in a fund offering document is classified as legal information or compliance information. The important point to remember is that the information contained in the offering documents is directly relevant to compliance management, regardless of the classification employed. The focus should be on the content of the information and not the classification nomenclature employed.

8.5 KEY GP COMPLIANCE DOCUMENTATION

We turn our focus to the compliance documentation that outlines compliance policies that are primarily focused around GP compliance as opposed to fund-level compliance.

All GPs have a series of compliance documents that constitute the outline of its compliance program. A private equity compliance program is not limited only to a series of documentation. The compliance documentation is merely the foundation upon which a strong private equity compliance program is built. As we outlined earlier, while the documents are certainly beneficial to a GP's compliance program, even well-thought-out best-practice compliance policies must actually be implemented and monitored, otherwise they will ultimately fail.

8.5.1 Compliance Manual

A *compliance manual* is a core document that is the central cornerstone of a private equity firm's compliance program. From a practical standpoint, different jurisdictions typically impose specific minimum regulatory requirements as to what types of information must be contained in the manual (i.e. *regulatory required documentation*). Beyond these minimums, compliance manuals often contain additional information related to the specific activities of a fund or specific practices employed by the GP (i.e. *demonstrative documentation*).

These may be complemented by further explanatory manuals that provide more topics specific to day-to-day guidance. Compliance manuals may also include a variety of information that is not focused exclusively on compliance, such as information on the investment opportunity the fund anticipates. With this understanding in place, there are certain compliance-related topics that are generally addressed in the majority of compliance manuals. The following example table of contents of a compliance manual demonstrates the wide range of topics typically covered in compliance manuals:

I. Introduction
II. Executive Summary
III. Market Opportunity/Investment Strategy
IV. Identification of CCO and Supervised Persons
V. Compliance Policies and Procedures:
    A. Disclosures and risk assessments
    B. Contracts
    C. Portfolio management processes
    D. Trading and brokerage practices
    E. Valuation
    F. Fees
    G. Insider trading prevention
    H. Safeguarding of client assets
    I. Media relations
    J. Advertising and marketing
    K. Use of third-party marketers
    L. Privacy policy and protecting client information
    M. Proxy voting
    N. Conflicts of interests
    O. Business continuity and disaster recovery
    P. Books and records
    Q. Electronic communications policy
    R. Complaints and rumors

S. Business entertainment
T. Political contributions
U. Oversight of third-party service providers
VI. Annual Review of Policies and Procedures

8.5.2 Code of Ethics

The *code of ethics*, sometimes referred to as a *code of conduct*, is a document that provides additional information on compliance policies. In practice, there may be some degree of overlap between the code of ethics and compliance manual, but generally one complements the other and when combined the two documents summarize the key aspects of a GP's compliance program. The code of ethics, as opposed to the compliance manual, is traditionally less technical and written in a more user-friendly format for employees' use.

In addition, code of ethics documents typically contain more specific details regarding the actual practices employed by a particular private equity firm in certain areas rather than the more technical regulatory descriptions contained in compliance manuals. Code of ethics documents may also be shorter in nature as compared to compliance manuals, and instead focus not on the actual compliance practices employed at the firm but rather highlight the need of employees to act in an ethical manner. In these types of shorter-form codes of ethics guidance is often given along the lines of advising employees to:

- Carry out their duties in an ethical manner.
- Perform their duties with integrity and in good faith.
- Avoid actual conflicts or the appearance of conflicts.
- Encourage others to act in a professional manner.

The problem with this type of guidance is that it is often lacking in specificity. As such, when utilizing these shorter-form codes of ethics, the GP's compliance manual often contains much more detailed information on the step-by-step implementation of compliance practices. If this is not the case, then as outlined earlier this more detailed guidance would be contained in stand-alone policy or topic-specific manuals.

It should also be noted that a private equity firm may also decide to combine their compliance manual and code of ethics into a single document. Another option would be for the GP to incorporate the code of ethics into another document as part of a larger combined manual such as an employee handbook.

8.5.3 Electronic Communication and Social Media Policies

Increasingly, private equity firms are faced with challenges and potential compliance liabilities surrounding their employees' use of electronic means of communication, such as email and social media. While a GP's compliance manual or code of ethics may provide general guidance in this area, increasingly GPs are creating specific stand-alone policies to focus on these issues. In drafting these policies GPs must also be careful not to overly restrict employee rights in areas such as free speech. The following is a representative sample of language that would be contained in these policies in regard to a private equity firm's social media policy:

Prior to making any posts made on social media by the firm's employees they should consider whether it would reflect negatively on themselves or the firm. Any posts by employees must make clear that they are making the post on behalf of themselves and not on behalf of the firm, its partners or affiliates. Senior management of the firm are subjected to enhanced scrutiny in this regard as their seniority within the firm could be interpreted in a manner such that they are speaking on behalf of the firm. Regardless of an employee's position they must not in any manner reference the firm, other employees, funds managed by the firm. Furthermore, no links should be included to the firm's websites. In the event an employee is making a comment or posting that could in any way be construed to relate to the firm in any capacity or potential business or investment activities in which the firm or its funds may be involved employees should include a disclaimer that makes it clear that they are not representing the firm. An example of such a disclaimer would read as follows: "The views expressed here are solely my own and do not reflect the views of my employer." Firm employees should also consider tailoring any profiles that they may maintain on social media websites to indicate that their profile only reflects their own activities. Postings on social media are also subject to all other applicable policies. As an example, firm employees are precluded from posting in any manner confidential information of any kind including about the firm, underlying portfolio companies or the funds. The firm disclaims any liability for errors or damages incurred by employees due to social media posting.

8.5.4 Other Compliance Documents

Other common policies may include those in the following areas:

- Advertising
- Affiliate Transactions Policy
- Deal allocations

- Insider trading
- Monitoring of service provider and vendors
- Political Donation and Activity Policy
- Valuation policies and procedures
- Anti-Bribery Policy and Procedures
- Conflicts of Interest Policy
- Gifts and Entertainment Policy
- Whistleblower and Anti-Retaliation Policy and Procedures
- Custody Policy and Procedures
- Soliciting Prospective Investors Policy
- Privacy and Data Confidentiality Policy
- Market Rumors Policy
- Personal Account Dealing Policy
- Pay to Play Policy
- Proxy Voting Policy and Guidelines
- Fair Credit Reporting Act
- Outside business activities
- Expense allocation
- Travel and expenses
- Identity theft
- Environmental, social, and governance

In addition, other policies may focus on the compliance aspects of technology-related matters, many of which were introduced in Chapter 7. Examples of those policies include the following:

- Data Backup Policy
- Cybersecurity Policy
- Telephone Recording Policy
- Business continuity and disaster recovery plan

8.6 CASE STUDY: WL ROSS & CO. LLC

Consistently outlining the firm's compliance policies in a sufficiently transparent way in compliance documentation is an area that financial regulatory agencies have increasingly sought to enforce when scrutinizing both GP- and fund-level compliance information. Private equity regulators also increasingly focus on the specific terminology in fund-level formation and offering documentation to ensure that a fund's compliance policies are documented in a clear way across a wide variety of topics.

A recent case relating to the specificity of language contained in a private equity fund's OM was the US SEC in August 2016 against WL Ross & Co. In that case, the Securities and Exchange Commission (SEC) alleged that the firm's LPAs were ambiguous about management fee offsets in situations where ownership was shared by multiple funds and other co-investors.[1]

What follows is an excerpt of the allegations as outlined in the SEC Administrative Proceeding in this matter, which provides background on the allegations in this case. As you read it consider the nature of what information may have been included or omitted in fund documentation and its potential legal and compliance implications (numbering has been left as it appeared in the original administrative proceeding):[2]

A. Background

7. WL Ross is a New York-based private equity firm that advises the WLR Funds and other private equity funds, as well as separately managed accounts and co-investment vehicles, with a focus on investing in and restructuring financially distressed companies. The limited partners in the WLR Funds include pension funds, university endowments and other large institutional investors, and high net worth individuals. The limited partners typically commit a specified amount of capital to a fund for its use to make qualifying investments during the investment period of the fund. Each WLR Fund has an Advisory Board, comprised of certain limited partners, to advise regarding conflicts of interest, valuations of securities, and other issues.

8. Each WLR Fund is governed by an LPA setting forth the rights and obligations of its limited partners, including their obligations to pay advisory and other fees and expenses to WL Ross pursuant to a separate management agreement between the fund and WL Ross. Among other fees and expenses, WL Ross charges each WLR Fund an annual advisory or management fee, which generally ranges from 0.75% to 1.5% of committed capital during the investment period.

---

[1]J. Beckerman, "WL Ross in SEC Settlement over Fee-Allocation Disclosure," *Wall Street Journal*, August 24, 2016.

[2]United States of America Before the Securities and Exchange Commission, Investment Advisors Act of 1940, Release No. 4494/August 24, 2016, Administrative Proceeding File No. 3-17491, In the Matter of WL Ross & Co. LLC, Respondent, ORDER INSTITUTING CEASE-AND DESIST PROCEEDINGS PURSUANT TO SECTION 203(k) OF THE INVESTMENT ADVISERS ACT OF 1940, MAKING FINDINGS, AND IMPOSING A CEASE-AND-DESIST ORDER.

9. From time to time, WL Ross also receives Transaction Fees directly from certain portfolio investments of the WLR Funds for providing monitoring, financial advisory, and other services, as contemplated by the LPAs in certain circumstances. The Transaction Fees paid by portfolio companies to WL Ross are in addition to the management fees paid by the WLR Funds to WL Ross. WL Ross allocates a percentage of the Transaction Fees it receives from the portfolio companies to the WLR Funds in order to offset the quarterly management fees payable by the WLR Funds. The offset percentage is set forth in each fund's LPA. All of the WLR Fund LPAs provide for a 50% management fee offset with the exception of the WLR Recovery Fund, L.P. ("Fund I"), which provides for an 80% management fee offset.

10. The LPA provisions concerning the management fee offsets for the WLR Funds are all substantially similar to the language in the WLR Recovery Fund II, L.P. LPA, which provides at Section 5.03, Management Fees, that:

   The Management Fee shall be reduced in any given quarter by an amount equal to fifty percent (50%) of any break-up, origination, commitment, broken deal, topped bid, cancellation, monitoring, closing, financial advisory, investment banking, director or other transaction fees received by the General Partner or any Affiliate thereof during the prior quarter from Portfolio Investments.[3]

11. WLR omitted material information regarding how Transaction Fees shall be allocated when multiple WLR Funds and co-investors are invested in the same portfolio company.

B. WL Ross' Historical Transaction Fee Allocation Practice

12. WL Ross' Transaction Fee allocation practice originated in 2001 in connection with the allocation of co-investment fees arising from a certain transaction (the "2001 Transaction").[4] In 2001, WL Ross formed a special purpose limited partnership

---

[3] *Portfolio investments* is defined in the LPA as "assets of the Partnership" that are invested in securities of companies.
[4] Although WL Ross later determined that the LPAs did not require that co-investment fees paid to WL Ross by coinvestors be allocated to the WLR Funds

("SPLP") for the sole purpose of investing in the 2001 Transaction. The SPLP was comprised of three WLR funds – Asia Recovery Fund, L.P., Asia Recovery Co-Investment Partners, L.P. (collectively, "Asia Funds"), and Fund I – as well as other co-investors. Together, Fund I and the two Asia Funds contributed approximately 40% in capital to the SPLP, while the co-investors contributed the remaining 60% in capital. Upon acquiring the portfolio company, the SPLP co-investors paid WL Ross a one-time $3.9 million fee as compensation for negotiating, advising, and structuring the 2001 Transaction.

13. Allocating the entire $3.9 million co-investment fee to each of the three funds in the 2001 Transaction would have resulted in WL Ross providing total management fee offsets to the funds greater than the actual co-investment fee it received in connection with the "Portfolio Investments" is defined in the LPA as "assets of the Partnership" that are invested in securities of companies. Although WL Ross later determined that the LPAs did not require that co-investment fees paid to WL Ross by coinvestors be allocated to the WLR Funds for offset purposes, it devised the allocation practice at the time of the 2001 Transaction and applied it consistently to both co-investment fees and Transaction Fees until 2014 transaction.[5] WL Ross instead determined to allocate the $3.9 million co-investment fee to the two Asia Funds and Fund I based on their relative ownership percentages of the portfolio company. Because the three funds collectively owned 40% of the portfolio company, WL Ross allocated 40% of the $3.9 million co-investment fee to the funds (approximately $1.6 million), and then offset the funds' management fees according to the fee offset percentages specified in each fund's LPA (80% for Fund I, 50% for each Asia Fund), resulting in a combined management fee offset of $962 000 for the three funds.

14. By interpreting the ambiguous language in the relevant LPAs as permitting it to adopt this allocation methodology, WL Ross

---

for offset purposes, it devised the allocation practice at the time of the 2001 Transaction and applied it consistently to both co-investment fees and Transaction Fees until 2014.

[5]Using that approach, WL Ross would have been required to allocate fee offsets to Fund I of $3.12 million (80% of $3.9 million) and fee offsets to the two Asia Funds of $1.95 million each (50% of $3.9 million), totaling $7.02 million in management fee offsets on the $3.9 million co-investment fee received by WL Ross.

retained 60% of the fee that was based on the coinvestors' 60% ownership share of the portfolio company. If WL Ross instead had adopted a methodology allocating all of the fees pro rata among the investing WLR funds, the three WLR funds investing in the 2001 Transaction would have received management fee offsets totaling $2.35 million rather than the $962 000 they actually received.[6]

15. Beginning with the 2001 Transaction and through 2011, WL Ross consistently allocated Transaction Fees it received from portfolio investments to the WLR Funds according to their ownership percentages of the portfolio companies. If WL Ross had instead allocated Transaction Fees pro rata between the investing WLR Funds, the WLR Funds would have received a larger credit for purposes of management fee offsets. By retaining the portion of the Transaction Fees allocable to co-investors' relative ownership share of the portfolio companies, WL Ross received approximately $10.4 million in additional management fees from the WLR Funds during the 10-year period between 2001 and 2011.

16. As noted above, WLR did not disclose how to allocate Transaction Fees when multiple WLR funds and co-investors are invested in a portfolio company. WL Ross did not disclose to the WLR Funds, the Funds' Advisory Boards, or the Funds' limited partners its chosen practice of allocating Transaction Fees based upon the WLR Funds' relative ownership percentages of the portfolio company. As a result, the WLR Funds, their boards, and limited partners may not have been aware that the WLR Funds did not receive that portion of the Transaction Fees allocable to co-investors' ownership percentages of the portfolio companies, or that WL Ross retained for itself that portion of the Transaction Fees instead.

---

[6]Fund I held approximately 14% and the two Asia Funds collectively held approximately 26% of the three funds' combined 40% ownership in the 2001 Transaction. If WLR had adopted a pro rata allocation methodology, Fund I would have been allocated approximately 35% (or 14% of 40%) of the $3.9 million co-investors' fee, or $1.4 million, and the two Asia Funds collectively would have been allocated 65% (or 26% of 40%) of the $3.9 million fee, or $2.5 million. Those allocations would then have been subject to the offset provisions of the LPAs, and the funds would have received management fee offsets of $1.1 million (Fund I, 80% offset), and $1.25 million (Asia Funds, 50% offsets), for a combined management fee offset of approximately $2.35 million between the three funds.

C. 2014 OCIE Examination, WL Ross' Remediation, and Implementation of New Allocation Methodology

17. In 2014, staff from the Commission's Office of Compliance Inspections and Examinations ("OCIE") conducted an examination of WL Ross. In reviewing management fee and fee offset data produced to the OCIE staff, WL Ross determined to revisit the methodology used to allocate Transaction Fees to WLR Funds that had invested with co-investors in portfolio companies. On August 20, 2014, WL Ross brought the issue to the attention of the OCIE staff.

18. After conducting an internal review, WL Ross voluntarily proposed and adopted a new methodology allocating all Transaction Fees received from a portfolio company pro rata across the WLR Funds that participated in the portfolio investment and recognized that it had not done so in the past. WL Ross then voluntarily retroactively applied this methodology to recalculate all historical management fees and offsets dating back to the inception of the funds. WLR adopted this new methodology even for its later funds where the LPAs specifically contemplated the use of the older methodology. WL Ross submitted its reimbursement calculations for review and verification to the WLR Funds' independent auditor, as well as to Invesco's Internal Audit Group, an independent accounting firm, and a forensic accounting firm.

19. WL Ross voluntarily reimbursed the WLR Funds approximately $10.4 million in management fees and $1.4 million in interest during the course of the OCIE exam and the staff's investigation as a result of retroactively applying its corrected Transaction Fee allocation methodology to the inception of the funds. WL Ross also disclosed the new methodology and reimbursement to the WLR Funds' investors in a series of written communications and meetings.

20. Since the OCIE exam, WL Ross has voluntarily taken a number of actions to strengthen its controls and compliance systems. WL Ross hired a new "CCO" and the CCO now participates in all of WL Ross' key committees. WL Ross also engaged an independent accounting firm to perform an internal controls review of its back-office functions, and implemented the firm's recommendations for enhancements to its processes and internal controls, including to the expense review and approval process and the tracking and monitoring of Transaction Fees.

21. WL Ross also implemented new controls concerning the review and approval of expense reimbursements and fee offsets. In December 2014, WL Ross revised the Expense Processing and Allocation Policy it had adopted in 2011. Under the revised policy, management fee calculations as well as Transaction Fees from portfolio investments and related fee offset calculations must be reviewed and approved by the Chief Financial Officer and the Expense Review Group, a new group comprised of senior management, the Chief Financial Officer, and legal and compliance representatives, to ensure appropriate allocations and compliance with the relevant fund offering documents and agreements.

Ultimately without admitting or denying the SEC findings, the firm agreed to pay a civil penalty of $2.3 million as well as voluntarily reimburse the funds approximately $10.4 million in management fees and $1.4 million in interest.[7]

8.7 SUMMARY

This chapter focused on private equity compliance documentation. We began by discussing the purposes of developing GP compliance documentation. Next, we addressed the benefits of documenting compliance, including complying with regulatory requirements, communicating compliance employees to GP employees, facilitating investors' understanding of compliance, and providing service providers with documented compliance guidance. The role of compliance documentation in facilitating ongoing change management of compliance functions and policies was also discussed. Key private equity compliance documentation, including the compliance manual and code of ethics, was examined. A range of other documented compliance policies was outlined, including electronic communication and social media policies. Finally, a case study in the ways in which the language in fund legal and compliance documentation is interpreted and applied in multiple areas, including the use of fee offsets, was presented. Now that we have an understanding of the core documentation that makes up a GP compliance program, in the next chapter we build upon this foundation to discuss the ongoing implementation of compliance through training, surveillance, and testing.

---

[7]A. Jacobius, "WL Ross to Pay $2.3 Million Penalty to SEC over Fee Allocation Practices," *Pensions & Investments*, August 25, 2016.

CHAPTER 9

Compliance Training, Surveillance, and Testing for Private Equity Firms

9.1 INTRODUCTION TO PRIVATE EQUITY TRAINING, SURVEILLANCE, AND TESTING

In previous chapters we introduced the key concepts related to the creation, documentation, and implementation of a private equity compliance program. Once a compliance program is up and running, however, this is not where a general partner's (GP's) compliance obligations end. The next stage in compliance management relates to ongoing compliance obligations in order to maintain and improve upon the existing compliance function. There are three main components to this ongoing compliance management: training, surveillance, and testing (TST), collectively referred to as *compliance TST*. We now proceed to discuss each aspect of TST in more detail.

9.2 GROWTH OF TST

In the early days of the private equity industry the rigor of the overall compliance function was relatively weak as compared to today. As compliance obligations of GPs as well as the oversight of private equity compliance-related duties by regulators and investors have steadily increased, so have the resources dedicated by GPs to compliance similarly increased. With this broader compliance increase has come an accompanying focus on compliance TST.

In regard to training specifically, as compliance has become more complex and GP compliance policies have become more rigorous, more resources have been devoted by GPs toward not only explaining compliance policies to employees but also making sure they know how to effectively implement them. Turning to testing and surveillance, traditionally this work was not performed by the compliance function at all but by a different department, known as the *internal audit function* (*IA*). The IA function typically picks a number of issues or departments throughout the firm related to funds and conducts testing and surveillance on them on an ongoing basis. The difference between the testing and surveillance work of IA versus that performed by the compliance function today is that the work of the internal audit function is not necessarily limited to compliance issues and may cover a wide variety of other issues throughout a firm. Over time the overlap between the internal audit and compliance training and surveillance function has led many GPs that previously maintained dedicated internal audit personnel to integrate many aspects of the internal audit function into the compliance function.

That being said, internal audit has not been completely eliminated and today larger private equity firms may still maintain their own in-house internal audit functions. In other cases, certain audit work may be outsourced to third parties. Increasingly fund managers have taken to pursuing third-party audit certifications that may have been pursued by fund administrators such as the International Standard of Assurance Engagements (ISAE) 3402 or Statement on Standards for Attestation Engagements (SSAE) 16. In the past decade there was a trend among certain large asset managers, such as hedge funds, to pursue these types of certifications in order to demonstrate enhanced auditor oversight over certain functions. More recently the popularity of these reviews in the hedge fund space has waned. While a GP may opt to undergo this review, such third-party audit certifications have gained less traction in the private equity space.

9.3 COMPLIANCE TRAINING

Compliance training refers to the practice of a private equity firm ensuring that its employees are informed about the key aspects of the firm's compliance program. The carrying out of training itself for employees is typically spelled out in the firm's policies and is a key aspect of the implementation of best practice compliance.

Compliance training typically takes place at two stages during the life of an employee. The first is when a new employee joins a private equity firm. In addition to standard new-hire orientation, the compliance department will also typically conduct *initial compliance training* or *new-hire compliance training* on the firm's compliance policies contained in these compliance documents.

In addition to compliance training for new employees, *ongoing training* is also performed for existing employees. This ongoing training takes three primary forms:

1. Firm-wide compliance meeting
2. Department-specific compliance training
3. Issue-specific compliance training

Training may be conducted through in-person meetings or through the use of computer-based training programs. Depending on the nature of the training, it may be more efficient for a GP to utilize a third-party's off-the-shelf training program, typically given through the Internet. These sessions are generally performed on broader industry-wide compliance matters, such as anti–money laundering, rather than on compliance matters more directly relevant to the unique aspects of each GP's funds. In practice, a combination of both in-person and computer-based training methods is typically employed.

9.3.1   Firm-Wide Compliance Training

Firm-wide compliance training refers to when all the employees of the GP undergo training on the firm's compliance policies and procedures. For GPs with multiple offices, or when it is not practical to conduct a single session for all employees, multiple firm-wide training sessions are performed. In this situation, it is generally advisable to perform all training around the same general time period in order to ensure the consistency of the dissemination of compliance information distributed throughout the firm.

On at least an annual basis it is considered best practice for a private equity firm to perform annual training for all employees. Even if annual training is not mandated by regulators in a particular jurisdiction, these meetings are typically encouraged. Furthermore, a regulator may inquire about the frequency and depth of employee compliance policy and procedure training. Key features of this annual compliance meeting generally include:[1]

- *Agenda development and documenting meeting attendance.* It is advisable for attendance to be taken at these annual mandatory meetings. Additionally, most compliance policies outline that the private equity firm should develop a meeting agenda to be distributed prior to

---

[1]J. Scharfman, "Hedge Fund Compliance: Risks, Regulation and Management" (Hoboken: Wiley Finance, December 2016).

the meeting. These procedures create a record for the private equity firm to use in analyzing future training efforts. Furthermore, this documentation facilitates the creation of a paper trail should a regulator require evidence of training procedures in more detail.

■ *Meeting led by chief compliance officer (CCO) or third party.* Either the CCO or a third-party service provider, such as a compliance consultant or law firm, typically leads the annual training meeting.

■ *Virtual participation.* If a GP has multiple offices in different locations, and the firm wishes to conduct fewer firm-wide training sessions, it may be more cost efficient to conduct the annual meeting in person for the bulk of the firm's employees and allow other employees to participate in the meeting virtually via conference call or videoconference.

■ *Recap of compliance policies and procedures.* The annual meeting should include an overview of the firm's compliance policies and procedures. This provides employees an opportunity to re-familiarize themselves with compliance policies.

■ *Updates on compliance changes.* Changes to compliance policies implemented in the past year are discussed at the annual meeting.

■ *Updates on compliance trends and anticipated changes.* The annual meeting is an opportunity to provide an update on emerging compliance issues as well as introduce anticipated compliance changes that may be implemented in the coming year.

■ *Question-and-answer session.* The annual compliance meeting also affords employees the opportunity to ask any questions regarding compliance matters.

Annual training meetings are also an opportunity to collect what are known as *employee acknowledgments*. These acknowledgments are typically mandated by regulators as well as a private equity firm's internal policies. Employee acknowledgments are compliance forms employees are required to complete acknowledging they have received the firm's compliance policies and procedures.

Either as part of the acknowledgment form or as a separate form, employees are also typically tasked with affirmatively stating that they have complied with the GP's policies over the last reporting period. This is referred to as a *compliance attestation*, because the employees are attesting (i.e. affirmatively stating) that they have complied with the policies. Exhibit 9.1 is an example of a combined acknowledgment and attestation form. In certain instances, employees may complete multiple additional acknowledgment and attestation forms to demonstrate adherence to specific compliance policies, such as the firm's code of ethics.

Acknowledgment Form for Code of Ethics

By affixing my signature in the indicated areas that follow, I certify that I have received this compliance manual. I further certify that I have fully read and understood the material contained in this manual. Additionally, I acknowledge that I have fully abided by this manual and will continue to do so.

I also acknowledge that I understand that should I have any questions about this compliance manual, I should direct them to the chief compliance officer.

Print: _____.

Signature: _____.

Date: _____

Exhibit 9.1 Example code of ethics acknowledgment for a private equity employee.

Another example would be an acknowledgment that an employee has agreed to adhere to a private equity's policies relating to the protection of investor data. An employee may also need to attest that he has complied with a GP's personal securities transaction policies, including the disclosure of any covered employee securities transactions throughout the reporting period. Compliance oversight of employee personal account trading is discussed in more detail in Chapter 5.

Employees are typically asked to complete these acknowledgments and attestations on at least an annual basis, if not more frequently, which is why it is convenient to time their collection around the annual compliance meeting. Some firms require signed hardcopies while others accept electronic signatures.

9.3.2 Department- and Issue-Specific Training

In addition to annual firm-wide compliance training, a GP may conduct more focused training for different departments. This is known as *department-specific training*. The purpose of these sessions is to focus on specific compliance rules that may be more applicable to certain job functions as compared to others. An example of this would be rules related to the ways in which investment analysts should manage expenses related to travel associated with investment research conducted on portfolio companies.

This training would obviously be more relevant to an investment analyst actually performing this type of research as opposed to a fund accountant in the back office.

Continuing our example, of course there is nothing wrong in providing a general introduction to travel expense policies to all employees of the firm; however, the goal of department-specific training is to provide further detail and emphasis on the rules that are most relevant to specific employees.

The third category of compliance training is known as *issue-specific training*. This is training focused around a certain specific topic. An example would be a training session limited to insider trading practices, how to comply with the employee cybersecurity policies, or a session on new regulations that were recently put into place. Issue-specific training may be offered either on a firm-wide or departmental basis as relevant. If offered firm-wide, it could be bundled into the annual firm-wide training that would already be taking place. However, in practice issue-specific training tends to delve into more detail than would be appropriate to cover in a larger firm-wide training session, so breakout issue-specific training sessions are preferred. The same holds true for issue-specific training on a departmental basis as well, where a stand-alone deep-dive into the specific issues is preferable to a more broadly focused departmental session.

9.4 DISTINGUISHING COMPLIANCE TESTING AND SURVEILLANCE

It is important to understand the distinction between compliance testing and surveillance. *Compliance testing* refers to a historical analysis of the ways in which actual procedures were carried out at the firm. *Compliance surveillance* refers to ongoing monitoring or a firm's activities to determine if a compliance violation occurs in or near real-time. To be clear, even though many private equity investment strategies are not actively executing trades or other transactions on a daily basis, a host of compliance policies and procedures address non-investment-related activities. As such, surveillance of these non-investment activities can be performed on an ongoing basis even though no other fund-level investment activities may be occurring. Furthermore, even if a private equity fund is not actively allocating new capital or selling out of a position, there may be follow-on investment activity related to current fund holdings. The reason this distinction is important is because a GP's compliance department, as well as any consultants utilized, must take care not to focus on the consequences of the violations when determining if any compliance violations occurred. Any subsequent profit or loss incurred is secondary to the concept of whether a violation occurred to begin with.

9.5   TESTING AND SURVEILLANCE SCOPE

When testing and surveillance are performed, it is important to understand that a compliance test can be differentiated from a full-compliance audit. For the purposes of this discussion, a compliance test means the utilization of a process, known as *compliance sampling*, whereby a portion of the activity in a specific function is tested. This can be distinguished from testing all of the activity in a specific area. Depending on the volume and scope of a compliance audit, an audit may utilize sampling or test all of the activity over a specific time period.

9.6   IMPLEMENTING COMPLIANCE TESTING

Due to the historical focus of compliance testing, it is also sometimes referred to as *compliance back testing*, because of its backward-looking nature. When performing testing, the first consideration is what area testing should focus on. It is recommended that testing is performed throughout all areas of the firm, including the investment and operational functions. In practice, however, compliance testing is not performed across all sections of the firm at a single point in time. One reason for this is that compliance resources are limited and it would often not be practical to conduct all this compliance testing at one time. Additionally, there is an added benefit to spreading out the compliance testing so that multiple points in time are covered. As such, GPs are faced with the challenge of prioritizing the testing of the implementation of compliance policies and procedures in certain areas of the firm ahead of others. In making this determination the GP will typically begin by placing emphasis on what are perceived to be the higher risk areas. This is known as a *risk-weighted assessment*.

While risk-weighted assessments are often backward looking, a GP will typically place more emphasis on the areas that are perceived to be at higher risk of compliance violations. As such, due to their importance in the landscape of private equity compliance, two of the most common examples of items often subject to prioritized testing by GP compliance functions are conflicts of interest and deal allocation.

9.6.1   Testing Schedules

Based on a GP's priorities, a list would be developed to schedule the order in which other items would be tested. This arrangement would then be placed on a *compliance testing calendar* or *testing schedule*. Regularly scheduled compliance events, such as the testing schedule, as well as any pre-planned training sessions would then be combined to form a *master compliance calendar* or simply *compliance calendar*. Compliance calendars are useful planning tools to outline pre-planned compliance events for the year.

Of course, these calendars are merely meant to be outlines and are subject to change. One example of the ways that a master compliance calendar may change from a training perspective would be if a new regulation is passed that the GP feels it would be useful to conduct a training session about. This issue-specific training would likely not have been anticipated and then could be added to the compliance calendar as needed. From a testing perspective, an example of the ways a compliance calendar could be amended would be if a new compliance violation is noted.

For example, consider a situation where a violation or series of violations come about with regard to the appropriate process for the compliance to review any marketing materials prior to their distribution to investors. Due to the increased violations in this area, the GP may deem it appropriate to move testing in this area ahead of other items and would therefore reorganize the compliance testing calendar. Similarly, the frequency of testing and training in this area would also likely increase.

9.6.2   Testing Frequency

The next consideration is how frequently testing should be performed. Several factors influence this determination, including:

- When was testing last performed in this area?
- Have any recent near-misses or actual violations been noted in this area?
- Have there been recent changes in regulations or laws influencing this area?
- Have market practices in this area significantly changed recently?
- Has the GP recently amended its compliance policies in this area?

To better understand the way testing works in practice, let us consider how testing in the area of deal allocation may work. The first place to start would be to understand the GP's policy in this area. The trade allocation policy in this place would be the *compliance benchmark* against which testing would be performed.

For the purposes of our example let us utilize the following sample GP trade allocation policy:

Under specific circumstances, an individual investment opportunity may be deemed to be appropriate for more than one fund managed by the firm. For the avoidance of doubt this could include, but is not limited to, co-investments. In making a determination as to how to allocate these opportunities the firm will first prepare an allocation memorandum outlining whether the allocation methodology employed is on a pro rata basis. By default, the use of a pro rata basis is preferred. In situations where a determination is made that a pro rata allocation would not be in the best interest of a particular investment, the allocation memorandum must also specify the basis for the decision not to utilize a pro rata methodology. The allocation memorandum shall also specify the factors considered in making an allocation determination including but not limited to consideration for existing fund holdings, fund risk profile, and investment strategy. Additionally, the fund's offering documents will also be consulted prior to any allocation recommendations being made. The allocation memorandum must also specify the proposed amounts to be allocated to each fund or entity. After the preparation of a memorandum a review shall be performed by the firm's allocation committee as to the appropriateness of the allocations methodology.

With this policy in place the compliance function of the GP could then select several instances in which deals were allocated across multiple funds to determine if the procedures outlined in the policy were indeed followed. The steps of each allocation as they were implemented in practice would then be compared to the steps followed as outlined in the policy. If a step in the process was omitted or incorrectly applied, or a near-miss took place, the GP would then take corrective action.

Which historical instances of deal allocation to select is in the discretion of the GP. One option would be to test a certain selection of recent deal allocations. An example of this would be to test the most recent five deal allocations. Another option would be to perform testing over a broader time period, such as the first deal allocation each year over the last three years. Yet another option would be to randomly select deals of trades over a broader period of time. This is commonly referred to as *random selection*. The specific resources of the GP, the periodicity of previous testing, and the overall risk weighting can all be factors considered by the GP in determining the methodology utilized to test in each area.

It should also be noted that a GP may wish to employ a different frequency and methodology of testing across different areas. For example, there will be a greater volume of emails sent among employees as compared to the number of deals allocated by private equity funds. In these instances, due to the differences in volume a testing program more focused around random selection may be preferred that casts a broader net as compared to a more focused, deeper-dive testing program on a lower-volume deal allocation.

9.7 INCORPORATING MOCK AUDITS INTO TESTING

As we referenced earlier in this book, a GP's compliance function may consist entirely of internal personnel, the compliance function may be entirely outsourced to third parties, or third-party resources may be utilized in conjunction with internal resources. This latter option is the most common construct as it allows the GP to maintain direct involvement with the compliance function while still benefiting from the expertise of third-party specialists. The two most common third-party service providers that offer compliance-related services are legal counsel and a compliance consultant.

One of the services typically offered by compliance consultants is a *mock audit*. A mock audit is a compliance review meant to simulate the examinations a regulator would conduct of a private equity fund. This is why mock audits may also be referred to as *regulatory mock audits*. Typically, mock audits simulate routine regulatory examinations as opposed to more targeted issue-specific regulatory examinations. Mock audits are backward-looking tests of how well a firm has adhered to their compliance policies and procedures with a specific focus on how a regulator would view a GP's compliance framework and subsequent adherence to that framework.

Mock audits involve the same procedures as GP-led compliance testing would, including compliance sampling, risk-weighted assessments, and random selection. Additionally, depending on their resources and in-house expertise GPs may opt to perform a mock audit themselves, rather than outsource the work to a third party, to complement existing testing procedures. However, based on their knowledge and experience with industry-wide practices, working with a third-party compliance consultant in some capacity to either design or perform the review process is often considered to be beneficial.

9.8 COMPLIANCE SURVEILLANCE IMPLEMENTATION

As outlined previously, the key differentiator between testing and surveillance relates to the time period being analyzed. Testing is backward looking while surveillance focuses on monitoring a private equity firm and funds' actual practices being employed in real time or near real time to determine if they are in compliance or deviating from the firm's policies. For a firm that trades actively, such as certain hedge fund strategies, compliance surveillance is typically focused heavily on fund-level trading activity. This can be contrasted with private equity firms that typically transact in deals and have relatively low trading volumes by comparison.

The different trading structures of private equity firms does not mean that surveillance adds no value; instead, its implementation is different. Surveillance can be conducted by compliance on non-operational issues when a private equity fund is not actively making any new allocations. An example of this would be compliance oversight of a fund's month-end accounting processes.

One way surveillance could be implemented in practice would be for the compliance function to compare any deal allocations made throughout the month to the month-end work on the day the work is completed (or shortly thereafter). Another example would be for the GP compliance department to make a random selection of any electronic communications sent throughout a particular day and monitor them for any compliance violations such as promising investors certain guaranteed performance or sharing confidential information. Compliance surveillance is typically conducted electronically; however, depending on the nature of the area being surveilled it could also be conducted through interviews or the review of physical documents as well.

9.9   ANALYZING TESTING AND SURVEILLANCE DATA

After compliance testing and surveillance have been completed, the compliance function will then have to proceed with analyzing the data about actual practices being employed. The first step in this process is to perform a *gap analysis*. This process compares the compliance benchmark (i.e. a specific compliance policy) to the data gathered during the testing and surveillance to determine if indeed the procedures were performed in adherence to the firm's policies (i.e. in compliance) or if a deviation from those prescribed policies occurred (i.e. out of compliance). There are three possible outcomes from the testing and surveillance data:

1. No violation occurred.
2. A near-miss occurred.
3. A violation occurred.

Under the first potential outcome, if no compliance violations occurred, then the training and surveillance data must next be analyzed to determine whether a violation almost occurred. These are known as *near misses*. Near misses are not technical compliance violations but the actions in question almost violated the policy. Private equity regulators may require or encourage GPs to maintain a record of these near-miss events, which are often noted as a result of training and surveillance. This is known as a *near-miss register*. A key purpose of this log is to allow the GP to study near misses, identify where potential weaknesses may exist in the compliance program, and determine if any future policy amendments or corrective action should be taken prior to any actual compliance violations occurring. Additionally, as part of their promotion of an open reporting framework by which employees can raise either actual knowledge of potential violations or concerns regarding potential violations, the reporting of near misses is similarly encouraged.[2]

The third outcome would be to note if a violation occurred. In this case the next step would be to determine the severity of the violation and then take corrective action.

9.10 CORRECTIVE ACTION

When determining the severity of a compliance policy breach, a GP typically distinguishes the nature of the violation based on the anticipated consequences. The three typical outcomes of compliance violations are not mutually exclusive:

1. Involving limited partners (LPs)
2. Involving regulators
3. Contained to the GP

As the list above indicates, not all compliance violations lead to actions by the regulator or legal consequences for a fund. The reason for this is because the GP's compliance policies may be stricter than required by law. In these cases, depending on the nature of the violation the GP may be able to simply note the compliance violations occurred and may be required to take corrective action or amend policies. In other instances, however, even though the GP's compliance policies were stricter than the law because the GP committed to a certain standard, the violation may have the same material effect as if the stricter policy had been law.

9.11 COMPLIANCE VIOLATIONS DO NOT NECESSARILY IMPLY GP OR FUND PROFITS

One common point of confusion among investors and fund managers relates to the notion that if a compliance violation occurs, it means that the GP, its employees, or funds benefited financially, and by association that a fund's

---

[2]UK Financial Services Authority, "Enhancing Frameworks in the Standardised Approach to Operational Risk: Guidance Note," January 2011.

investors were financially disadvantaged, from the actions that caused the violation. This is not always the case.

When a compliance violation occurs, it does not necessarily imply that the GP or funds profited from the violation. Indeed, violations can also occur where a GP, its employees, or the funds either lost money or no financial impact transpired. The issue of profit or loss is important to determining the impact of the violation, but not whether a violation actually occurred.

We can demonstrate this concept through an example. Consider a GP that maintains a compliance policy relating to restrictions on the personal security transactions of its employees.

For our example, let us assume that this GP's compliance policy requires that employees hold all purchases of securities for 30 days. In the event they want to sell a security purchased in less than 30 days, pre-clearance from the compliance department would be required. Let us further assume that an employee simply makes a mistake and sells the security on day 29 instead after the 30-day limit. At this point we do not care whether the employee made money. A violation occurred simply because the rules as outlined were not followed.

If instead the GP's policy had only provided for a required 15-day holding period window, then this would not be a violation. Continuing our example, we can then determine if the employee profited or lost money and what to do about. The common approach taken is if an employee profited, she is required to donate the profits to charity, and if a loss occurred, no action is taken; however, the employee is typically warned and potentially subject to further disciplinary action.

The results of this gap analysis are then to take corrective action. This corrective action focuses on two primary tasks. The first is to determine if any damage has been done. For example, if a certain type of trading limit was breached, a misallocation of trades occurred, or employees inadvertently acted on material non-public information, a GP may need to proactively reach out to a financial regulator as well as investors to disclose this breach and place LPs back in the position they were before the error occurred. The second focus of corrective action would be to determine if the firm's compliance policies need to be amended to ensure that there is a sufficient match between the firm and fund's current practices. Perhaps the reason that the compliance policies were violated was because the activities of the firm and funds have changed such that the compliance policies need to be amended to properly reflect this.

An extreme example of this would be if a fund's compliance manual outlined that employees were not allowed to access information from outside the firm's main offices. Let us further assume that since this policy was written the firm has opened several other offices and significantly expanded its investment scope. The chief investment officer (CIO) of the firm may be traveling much more and need to access information remotely. Furthermore, advances in information security software may have increased the security surrounding the access of information from outside the firm's primary office setup and the GP may determine that the benefits of this type of access outweigh the risks. However, the firm may have not yet updated its compliance policies, and a subsequent technical breach may have occurred. As such, after a technical breach would have been noted by having the CIO log into the firm's network remotely, the GP could decide that the corrective action would be to amend the compliance manual to now reflect that accessing the systems remotely under certain conditions, subject to oversight by the information technology function, would now be acceptable.

9.12 SUMMARY

This chapter introduced the concepts of compliance TST for private equity firms. We began with an analysis of why GPs are increasingly devoting more resources to TST. Next, we examined the various methods of compliance training, including new-hire and ongoing compliance training. We then addressed firm-wide, department-specific, and issue-specific compliance training approaches. The differences between testing and surveillance were examined. The implementation of compliance testing was then discussed in more detail, including the frequency by which tests should be conducted and the role of mock audits in testing. We then discussed private equity compliance surveillance and techniques for analyzing testing data through gap analysis protocols. In the next chapter we build upon our understanding of the GP TST techniques to understand how a private equity fund's LPs analyze the strength of a GP compliance program.

CHAPTER 10

Limited Partner Analysis of Private Equity Compliance Functions

10.1 A COMPLIANCE EVALUATION IS PART OF THE OVERALL DUE DILIGENCE PROCESS

When an investor in a private equity fund is considering allocating to a general partner (GP) they go through a process of collecting and reviewing information from the GP. This process is known as *due diligence*. At a high level, due diligence can be segregated into two distinct areas. The first is *investment due diligence* (IDD). IDD focuses primarily on the investment-related aspects of the private equity funds. The second category is *operational due diligence* (ODD).

As contrasted with IDD, ODD focuses primarily on non-investment-related aspects of a fund's management. This due diligence process should also include an analysis of the compliance function in place. These compliance reviews have traditionally been more centered in the realm of ODD as opposed to IDD; however, there is increasingly an overlap between the two areas. The reason for this is many of these other areas covered during the larger due diligence process, while not directly part of the compliance function, have compliance elements or directly overlap with compliance.

10.1.1 Focus on GP Compliance

Throughout this book we have outlined the three tiers across which compliance procedures can be implemented:

1. GP level compliance
2. Fund level compliance
3. Portfolio company compliance as it relates to the GP and funds

When a limited partner (LP) sets out to evaluate the compliance function, the primary focus will be on GP-level compliance procedures. This is
because, as we have previously noted, the GP procedures have direct influence on the other two tiers. Once an LP has a firm understanding of the
GP-level compliance framework, then an analysis of fund-level compliance
procedures can ensue. While there may be common shared elements among
different funds, the fund formation documents will dictate the essential elements of fund-level compliance obligations and these will be specific to each
fund. Finally, any portfolio company compliance considerations can then
be evaluated.

10.2   GOALS OF INVESTOR COMPLIANCE ANALYSIS

Investors have a number of different goals when performing due diligence
on a private equity fund. From an investment perspective a primary goal is
for investors to develop an understanding of the firm's investment strategy
and research process. From an operations perspective, a key goal for LPs is
to determine if a fund maintains a strong operational infrastructure. With
regard to the ODD processes in particular a core theme of the due diligence
process is to not only determine where a GP's strength may lie, but also
where there may be weaknesses as well as room for improvement as part of
the overall risk assessment process.

10.2.1   Signaling Effect of Compliance Due Diligence

The strength of the compliance function can often be a key indicator as to
the overall strength of the firm's operations, as well as the seriousness with
which they approach issues outside of those directly related to managing
the firm's investments. In a due diligence construct, the concept of looking
at one area of a fund's operations for cues as to strengths or weaknesses in
other areas is known as the *signaling effect*. Therefore, an LP who during
the ODD process notes weaknesses in the compliance process might utilize
this information to tailor the rest of his due diligence process based on the
weak compliance signals generated during the compliance review.

10.2.2   Evaluating the GP's Compliance Culture

When conducting due diligence on the GP's compliance framework,
investors seek to evaluate the quality of the overall compliance function.
A firm with a strong compliance function is often deemed to have a strong

culture of compliance. Qualitative terms such as *quality* and *culture,* however, can be difficult to define when LPs attempt to make a detailed due diligence evaluation of the compliance function.

A key element of the culture of compliance is not only whether a firm has well-documented compliance policies, but also whether they are actively implemented in practice. An accompanying element of a strong culture of compliance relates to how well compliance policies are reinforced among employees through avenues such as frequent training on compliance matters. Other specific elements LP investors traditionally look for when evaluating the culture of the compliance include:[1]

- Strength of compliance controls
- Independence of the compliance function
- Appropriateness of resources devoted to the compliance function
- Frequency and comprehensiveness of compliance training
- Robustness of ongoing compliance oversight and testing
- Presence of a history of any violations of internal compliance policies or regulatory violations

10.3 DISTINGUISHING INITIAL VERSUS ONGOING COMPLIANCE DUE DILIGENCE

Due diligence, including a review of the compliance function, can be performed by LPs at multiple stages in the investment process. The most common time LPs first perform compliance due diligence on a GP is prior to when they allocate capital. This is known as *initial compliance due diligence,* that is, when an investor analyzes a GP's compliance function for the first time. This can be contrasted with *ongoing compliance due diligence,* which refers to when an investor performs continued evaluations of a GP's compliance function after an initial review has been completed.

There may be unusual instances where an investor may have already invested in a private equity fund and, in deviation of best practices, performed little or no due diligence on the compliance function prior to investing. There are a variety of reasons why this may have occurred, including a historical bias against compliance due diligence for a particular investor and a lack of due diligence of resources for an LP. Furthermore, an LP may have

---

[1]J. Scharfman, "Hedge Fund Compliance: Risks, Regulation and Management" (Wiley Finance, December 2016).

simply lacked the specialized knowledge required to evaluate the compliance function in-house and have chosen not to work with an ODD consultant, which often possesses such expertise.

While certainly not advisable, this could result in a situation whereby an existing investor, realizing the error of her ways in not performing initial due diligence, could decide several years after making an investment in a private equity fund to analyze the compliance function for the first time. This special case, therefore, would be considered initial compliance analysis for an existing investor rather than ongoing monitoring.

The reason it is important to distinguish between initial analysis and ongoing monitoring is because initial and ongoing compliance analyses typically operate on different timelines and require different allocations of resources from investors. Additionally, there are often slightly different goals associated with the two different stages of compliance analysis. Initial compliance analysis is more focused on making an initial determination as to the strengths and weaknesses of a compliance function, whereas ongoing compliance monitoring is focused more on analyzing the change in a compliance function over time.

10.4   INITIAL COMPLIANCE DUE DILIGENCE PROCESS

The initial compliance due diligence process can be broadly categorized into three steps:

- *Step # 1: Compliance documentation collection and review.* To begin the initial analysis of the compliance function, an investor starts by collecting documentation from a private equity fund. The documents collected are the compliance policies and procedures described in the previous chapter, and should include key compliance documentation, such as the compliance manual and code of ethics as applicable.

  After this documentation is collected from the GP, an investor would then proceed to review it and develop an initial understanding of the private equity firm's compliance function. As compliance evaluations are typically conducted in conjunction as part of the larger due diligence process, there may be other additional documents that are reviewed that cover a wide variety of topics, such as a GP's marketing pitchbook or due diligence questionnaire. These other documents can often provide valuable insights into compliance practices and procedures.

- *Step #2: Interviews with compliance personnel.* Once the relevant compliance documentation has been collected and reviewed, an LP would then proceed to conduct an interview with compliance personnel. These interviews serve two primary functions. First, they afford an investor with the opportunity to confirm the information outlined in the collected documentation. Second, they allow LPs to fill in any gaps in their understanding of a GP's compliance program, as well as gain additional insights into the function of compliance programs. If possible, it is considered a best practice for an investor to conduct these interviews in person and onsite in the fund manager's office.

One benefit of conducting an in-person interview is that it provides the opportunity for an investor to review additional compliance documentation directly in the GP's office. In certain instances, citing primarily confidentiality concerns, a private equity fund may only provide investors with limited excerpts or the table of contents of certain compliance documentation that they may have requested. For example, this is common practice with a GP's compliance manual. To review the entire document an investor may be required to visit the fund manager's office and review it there. A second benefit to an in-person onsite interview is that an investor will also have the direct opportunity to review a demonstration of the GP's compliance-related systems operating in practice. While not preferred, in certain instances, investors do not have the resources to visit a manager onsite, and instead opt to conduct these interviews remotely through a videoconference or through screen-sharing technology.

- *Step #3: Confirm and analyze compliance-related service provider relationships.* Service providers can play a critical role in the compliance process. It is important that investors do not neglect analyzing these service providers when performing due diligence on the compliance function. The service provider review process can be categorized into three general stages:

  1. *Relationship confirmation.* To ensure a GP and its funds are not fraudulently fabricating its relationships with a particular compliance service provider, investors should first attempt to independently confirm that an actual relationship is in place.

  2. *Document collection.* After the relationship is confirmed an investor would next proceed with collecting documentation from the service provider relevant to their relationship with the GP. Examples of this could include marketing materials that provide an overview of the service provider's firm and service level agreements (SLAs) detailing the compliance services provided to the GP.

  3. *Interview.* After the relevant documentation has been collected and reviewed, an investor would next conduct an interview with the service provider. Similar to the interview conducted with the private equity firm, the goals of this interview are to confirm the information

obtained in the documentation as well as to gain additional insights into the way the service provider works with the GP's compliance function. While it is beneficial to conduct these meetings on site, it is common industry practice for investors to conduct these service provider meetings remotely via phone or videoconference in most cases.

10.5 INCORPORATING VENDORS INTO COMPLIANCE POLICIES

A GP's in-house compliance department is typically also involved in drafting procedures that address the role of third-party service providers. Depending on the particular compliance procedure being addressed, in many instances compliance policies will detail the procedures for matters that cover both the in-house work of the GP as well as the services of a vendor in the same document. For example, a private equity fund's valuation policy would likely address a GP's policy for overseeing in-house valuations through mechanisms such as a valuation committee, but may also address the role of third-party service providers in this process, such as valuation consultants and auditors, in determining and documenting valuations.

10.5.1 Valuation Policy Vendor Example

If a GP's compliance function limits their compliance procedures to primarily focus on in-house work, and does not incorporate the roles of service providers, they may be exposing themselves to unnecessary risks and the potential of ongoing confusion. One issue for the employees of the GP is that a lack of clearly documented guidance may leave the specific compliance requirements of vendors open to interpretation. This could result in inconsistencies in the process.

Returning to our valuation policy example, consider the situation where a fund is intended to receive certain documentation from a valuation consultant that details the sources used in determining a value for a specific portfolio holding on a quarterly basis. Let us further assume that the common practice in place between the valuation consultant and the GP was that this information would be sent in an email accompanying a separate fund valuation report sent by the valuation consultant. For the purposes of this example, we will also further specify that the GP's valuation policy does not address in detail the common practice between the GP and valuation consultant that the valuation sources are to be received quarterly.

Now let's assume that a key employee at the valuation consultant responsible for writing and sending these emails on a quarterly basis has now left the firm. A new employee takes over who is not familiar with the procedures and could simply send the valuation report without the email containing the valuation sources. Alternatively, we could have a situation where the individual at the GP who received and logged the emails may have left the firm, and his replacement may not know about the specific previous procedures employed. If the process was addressed in detail and specified appropriately in the valuation policy of the GP, then this confusion would likely have been avoided. Furthermore, even if the receipts of these emails were not overlooked initially due to employee turnover at either the GP or the valuation consultant, then, as a backstop, testing of the documented procedures by the compliance department would likely have caught the oversight.

10.5.2 Potential Penalties for Lack of Vendor Oversight Procedures

Another compliance-related issue facing GPs whose policies do not incorporate the role of vendors relates to regulatory liability. In some instances, GPs may be required to draft and implement compliance procedures that not only detail the scope of services performed by service providers, but also outline the procedures by which a GP will oversee the implementation of these services.

One example from the funds management industry that highlights the importance of GP compliance policies for oversight of vendors was a 2016 incident involving a fund manager named Tillage Commodities, LLC ("Tillage") and its fund administrator SS&C Technologies ("SS&C"). For reference, this case was first introduced in Chapter 7. As background, in this case Chinese hackers tricked SS&C into processing fraudulent wire transfers of funds, including one wire transfer totaling $3 million.[2] In total, fake wire requests were received resulting in fraudulent transfers of $5.9 million.[3] In September 2017, the US Commodity Futures Trading Commission (CFTC) issued an order that in part required Tillage to pay a $150,000 civil monetary penalty. In a release announcing the order, the CFTC stated, "Although only the fund administrator had the right to

---

[2] *See Tillage Commodities Fund, LP v. SS&C Tech., Inc.*, 2016 N.Y. Misc. LEXIS 4834 (Dec. 22, 2016) and associated filings.
[3] Jon Marino, "China Hackers Swipe Millions in Data Breach Penalty for Supervision Failures," *CNBC.com*, September 16, 2016.

make withdrawals from the pool bank account, Tillage had no procedures in place to monitor the administrator's operation of this account and no system in place to alert it when transactions cleared from the account."[4]

This case highlights the importance of having a fund manager:

- Design compliance policies and accompanying operational procedures to incorporate appropriate oversight of service providers.
- Develop ongoing testing and monitoring procedures that oversee the actions of service providers.

As this case demonstrates, this oversight also includes fund administrators and movements of cash from fund bank accounts. It should be noted that in a private equity context, even though a GP may self-administer their own funds, the same lessons regarding the oversight of other service providers, even if no third-party fund administrator is present, are likely still applicable.

10.6   CASE STUDY: BLACKSTREET CAPITAL MANAGEMENT

One of the basic goals in performing ongoing testing and surveillance is to ensure that a private equity fund is operating in compliance with the fund's governing formation documents.

Upon formation of the fund, another key compliance obligation of GPs, and by association their chief compliance officer (CCO), is to ensure that the fund has gone through the process of filing the appropriate regulatory registrations with regulators. If the fund's activities were to change over time, then based on this new activity the GP may need to apply for additional regulatory registrations and in some cases may also be required to make additional filings as well. A critical function of testing and surveillance is, therefore, for the compliance function to monitor both the fund's adherence to the offering documents as well as to determine if they venture into these new areas that require additional registration or filing activity.

In June 2016, the US Securities and Exchange Commission (SEC) investigated the actions of Blackstreet Capital Management (BCM), a Maryland-based private equity firm. What follows is an excerpt from the SEC Administrative Proceeding in this matter, which details allegations

---

[4]CFTC Release: pr7620-17, "CFTC Orders Connecticut-based Tillage Commodities, LLC to Pay a $150 000 Civil Monetary Penalty for Supervision Failures," September 28, 2017.

related to issues including both deviations from the fund offering documents and unregistered brokerage activity by a private equity firm. A host of associated issues relating to conflicts of interest and expense management are also discussed as well:[5]

FACTS

A. Background

15. BCM provides investment advisory and management services to Fund I and Fund II (collectively, the "Funds"). The Funds are each governed by a limited partnership agreement (LPA) that sets forth the terms and operation of the fund. Pursuant to each LPA, BCA, and BCA II, GPs are responsible for management of their respective funds, but each is permitted to, and did, appoint BCM to serve as manager.

16. The Funds invest primarily in undervalued portfolio companies that are mismanaged, unprofitable, orphaned by a parent conglomerate, or have limited earnings potential in a declining market. The Funds call capital from their respective LPs, which may be used to fund the acquisition of the portfolio companies, including related turnaround fees and other transaction fees and costs, or to pay "Partnership Expenses," which include management fees and all fund costs and expenses (as distinctly defined in each LPA). LPs failing to satisfy capital calls may be defaulted, subjecting them to possible forfeiture of their interests in the fund.

17. BCM earns a management fee equal to 2% of the aggregate capital commitment, which is then reduced by 0.2% per year following expiration of the commitment period. BCM also is entitled to a "carry" of 20% of the sum of all distributions in excess of the sums contributed by the LPs in Fund I and up to 25% in Fund II.

---

[5]United States of America Before the Securities and Exchange Commission, Securities and Exchange Act of 1934 Release No. 77959 / June 1, 2016, Investment Advisors Act of 1940, Release No. 4411 / June 1, 2016, Administrative Proceeding File No. 3-17267, In the Matter of Blackstreet Capital Management, LLC and Murry N. Gunty, ORDER INSTITUTING ADMINISTRATIVE AND CEASE-AND-DESIST PROCEEDINGS, PURSUANT TO SECTIONS 15(b) AND 21C OF THE SECURITIES EXCHANGE ACT OF 1934, AND SECTIONS 203(e) AND 203(k) OF THE INVESTMENT ADVISERS ACT OF 1940, MAKING FINDINGS, AND IMPOSING REMEDIAL SANCTIONS AND A CEASEAND-DESIST ORDER.

B. Unregistered Broker–Dealer Activity

18. Although the LPAs expressly permitted BCM to charge transaction or brokerage fees, BCM has never been registered with the Commission as a broker nor has it ever been affiliated with a registered broker. Rather than employing investment banks or broker–dealers to provide brokerage services with respect to the acquisition and disposition of portfolio companies, some of which involved the purchase or sale of securities, BCM performed these services in-house, including soliciting deals, identifying buyers or sellers, negotiating and structuring transactions, arranging financing, and executing the transactions. BCM received at least $1,877,000 in transaction-based compensation in connection with providing these brokerage services.

C. Undisclosed (Operating Partner Oversight) OPO Fees

19. In 2011 and 2012, BCM charged two Fund I portfolio companies at least $450,000 in OPO fees. These fees were paid directly to BCM pursuant to a written agreement between BCM and the portfolio companies for various BCM employees to provide certain senior-level operating and management services to these companies in circumstances where the companies were having difficulty recruiting suitable talent to work directly for them. The fees were intended to remain in place until the portfolio companies were able to attract suitable personnel to perform these services. The OPO fees resulted in a conflict of interest between the fund and BCM because BCM used the fund's assets to compensate itself and BCM employees. Fund I's LPA did not expressly address OPO fees or specifically authorize BCM to charge these fees to the portfolio companies (and, indirectly, to the fund). BCM did not disclose the OPO fees to the fund's LPs until after the LPs committed capital and the fees were being charged.

D. Unauthorized Use of Fund Assets

20. In several instances between 2005 and 2012, BCM used fund assets for purposes that were not expressly authorized by the Funds' LPAs. In particular, the LPAs did not address using fund assets to pay for political contributions, charitable contributions, and entertainment expenses.

(i) Political Contributions

21. Beginning in 2005, BCM used fund assets to make political contributions to a Maryland political candidate's campaigns. Fund I contributed a total of $12,000 to the candidate's campaigns, including $4,000 in each of 2005, 2009, and 2011.

(ii) Charitable Contributions

22. From 2009 to 2011, BCM used Fund I assets to make more than $23,000 in charitable contributions to a variety of charities. BCM subsequently reimbursed Fund I for these contributions, plus interest.

(iii) Entertainment Expenses

23. From 2010 to 2013, BCM charged Fund I and Fund II each one-third of the cost of the lease and event tickets associated with a luxury suite at the Verizon Center in Washington, DC; BCM paid the remaining one-third of the cost. BCM and Gunty did not take sufficient steps to ensure that the costs of the lease and event tickets were allocated appropriately among BCM and the Funds. BCM and Gunty also did not adequately track or keep records of their usage of the lease or event tickets, including adequate records of personal use. BCM reimbursed the Funds, with interest, for their costs of the suite and tickets.
24. Although BCM disclosed to the Funds' LPs that fund assets had been used to make political and charitable contributions, and to pay entertainment expenses, the disclosures were not made until after the LPs committed capital and until after the contributions were made and the expenses were incurred. BCM neither sought nor obtained appropriate consent for these expenditures.

E. Purchase of Portfolio Company Interests
25. BCM provided incentive-based compensation to employees assigned to perform services on behalf of portfolio companies. Such incentives included the opportunity to invest

alongside the Funds and purchase shares in the portfolio companies. In those instances, the employees signed share purchase agreements that granted the portfolio companies exclusive rights to repurchase the employees' shares at fair market value in the event of the employees' departure or termination.

26. Despite that term of the share purchase agreements, in 2010, BCM purchased a departing employee's incentive-based shares in Fund I portfolio companies. By acquiring the shares, BCM engaged in a conflicted transaction because it purchased shares in portfolio companies owned by Fund I without disclosing its financial interest or obtaining appropriate consent to engage in the transaction. BCM later transferred the shares and associated distributions, plus interest, to Fund I.

F. Acquisition of LP Interests

27. Between 2010 and 2012, Gunty, through an entity he controlled, acquired interests in Fund II from two defaulted LPs and from six LPs who were seeking to sell their interests and exit the fund.

28. As to the two defaulted LPs, Fund II's LPA permits the GP – BCA II – to require defaulted LPs to forfeit all but one dollar of their interests, and then the GP shall purchase the defaulted partner's remaining interest for one dollar. Gunty, however, paid only one dollar to acquire each defaulted LP's entire forfeited interest for himself rather than forfeiting all but one dollar of their interests to the fund. Gunty later relinquished to Fund II the forfeited interests that he acquired. As to the six LPs who sought to sell their interests and exit the fund, Gunty and the LPs agreed on a negotiated price at which Gunty would pay for their interests.

29. Fund II's LPA states that anyone who acquires the interest of another LP assumes that LP's obligation to make future capital contributions. Despite this disclosure, BCA II, at Gunty's direction, waived Gunty's obligation to make future capital calls on any new investments that would have been associated with the interests he purchased from the two defaulted LPs and the other six LPs. The waivers of Gunty's obligation to make future capital calls on new investments were not disclosed to the Fund II LPs. Accordingly, BCM's failure to disclose the waivers rendered the LPA's disclosures concerning LPs' obligations to make future capital calls materially misleading.

30. Although Gunty did not participate in the gains resulting from new investments made in Fund II subsequent to acquiring the defaulting and non-defaulting LP interests, his failure to make future capital calls reduced the capital available for investment opportunities and increased the pro rata share of future capital calls borne by the remaining LPs.

G. Failure to Adopt and Implement Policies and Procedures Reasonably Designed to Prevent Violations of the Advisers Act and its Rules

31. As a registered investment adviser, BCM was subject to the Advisers Act's rule requiring it to adopt and implement written policies and procedures reasonably designed to prevent violations of the Advisers Act and its rules.

32. BCM adopted and implemented written policies and procedures in the form of its Investment Adviser Supervisory Procedures and Compliance Manual. BCM, however, did not adopt or implement any policies and procedures designed to prevent violations of the Advisers Act or its rules arising from the improper use of fund assets, undisclosed receipt of fees, or purchase of LP interests. Furthermore, despite BCM's policies and procedures designating Gunty as BCM's "Designated Supervisor" responsible for ensuring compliance with BCM's policies and procedures and the federal securities laws, BCM failed to adopt and implement any policies and procedures designed to address conflicts of interest arising from Gunty's supervisory role. Thus, BCM's policies and procedures were not reasonably designed to prevent the violations of the Advisers Act and its rules described herein.

Without admitting or denying the findings, Blackstreet agreed to be censured, and Blackstreet and Mr. Gunty were to cease and desist from further violations while paying combined disgorgement of $2.339 million, including $504,588 that was to be distributed back to affected clients, $283,737 in interest, and a $500,000 penalty.[6]

Concept Questions:

1. If you were the CCO of this firm, and as part of your testing and surveillance procedures had uncovered the items noted in the SEC investigation

---

[6]US Securities and Exchange Commission, "SEC: Private Equity Fund Adviser Acted as Unregistered Broker," June 1, 2016.

prior to the investigation, what would you have done? Was there anything you were legally required to do?

2. The use of fund assets for contributions and expenses:

   a. One of the issues raised by the SEC related to the use of fund assets for political and charitable contributions. If you were the CCO of this firm, what testing and surveillance protocols would you have suggested implementing regarding oversight of any such contributions by the firm's funds? What about oversight of these types of contributions by individuals?

   b. A related finding by the SEC was that fund assets were also utilized to pay entertainment expenses. If you were the CCO of this firm, would your testing and surveillance protocols differ for expense oversight (as compared to political and charitable contributions), or would the same procedures be followed? Why?

   c. As CCO, what training would you have recommended implementing prior to the SEC investigation related to political and charitable contributions and entertainment expenses? How might this training have changed after the SEC settlement?

Interestingly, until the Blackstreet Capital settlement, it had been reported that private equity firms believed they could avoid registering as a broker–dealer if they refunded 100 percent of transaction fees to investors.[7] The Blackstreet settlement caused private equity firms to consider taking a more conservative approach in this area as more attention was drawn to the transaction fees earned by managers from funds and portfolio companies in particular.[8]

In this way it is important for GPs to acknowledge that previously established beliefs about regulatory interpretations of rules may shift over time. By developing a series of ongoing dialogues with other private equity firms, regulators, and legal and compliance practitioners, GPs can work to ensure they are not being too aggressive or conservative with their compliance practices. Similarly, when GPs conduct ongoing testing and training on these types of issues as they are brought to the forefront, such as through regulatory enforcement actions, GPs may further mitigate their compliance risk exposures in these areas.

---

[7] A. Jacobius, "Private Equity Firms Fear Broker-Dealer Registration," *Pensions & Investments*, July 11, 2016.
[8] D. Lim and C. Crumming, "SEC Official Puts Broker-Dealer Issue Back on Private Equity's Radar," *Wall Street Journal*, June 7, 2016.

10.7 SUMMARY

This chapter focused on the LP analysis of private equity compliance functions. We began with a discussion of the increased focus on GP compliance during the LP due diligence process. Next, we discussed the goals of investor compliance analysis and the signaling effect at play during the due diligence process. Considerations relating to an LP's analysis of the culture of compliance in place at a private equity firm were next addressed. An overview of the initial and ongoing compliance due diligence processes was analyzed. Next, the motivations for incorporating vendors into compliance policies were discussed. Finally, a case study was presented, showing regulatory activity relating to multiple compliance issues LPs may come across when analyzing a GP's compliance function. The next chapter focuses on the practical application of compliance concepts and trends through interviews with practitioners in this area.

CHAPTER 11

Interviews with Private Equity Compliance Professionals

Throughout this book we have incorporated practical real-world examples of the implementation of compliance policies and procedures in private equity funds. This has been completed by case studies in regulatory actions related to private equity general partner (GP) and fund-level compliance. To continue this practical focus, this chapter provides interviews with three leading private equity professionals on trends and best practices in global private equity compliance.

11.1 BIOGRAPHY AND INTERVIEW WITH DR. THOMAS MEYER

Dr. Thomas Meyer's focus is the development of risk measurement models and investment strategies for private equity funds, funds-of-funds, and institutional investment programs. Related to this, he has years of practical experience and has researched and published on public policy approaches to the development of venture capital markets. Thomas is a member of the Risk Management for Alternative Investment Funds (AIFs) Working Group, of ALFI (Association of the Luxembourg Fund Industry), and of the Private Equity Fund Risk Measurement Guidelines Working Group of Invest Europe (former EVCA, European Venture Capital and Private Equity Association).

After 12 years in the German Air Force he worked for the German insurance group Allianz AG in corporate finance and as the regional chief financial officer of Allianz Asia Pacific in Singapore. He was responsible for the creation of the risk management function at the European Investment Fund (EIF). Thomas was a director of the European Private Equity and Venture Capital Association. He is a member of the private equity subcommittee of the Chartered Alternative Investment Analyst® Program.

Thomas authored *Private Equity Unchained: Strategy Insights for the Institutional Investor* (Palgrave MacMillan) and co-authored *Beyond the J Curve* (also translated in Chinese and in Japanese), *J Curve Exposure*, and *Mastering Illiquidity* (all John Wiley & Sons), and two Chartered Alternative Investment Analyst (CAIA) Level II books, the required readings of level II of the Chartered Alternative Investment Analyst Program.

Thomas studied computer science at the Bundeswehr Universität in Munich and holds a Dr. rer. nat. from the University of Trier. He graduated with an MBA from the London Business School and with an MA in Japanese Language and Society from the University of Sheffield's School of East Asian Studies. He was a visiting researcher at Hitotsubashi University in Tokyo and the Development Bank of Japan's Research Institute of Capital Formation. Thomas is a Shimomura Fellow of the Development Bank of Japan.

Jason Scharfman   On a global basis, do you feel that private equity funds are subject to an appropriate amount of global regulation? Or instead are they overregulated (or underregulated)? Why do you come to this assessment?

Thomas Meyer   To avoid any misunderstanding, I agree with the objective that all parts of the financial system need to be regulated. However, when it comes to alternative assets I question whether regulators (in consultation with the financial industry) have taken the right direction. The choices made have resulted in contradictions and significant burdens in the wrong areas, with often unintended consequences.

Actually, some time ago I participated in a discussion among CAIA committee members. One participant questioned whether regulators should not focus on protecting unsophisticated investors from venturing into alternative assets. He observed that regulatory philosophy is unfortunately not developing in this direction. The thrust of regulation like the AIFMD is to make alternative assets "safe," which is almost comparable to the attempt to increase safety standards in Formula One by requiring to put a first aid kit and a spare tire on board of every racing car. This approach to regulate risk out of alternatives is counterproductive and almost absurd. Risks will continue to exist regardless, and this will just lead to a spiral of ever-tightening regulation. In my opinion, the right approach would be making sure that the investors in this asset class have the right skills, profile, processes, systems, experienced staff, and resources – to stay with the analogy, are qualified Formula One drivers instead of somebody with my driving skills.

Other participants feel very uncomfortable with regulating the kinds of investors who can access various investment products and saw this as a kind of discrimination. Because of their risk characteristics, strategies embraced by allegedly "sophisticated investors" would be off-limits to retail investors. Regulating differently according to type of investors does not strike me as radical as you see comparable approaches in many strands of life (for instance, driver licenses). My own bias is clearly private equity where attempts to make this asset class liquid and attract retail investors have arguably not met with great success. It is not about denying retail investors exposure to this asset class but about making sure that they involve intermediaries who know what they are doing and have sufficient skills, experience, and systems to deal with the risks. In any case, for the AIFMD and comparable regulatory initiatives it is still early days and the jury is still out.

Jason Scharfman Do you feel any countries' (or regions') regulatory regimes are better than others at balancing GP oversight without overburdening them from a compliance perspective?

Thomas Meyer My answer follows on from the previous question: Why focus on GP oversight and not become more stringent regarding limited partners (LPs)? The idea to focus on GPs, in my interpretation, stems from the perception that underperformance and failure is mainly caused by negligence and/or mistakes and that regulation is the right tool to address this. The interpretation of negligence and mistakes is arguing in hindsight, but for long-term-oriented investments change is inevitable – and in many situations change can be detrimental to investments without anybody at fault.

To maintain the integrity of the financial system does not seem convincing as a reason to regulate private equity as this asset class is hardly systemic. However, having grown from a few hundred private equity firms in the 1990s to by now about 10,000 private equity firms, more caution is clearly in order. Moreover, the financial industry is extremely innovative in finding loopholes and could certainly find ways to jump over the boundary to more liquid and systemic asset classes like hedge funds. So, it is sound to close all avenues to regulatory arbitrage and in this respect I personally welcome all-encompassing and sound regulation.

On the other hand, private equity as a niche area of the financial system never was the focus of regulation and more the troublesome exception. As a consequence, rules suitable to hedge funds are difficult to apply to private equity. Regulation also appears too much a reaction to the latest (perceived) scandal. Various regulatory initiatives overlap and there is no real architecture. For instance, in regard to private equity institutional investors are subject to Solvency II and Basel III, whereas the fund managers need to comply with the AIFMD, but these regulations do not talk to each other (or about the same thing).

Jason Scharfman   Recently the US Securities and Exchange Commission (US SEC) has increasingly focused on scrutinizing previously accepted practices in areas such as GP fee acceleration and the overall expenses GPs pass through to LPs. Based on a lack of similar enforcement actions in other jurisdictions, do you feel there is less focus on these issues by European regulators? Is this a good or bad thing?

Thomas Meyer   In many ways the US private equity market is still the most mature, sophisticated, and innovative, so it is no wonder that the Securities and Exchange Commission (SEC) often is the first regulator to focus on certain issues. On the other hand, private equity investors operate on a global basis, so practices quickly spread internationally and regulators worldwide sooner or later catch up with such trends. In any case, internationally operating US LPs are unlikely to continue accepting practices outside the United States that are no longer accepted in their own country.

Jason Scharfman   Does such scrutiny in the United States benefit the overall transparency of the private equity industry?

Thomas Meyer   The question of transparency in private equity continues to puzzle me as LPs always could ask GPs and – at least the experienced LPs – thus had full transparency, far more even than investors in publicly quoted companies.

The private equity industry is "private" and legitimately exploits opportunities associated with non-transparency, so I question whether increased transparency and disclosure would be the solution.

I interpret many aspects of regulatory initiatives as the result of a crisis of trust where suspicion about financial actors has become routine. However, private equity is operating in environments where information is difficult to get, non-standardized, and difficult to understand and where its interpretation requires professional judgment and experience. Any disclosure is likely to trigger a cycle of follow-on questions and increasing suspicion. As the philosopher Onora O'Neill observed, public distrust had grown in the "very years in which transparency and accountability had been so avidly pursued."

Jason Scharfman   The year 2018 has ushered in a host of new financial regulations that influence the private equity industry, including MiFID II, GDPR, and PRIIPs, with the majority of new regulations being implemented in Europe. How do you feel GPs in Europe, and those influenced by these new rules, are responding?

Thomas Meyer   These financial regulations aim to protect unsophisticated investors, which, as discussed before, may be the wrong policy avenue to take. In any case, the European GPs have, more or less grudgingly, accepted these regulations and the smaller players are searching for lowest cost and bare-minimum solutions. On the other hand, the large GPs even appear to embrace these regulatory initiatives as they have sufficient resources to deal with them and the complexity and effort to comply helps them to erect entry barriers that keep competition out. I fear that this development will accelerate and eventually lead to a fossilization of this asset class.

Jason Scharfman   What advice would you have for LPs seeking to invest in managers influenced by this new regulation to ensure their GPs are operating in compliance?

Thomas Meyer   In order to ensure their GPs' compliance with regulation LPs need to spend more effort on operational due diligence (ODD) and monitoring. In fact, the experienced LPs have always been doing this. This also has created a market for third-party AIFMs whose entire raison d'être is to assure the regulatory compliance on behalf of their clients.

Jason Scharfman　　Do you feel private equity managers and investors in regions with less restrictive regulations, such as Asia, are at an advantage compared to Europe and the United States?

Thomas Meyer　　As alternative assets could be considered as "experiments" and investment strategies aim to exploit inefficient and underexplored niches, in theory less restrictive regulation would be advantageous as it puts fewer obstacles in the way of such experimentation. However, many funds in Asia count on EU and US LPs. That requires them, in the case of the EU, to obtain individual country licenses (i.e. "passports") before marketing their funds to European investors. So they have no choice and need to comply with regulation. Also the registration with the US SEC is perceived to be a high hurdle. Asia and comparable markets therefore do not necessarily offer a "less restrictive" fund environment because many funds in both places would like to raise funds globally. A private equity manager in, say, Vietnam goes to Luxembourg, Zurich, and New York and recognizes that local legal assistance is needed to raise funds in these locations. For the bigger private equity houses that have legal teams and experience in this, it is just another cost. For smaller GPs it becomes a burdensome and risky issue.

Jason Scharfman　　Do you feel GPs do a good job managing and disclosing conflicts of interest? Why or why not?

Thomas Meyer　　Experienced and in particular institutional investors understand the relevance of conflicts of interest. For instance, they increasingly demand that a limited partner advisory committee (LPAC) – an important approach to address this concern – is part of a private equity fund's structure. In my experience, it is rather an issue for emerging firms where moving from to club deals with friends and family to first institutional funds often comes with legacy conflicts of interest, albeit not on purpose. Later and once firmly established this potential decreases as GPs understand that they need to be vigilant and don't want to jeopardize their relationship with LPs.

Jason Scharfman　　Some LPs and regulators have raised objections with the model of a lack of management fee offset typically applied to GP operating partners (as compared to the

	offsets typically applied for GP employees serving as directors of underlying portfolio companies). What are your thoughts on this?
Thomas Meyer	Private equity is about incentives and alignment of interests, without offsets for monitoring and transaction-related fees; for instance, investors are not paying anymore for performance. Here incentives get distorted and the alignment of interests gets weakened. In the extreme, this even can become a double charging for the same activities and services to LPs and portfolio companies. However, I wonder whether this is really something where the regulator should step in. It is rather a practice LPs should reject and experienced LPs will reject.
Jason Scharfman	Increasingly in the United States, LPACs have been given more transparency and oversight responsibilities in a host of areas, including compliance. Do you feel similar trends have taken hold in Europe? Do you feel the growth of LPACs is a good development for the private equity industry?
Thomas Meyer	With it becoming a global asset class also in Europe LPACs are increasingly becoming a feature of the private equity landscape. As the LPACs' role and responsibilities are clearly defined and as they are advising the GP particularly on conflict of interest–related issues, institutional investors see such committees are best practice. They increasingly will not invest in a private equity fund unless an LPAC is included in the fund's structure. On the other hand, smaller funds without institutional investors rarely have an LPAC (see also next question).
Jason Scharfman	In the United States, venture funds and private equity funds below certain minimum asset sizes are subject to exemptions from registrations and operate in a compliance-light environment. Do you feel that this exemption is necessary for venture funds and smaller private equity funds? Why?
Thomas Meyer	This, in my eyes, shows the major inconsistency of the approach taken by regulators in the United States but also in the EU. Such exemptions contradict one important purpose of the regulation, that is, to protect investors (the stated mission of the US SEC is to protect investors, maintain fair, orderly, and efficient

markets, and facilitate capital formation). Smaller funds tend to attract smaller investors that are less well placed to exercise oversight. Typically also less experienced investors need more protection than institutional investors that predominantly invest in larger funds that also fall under stronger regulation.

One could also interpret this as relying on "regulated" LPs. During my work for the EIF in the early 2000s we were continuously asked by policymakers to promote practices and push for investor protection clauses with the VC funds under EIF management. Many of the practices we developed and introduced later resurfaced in the AIFMD. In my interpretation at the time, EIF, due to its domineering position in the European VC market, acted as a "quasi-regulator," giving confidence to less experienced LPs to follow EIF's lead. This would be in line with a model for alternative assets where it is rather the LPs who have to meet standards and as experienced investors need to exercise proper care.

Jason Scharfman   What advice would you have for investors who want to invest in these funds, but raise concerns about the less strict required compliance obligations of these types of funds?

Thomas Meyer   Following on from the last point, such investors need to rely on their own team of skilled and experienced private equity professionals.

Jason Scharfman   Many new funds are burdened by the high costs of building an initial compliance infrastructure at launch. What advice would you offer to a new venture fund being started with regard to dealing with these compliance costs?

Thomas Meyer   In Europe the model of the third-party AIFM addresses these high costs. The Bank of New York suggested that full AIFMD compliance adds approximately US$300K to US$1M per annum to a GP's operating costs. The one-off setup costs are between $100K and $250K, the long delays for getting regulatory approval aside. A third-party AIFM can provide the substance needed for compliance with the AIFM – portfolio management and risk management professionals, systems, and procedures – much quicker and cheaper.

Jason Scharfman	Are there any types of expenses that GPs used to pass along to LPs but no longer should? How do you feel the area of GP expense management will continue to evolve?
Thomas Meyer	This is all about incentives and alignment of interests. It is the oversubscribed and established firms where LPs want to get in and thus tend to accept many fees, whereas the smaller and emerging players are faced with a much stronger push-back in this respect. It should be the other way around, but it comes down to supply and demand.
Jason Scharfman	What advice would you offer for investors seeking to better model GP compliance risk into their overall portfolio management process?
Thomas Meyer	When speaking about portfolio management and risk, I look at this from the perspective of taking necessary risks in order to get a higher financial return. Arguably when focusing on compliance and operational risks the perspective is different. Here it is rather the avoidance of problems with regulators and unfavorable reputation that matters. On the other hand, investors in private equity funds, say, a pension fund, should keep this in balance against underperformance as this is what really hurts pensioners. Looking at this from a purely financial perspective, the likelihood of compliance and operational risk–related events is not correlated between funds and thus less of a concern for investors with diversified portfolios.

At a certain point investors find this cheaper to diversify the impact of such risks away than paying higher management fees to funds in order to further reduce the probability of adverse events. This is what was reflected in a comment a managing director of a highly respected VC fund-of-funds made at a conference pre-2008 (those were the days . . .): "If we hear a GP talk about risk management, we walk away from the deal." Two caveats: First, also compliance and operational risk–related events can be correlated, for instance, in cases where flawed valuation or risk models are widely accepted in the industry. To tackle this, regulators should avoid being too prescriptive – strict adherence to regulatory requirements can also result in complacency, lack of attention, and systemic risk. Second, high diversification leads to higher probability that potentially embarrassing compliance failures happen, like the proverbial terrorist that is getting through. However, rather than aiming for funds being failsafe, investors should find ways to deal with public anger, admittedly not an easy task nowadays.

Jason Scharfman   There has been increased scrutiny of private equity valuation practices, as well as several regulatory enforcement actions in this area. How do you see GP valuation practices evolving in the future?

Thomas Meyer   Regulation (again, the EU AIFMD is an important example) requires that there are appropriate and consistent procedures concerning the valuation of private equity assets put in place and that the valuation process is independent from, for instance, portfolio management and remuneration functions, often involving external valuation agents. Since the beginning of the 2000 valuation practices in private equity have made great progress. Notably the development of the International Private Equity and Valuation (IPEV) Guidelines has been a significant step forward and I expect that such guidelines will become the standard worldwide.

Having said this, finding value and pricing it is the business GPs are in and if they would be always right in their assessments, the private equity asset class would be without any risk. Arguably, the valuation is more of an issue for auditors, regulators, and investors who are concerned about financial reporting errors and fair-value measurements that cannot be supported. But a value is not equivalent to a price and valuations are by definition subjective, even more so in the thin market that characterizes private equity. In my various publications I put forward as one argument why in private equity and particularly in venture capital we mainly see self-liquidating fund structures is because valuations relate to a large degree to intangibles and can only be proven as "true" by exiting the investments and turning them into liquidity. My concern is that with recent regulatory initiatives related to valuation we will see allegations of misbehavior in fair-value measurements where actually no wrong-doing happened.

Moreover, there are often conflicting objectives associated with "fair" valuations. The IPEV Guidelines see fair value as the "price that would be received to sell an asset in an Orderly Transaction between Market Participants at the Measurement Date," which is certainly the perspective GPs would take. LPs may be more interested in understanding how the investments are developing, that is, consistency of valuations over time. Here I have heard the argument that practices before 2000 (keeping values at cost and only writing them up after new capital rounds) made this easier for LPs as this disregarded market noise. Auditors and regulators, on the other hand, tend to have a conservative bias, but LPs are also concerned about safeguarding their assets and would certainly object to assets being exited at low prices in line with a conservative valuation but that jump in value subsequently.

Finally, as a previous risk manager I (and several others in the industry) disagree with the IPEV Guidelines view that the fair value of fund interests is based (as described in the Guidelines essentially equivalent) on the fund's attributable net asset value. An in-depth discussion of this point goes beyond the scope of this interview. Just one aspect: LPs are exposed to the uncertainty regarding timing and amounts of the fund's cash flow. From their perspective also, the fund's undrawn capital forms part of their exposure. When LPs commit to a fund, the fund has no net-asset-value (NAV) but forms a risk.

Jason Scharfman   Do you see an eventual move toward LPs demanding third-party administration (as they do in the hedge fund industry)?

Thomas Meyer   Ultimately it is a question of the cost/benefit relationship. While transactions in private equity are not as frequent as in the case of hedge funds, they are far less standardized and require a deep understanding of many different situations. This makes high-quality fund administration expensive, and only with economies of scale is this viable. This in combination with demands for timely and high-quality reporting, also to regulators, makes third-party administration a more sensible option from the LP perspective.

Jason Scharfman   What trends do you see in European private equity compliance going forward?

Thomas Meyer   While this was not the case only a few years ago, the private equity industry now is aware of compliance. It has recognized that something needs to be done and has moved toward better compliance practices. One important trend is an entirely new industry emerging around regulation, the third-party AIFMs as an example. On the other hand, the current move toward compliance was to a large degree motivated by the regulators' paranoia, ushering a wave of rules which addressed concerns relevant to hedge funds but not suitable and not meaningful for private equity. In Europe there is some hope that AIFMD II will take this lesson on board. Like in the case of the UCITS regulation, which was first very restrictive but over time became more open in regard to eligible assets and strategies to invest in, it is possible that the review will lead to a more reasonable regulation with more distinct rules for private equity that are more tailored for the asset class's specifics. I may be too optimistic here, as at the end of the day private equity is still small compared to the rest of the financial system and therefore it could take much longer before regulators feel the need to change anything.

11.2   BIOGRAPHY AND INTERVIEW WITH MATTHEW DEMATTEIS – INSTITUTIONAL LIMITED PARTNERS ASSOCIATION (ILPA)

Matthew DeMatteis is the Institutional Limited Partners Association's (ILPA's) Director of Research. His primary responsibilities include LP-focused research papers, the ILPA Private Markets Benchmark, and an annual LP compensation survey. Matthew also leads several ILPA best-practices initiatives, including the Fee Transparency Initiative, Reporting Best Practices, and Due Diligence Questionnaire. Prior to joining the organization in 2013, he was a director at LP Capital Advisors, where he managed their fund diligence, advisory, and fund monitoring/analytics services. Matthew received his undergraduate degree in finance from Syracuse University.

Jason Scharfman	Can you provide an introduction to ILPA and the organization's role in the private equity industry?
Matthew DeMatteis	ILPA is the only global, member-driven association comprised solely of institutional investors in private equity, typically through fund structures. Our 450+ member organizations manage approximately $2 trillion in private equity assets under management.

	These institutional investors join ILPA for access to best-in-class networking opportunities, education programs, and research, as well as to advocate for industry-wide best practices, including compliance.
Jason Scharfman	ILPA outlines three guiding principles to form an effective private equity partnership between LPs and GPs. These are alignment of interest, governance, and transparency. How do you feel these principles relate to the current state of private equity compliance? Can you provide examples?
Matthew DeMatteis	Transparency and governance are the tools used by LPs to ensure that the GP remains aligned with the best interest of the fund. For example, through greater transparency into the fees charged by GPs, LPs can gain confidence that the GPs are complying with the terms of the fund's LPA. Additionally, an engaged LPAC that's empowered to provide feedback on GP conflicts of interest, like investment valuations, can help ensure that a GP complies with its internal policies.
Jason Scharfman	What benefits do you feel the uniform reporting practices encouraged by the templates have for LPs seeking to evaluate GPs in the area of compliance? Similarly, how can GPs utilize these templates to more effectively communicate their compliance infrastructures with LPs?
Matthew DeMatteis	One of the greatest benefits from the standardized formats for fee reporting, capital calls, and distributions is the improved accuracy and uniformity of an LP's internal records, which are used to monitor fund activity and compliance. Without accurate data, even the simplest tasks, like reconciling their remaining commitment to a fund, can be problematic. Furthermore, using standard reporting templates allows LPs to compare funds in a way that utilizes the same definitions – apples to apples, if you will. In terms of how GPs can better communicate their cost structure, we certainly feel our Reporting Template on fees, expenses, and carried interest provides a roadmap to the GP's operations. This includes the services provided (to both the fund and its investments) by affiliated entities and third parties, all of which can represent potential conflicts

that must be addressed through oversight and sound compliance policies.

Jason Scharfman   The feedback I've heard from certain LPs is that they want more transparency from GPs regarding potential conflicts of interest when they arise, but they also don't want to micromanage GPs. What advice would you have with them to develop further meaningful dialogues in this regard?

Matthew DeMatteis   LPs are certainly not staffed, nor interested for that matter, to micromanage their GPs. If they were, they wouldn't invest in funds in the first place. To be efficient "managers of managers," LPs must conduct thorough operational and legal due diligence during fundraising. They must be comfortable that the fund provisions and GP policies designed to address agency conflicts are clear and impactful. During the life of the fund, LPs should leverage scheduled touchpoints (AGMs and quarterly update calls) to monitor any potential conflicts that are identified during their due diligence. The time invested before and during the life of the fund can help minimize LP-involvement in higher-touch issues, such as GP removal.

Jason Scharfman   Can you comment on the compliance roles you feel should be played by the limited partner operating committee? What are some best practices you would recommend in this area?

Matthew DeMatteis   LPACs can be most impactful when they serve as a sounding board for GPs to seek guidance on sensitive matters of conflict (e.g. valuation, potential amendments). However, they should not be used as a substitute for LP-wide engagement or as a proxy for the interest of all investors.

Jason Scharfman   Do you feel LPs have a responsibility to be actively involved in partnering with GPs to implement best practices in areas such as compliance and governance or instead does this responsibility lie primarily with GPs?

Matthew DeMatteis   All LPs have a responsibility to inform GPs of best practices, push for the implementation of best practices, and periodically monitor the progress of

	any implementation. Any further, more hands-on level of involvement can be highly inefficient for an LP and should only be used as a measure of last resort.
Jason Scharfman	Beyond being familiar with a fund's offering documents, what steps do you feel LPs should take to educate themselves about a specific GP's compliance practices? And what about larger private equity compliance best practices in general?
Matthew DeMatteis	Best practices in ODD include: (i) submitting a thoughtful set of questions that seek to clarify the statements made in offering documents and (ii) conducting onsite visits (ante- and post-commitment) at GP offices, including one-on-one conversations with compliance officers. The finer points of ODD are addressed during the educational opportunities provided to ILPA members.
Jason Scharfman	What issues in private equity compliance do you feel are the most important to LPs today?
Matthew DeMatteis	Compliance with fee and waterfall provisions is top of mind. There are also two other growing areas of interest: (i) the trend of increasing reliance upon credit facilities by certain types of equity-focused funds and (ii) that GPs are implementing and adhering to strong HR-level policies, including those preventing and identifying sexual harassment in the workplace.
Jason Scharfman	What areas of compliance do you feel present the biggest challenges for both LPs and GPs?
Matthew DeMatteis	The increasingly complex nature of multiproduct GPs, including those managing multiple funds at once and those with dedicated teams focused on operating improvements at portfolio companies, has created significant potential conflicts and compliance challenges that LPs must be mindful of. As a result, GPs have been beset with numerous bespoke requests for additional transparency on the fees they've charged. The inefficiencies created by these LP requests were among the primary reasons for the development of our Reporting Template.

11.3   BIOGRAPHIES AND INTERVIEW WITH CLAIRE WILKINSON AND LUDOVIC PHALIPPOU

Claire Wilkinson: Ms. Wilkinson is a UK solicitor. She trained at Slaughter and May and spent 11 years in total there advising on corporate finance, public, and private M&A, capital markets and a broad range of company law matters. She then worked as general counsel for 11 years in various in-house roles in private equity and venture capital. During this time, she founded and chaired the Private Equity Lawyers Forum, a best-practice knowhow and training organization for in-house lawyers, and served on the Invest Europe Professional Standards Committee, the BVCA's Responsible Investment Committee, and co-chaired the Invest Europe Responsible Investment Roundtable. She has contributed to a number of publications on private equity and participated on numerous panels and at numerous conferences. She teaches the Invest Europe Private Equity Foundation course. She now works for Grantham, Mayo, Van Otterloo & Co., LLC. She graduated from the University of Durham in French and German and holds a postgraduate diploma in Risk, Governance and Compliance from the University of Manchester.

Ludovic Phalippou: Mr. Phalippou is author of the bestseller *Private Equity Laid Bare*, published by the CreateSpace Independent Publishing Platform on September 7, 2017. He is a tenured faculty member of the Said Business School at the University of Oxford. He specializes in the areas of private equity that are of interest to investors in that asset class, such as fee tracking, interest alignment, and return benchmarking. Named as one of the "40 Most Outstanding Business School Profs Under 40 in the World" in 2014, and as one of the 20 most influential individuals in private equity in Europe in 2016, Ludovic has strong links with senior practitioners in the industry, routinely speaks at practitioner conferences, and appears in the media internationally. Ludovic's research papers have been widely cited in academia, in the press, and in regulatory circles. He worked with a number of large institutional investors on their private equity investment decisions and benchmarking systems. At Oxford, Ludovic teaches "Asset Management" and "Private Equity." Ludovic achieved a degree in Economics from Toulouse School of Economics; a Master in Economics and a Master in Mathematical Finance both from the University of Southern California; and a PhD in Finance from INSEAD.

Claire Wilkinson/ *Ludovic Phalippou*	Let us first provide context on the evolution of in-house lawyers and the compliance function in private equity houses. Prior to 2000, the largest fund in Europe was under €1 billion in committed capital.

The headcount of PE houses was small in comparison to today's staffing levels and specialization of function within PE houses was relatively unknown outside of the then–obviously essential investment professional, finance, and investor relations spheres. PE houses were more concentrated geographically, both in terms of the location of the investment management teams and investment hunting-ground. Fundraising, although already complex and protracted by 2000, followed conventional and recognized legal routes with limited co-investment opportunities and more passive LPs. Growth in the industry after 2000 was a catalyst for specialist recruitment within the PE houses themselves. Legislative changes imposed on the industry also played a role in the growth of specialist recruitment of lawyers and compliance personnel. In the UK, the Financial Services and Markets Act of 2000 was a driver for change by creating a new regulatory framework. In 2002, this was followed by the Sarbanes–Oxley Act, which had an impact beyond the United States on corporate governance practices. In 2008, the Markets in Financial Instruments Directive was a further key piece of legislation affecting conduct of business in PE houses, and in 2014, the AIF Managers Directive led to further legal complexity in the wake of demands for increased reporting coupled with curbs on remuneration.

Lawyers in private practice law firms became engaged in work arising as a result of these increases in complexity in fundraising and legislative landscape and in deal size. These lawyers made themselves indispensable to PE management teams. As fund sizes grew and number of closings with differentiation in terms increased, limited partnership agreements (LPAs) and ancillary documents expanded. Simply managing side letters became a full-time job.

Jason Scharfman How do you feel institutional investors (i.e. pension funds, sovereign funds, etc.) today approach the issue of compliance at private equity funds they are considering committing capital to?

Claire Wilkinson/ Track record and investment thesis are the con-
Ludovic Phalippou ventional fundamental elements for an investment

decision for any institutional investor. But we live in times where the basis for decisions and the decision-making process must be thoroughly documented. It is important to note that although called asset owners, the institutional investors committing to PE (LPs) are investing other people's money. As a result, they take a risk-averse view about the scrutiny they could face about their decisions. Due diligence into the compliance function has therefore become part of the overall review and paper-gathering exercise prior to investment. That said, the typically raised due diligence questions regarding compliance are frequently formulaic and can be seen as a bolt-on tire-kicking exercise rather than something meaningful. It is rare for an investor to ask follow-up questions on the compliance section of the due diligence questionnaire, or to ask to interview compliance personnel as part of due diligence.

Jason Scharfman Do you feel US, European, and Asian institutional allocators take different approaches in this regard?

Claire Wilkinson/ Ludovic Phalippou Investors' due diligence into compliance prior to investment is less dependent on the geography of the investor than on investor type. For example, large sovereign wealth funds in Asian and the Middle East and US public pension plans have detailed questionnaires. Investment consultants operating worldwide, potentially with the desire to demonstrate their own value-add through the production of volumes of paperwork, request particularly detailed, and lengthy analysis. Industry bodies and practices transcend borders. For example, the ILPA, while North American in origin, now has members worldwide and is influential in standards setting for LPs. When responsible investment first became a hot topic, it is true that Northern Europeans led the way in making this an issue and this had a knock-on effect on the involvement of Legal and Compliance. So, at the margin, it could be argued that some elements of compliance and governance scrutiny were driven by Scandinavian and Dutch investors before the rest of Europe, Asia, and ultimately North America took up the cause.

Jason Scharfman	What are your thoughts about how institutional investors can integrate an assessment of a GP's compliance function into their overall risk assessment and ongoing risk management processes?
Claire Wilkinson/ Ludovic Phalippou	Few LPs ask to interview the compliance officer and the general counsel (GC) on their own, or even at all as part of their pre-investment due diligence exercise. Few compliance officers and GCs of LPs actively interact with their counterparts in the GP – the communication takes place through outside counsel and through the IR teams and investment consultants. The industry is in a phase where the exercise of judgment through face-to-face meetings and a more interlocutory style of information exchange has been supplanted by the production and disclosure of reams of written information which may or may not be read and analyzed prior to investment but provides a thick paper security blanket.
Jason Scharfman	Anecdotally, certain LPs have expressed concerns that they feel GPs are behind the curve in regard to rigorous industry-wide compliance regimes as compared to hedge funds. What are your thoughts on this?
Claire Wilkinson/ Ludovic Phalippou	Yes, this observation is valid. Pockets of excellence in compliance do exist in PE houses and there are some excellent individual practitioners, including in PE houses, that have experience in regulatory censure. There is just not a culture of compliance in PE. This is actually often presented as one of the benefits of PE: Companies they run focus on generating money instead of compliance-related paperwork and discussions. This mindset percolates to the PE house itself. There is much anecdotal evidence of senior management failing in their support of the compliance and legal function and failing to set the tone from the top. Lawyers and compliance folk are there to plug gaps and to do the work the investment professionals do not want to do. Few in-house lawyers and even fewer legally trained compliance officers are partners, few are board members, and few are invited to participate in fund marketing and decision-making bodies other than to perform the company secretarial function.

	All these factors indicate an industry sector where compliance is tolerated rather than embraced.
Jason Scharfman	Can you comment on some of the differences you have seen develop between US and European private equity funds in regard to their approach to compliance? What implications do you feel this has had for the ways GPs approach compliance?
Claire Wilkinson/ Ludovic Phalippou	In my experience, US houses frequently exhibit a defensive style in answering LPs questions on compliance, very much adopting a minimal disclosure risk-averse and liability-limiting stance. European PE houses are more progressive and more open. GCs may have more power in the States, but Compliance has more power in Europe.
Jason Scharfman	Specifically, how do you feel GPs are dealing with the wave of new and evolving European regulations such as MIFID 2, GDPR, and PRIIPs?
Claire Wilkinson/ Ludovic Phalippou	Compared to asset managers, PE houses have got away with it lightly on MIFID 2, GDPR, and PRIIPs. The AIF Managers Directive was a much bigger issue. The PE sector in general adapts to new regulation with typical creativity. PE houses have proven themselves to be adaptable to opening new offices, relocating, outsourcing, creating governance structures that meet regulatory demands, and developing the infrastructure to handle more complex reporting.
Jason Scharfman	Do you feel GPs in general are responsive enough to institutional investors when they raise concerns in areas such as compliance and regulatory change impacting private equity funds?
Claire Wilkinson/ Ludovic Phalippou	LPs don't often raise these questions. From an in-house legal perspective, the lack of scrutiny could even be said to be disappointing. Where these concerns do arise, they are unlikely to be communicated directly to the in-house legal and compliance group. There are typically two responses. The first is to have the investor relations folk and CFO answer these queries, and the second response, where the compliance and legal functions are more integrated at senior management level, is to develop a written response in consultation with senior management, which is communicated through the investor relations function

	rather than through direct communication by the legal and compliance function with the institutional investor. This is not a satisfactory state of affairs and discourages transparency.
Jason Scharfman	What are your thoughts on whether a GP should maintain a compliance function primarily consisting of in-house resources (such as an in-house chief compliance officer) versus a compliance function that is primarily outsourced to specialist compliance consultants?
Claire Wilkinson/ Ludovic Phalippou	We believe in integrating compliance into the culture of a firm and into the senior management function. Many disagree, mainly because of the cost, and specifically, who should pay for this increased compliance presence? Outsourced costs are easier to quantify and easier to expense to the fund. Ideally, there would be a Compliance/GC function which reports to the LPAC and is paid for from the fund (hence the LPs). It makes the Compliance/GC functions harder in some respects as performing a law-enforcement and whistleblowing role vis-a vis colleagues is difficult and there is an increased risk of concealment by the deal teams of issues that should be brought to Compliance's attention. A semi-independent compliance function would add robustness to the governance of a PE house. Note that many internal counsel and compliance officers behave in this manner already and tread a difficult tightrope diplomatically.
Jason Scharfman	Do you feel a one-size-fits-all approach works for GP compliance?
Claire Wilkinson/ Ludovic Phalippou	No, but there are certainly common themes in almost every PE house. The regulator allows firms to adapt their compliance programs to suit the nature, scale, and complexity of that firm's business. GPs' compliance departments can leverage industry experience and apply it to their own model.
Jason Scharfman	As compliance has become more resources intensive, increasingly the costs of developing a compliance infrastructure for a private equity firm have gone up. From both a risk management and capital allocation perspective, do you feel institutional investors penalize start-up or younger private equity firms as compared

Claire Wilkinson/
Ludovic Phalippou

to larger firms that may benefit from economies of scale and lower compliance costs on a per-fund basis? Large PE houses seem to be happy to see these barriers to entry persist and encourage these barriers by appointing increasingly specialized teams that only they can afford. Yet, the PE sector has enjoyed a relatively light touch from regulators and the costs of compliance are not prohibitive to start-ups.

Jason Scharfman

What challenges do you find institutional investors most commonly face when approaching the issue of GP compliance?

Claire Wilkinson/
Ludovic Phalippou

LPs do not always have the access to the Compliance and Legal functions in the PE houses that they ought to have. However, few LPs are requesting this access, which deprives them of a valuable data source and safety valve. In addition, the Compliance and Legal function interface with institutional investors only through the investor relations or finance function and thus have imposed a degree of "party line" which is not conducive to full transparency and cooperation.

Jason Scharfman

What are your thoughts on current attitudes of GPs toward the levels and disclosures of transaction fees?

Claire Wilkinson/
Ludovic Phalippou

In recent years, a wide set of people became aware of the practice by PE houses of invoicing and claiming expenses directly from their portfolio companies – for example, transaction fees. As PE houses are in control of these companies but the ultimate equity holder is someone else (LPs), the potential for conflicts of interest and abuse is obvious. As boards and the public were generally quite surprised by the existence of such a practice, let alone how widespread it was, LPs had to act. Most LPs nowadays monitor how much is being charged to their portfolio companies and ask for full rebates. That appeases their boards but does not really solve the root of the problem and we can therefore be concerned that related issues will persist. When this topic became prominent (2012–2013), it was rather surprising to hear several prominent GPs saying that, yes, most of us have charged fees like this for many years, in large amounts, with LPs having little information about it, but we now refrain from charging such fees, we

	have moved on, so let's not talk about it anymore. In other contexts there might have been some follow-up questions.
Jason Scharfman	Do you feel LPs have been more vocal in expressing their concerns in this regard? Do you note any differences in US and European attitudes in this regard? Why?
Claire Wilkinson/ Ludovic Phalippou	LPs been more vocal with regard to disclosure of transaction fees and this matter has also been the subject of regulatory scrutiny and press coverage. PE houses on both sides of the Atlantic have had to respond to these concerns.
Jason Scharfman	Recently financial regulators have placed more attention on fee practices such as GP monitoring of fee extension and fee acceleration. Do you feel this will have a positive effect for institutional private equity investors?
Claire Wilkinson/ Ludovic Phalippou	Transparency and alignment do matter to LPs. The problem is that the alignment is often weak. Management and GPs have financial incentives that are quite aligned; LPs and GPs do not. It is also important to bear in mind that GPs are creative and entrepreneurial, and these traits are also put at work when it comes to writing an LPA or interpreting it. Obviously, in principle, this creativity and entrepreneurial activity should not be to the detriment of transparency. In practice, it varies from one PE house to the other.
Jason Scharfman	What are your thoughts on current LP attitudes to the practice of GPs not generally applying management fee offsets to GP operating partners, but they are applied to GP employees serving on underlying portfolio companies?
Claire Wilkinson/ Ludovic Phalippou	What fundamentally matters here is that the extent of the offsets are fully budgeted and disclosed prior to the fees being incurred. PE houses can add value to their underlying portfolio companies, but the basis of the cost of this intervention needs to be disclosed in advance to investors (if they are not included in the management fees).
Jason Scharfman	Regulators have increasingly focused on the allocation of GP expenses. One example was the SEC action relating to Kohlberg Kravis Roberts & Co. LP (KKR),

relating to broker fee expenses. Do you feel insti-tutional investors' attitudes toward (i) these types of expenses and (ii) the oversight of their allocation among funds has changed based on these actions? Do you feel attitudes are different in the United States as compared to Europe?

Claire Wilkinson/ Ludovic Phalippou This has always been important, but only large LPs were fully aware of the importance. As discussed earlier, it took a symbolic fine by the SEC to a famous GP (and the ensuing press coverage) to make everyone aware of the issue. Also, bodies such as ILPA and Invest Europe have been influential in setting global standards. There are no differences between Euro-peans and Americans. This is pretty much one market, they all read the same newspapers.

Jason Scharfman Are there any fund expenses that you feel institutional investors are increasingly skeptical of?

Claire Wilkinson/ Ludovic Phalippou An investor should be skeptical of any lack of clarity, reticence, or any over-complexity in the presentation of fund expenses, whatever their nature. In some funds the amounts are extraordinary, and it is sometimes dif-ficult to obtain a breakdown of the total amount. Also, the fact that these expenses are ex-post is problem-atic for any investor. Any expenses except the essential ones (legal and accounting) are to be analyzed with care. And even the essential ones need to be analyzed to make sure they are at arm's-length prices.

Jason Scharfman What advice would you have for institutional investors seeking to evaluate the compliance function at a pri-vate equity firm?

Claire Wilkinson/ Ludovic Phalippou Ask to see the legal and compliance team alone. Ask open-ended questions about the culture of the firm and also quantitative questions about the number of train-ing sessions, number of board meetings, strategy ses-sions, and involvement of the legal and compliance departments in the preparation of investment theses. Ask for the view of your own compliance folk and have them meet their counterparts to establish a dialogue.

Jason Scharfman The role of LPACs has increasingly expanded. What role do you feel LPACs should play from a compliance perspective? Do you feel attitudes about LPACs differ among institutional investors in the United States and Europe?

Claire Wilkinson/ Ludovic Phalippou	LPACs rarely demand to hear the General Counsel speak. This is an omission. LPACs should routinely be asking for a closed session with the head of legal or compliance. Note that LPACs can themselves comprise members with conflicts of interest without the same fiduciary duties as the GP toward the entire constituency of LPs. This is a danger to be monitored by any LP without an LPAC seat. Again, no difference between the United States and Europe.
Jason Scharfman	How do you feel institutional investors can develop dialogues with GPs about compliance and regulatory matters outside of formal LPACs?
Claire Wilkinson/ Ludovic Phalippou	An institutional investor with its own in-house legal capability should be encouraging its legal team to network in the industry with GP legal representatives. LPs and GPs have many legal and compliance issues in common and an increase in dialogue can help with benchmarking and increased understanding. The Private Equity Lawyers Forum and the International Bar Association welcome members from both LP and GP communities. Invest Europe has an LP forum. All these initiatives promote transparency and professional standards.
Jason Scharfman	US financial regulators have increasingly focused on the disclosure of conflicts of interest by GPs. What do you feel are current institutional investor attitudes toward whether GPs are doing a good job in this area?
Claire Wilkinson/ Ludovic Phalippou	There are bound to be pockets of unsatisfactory behavior. Also, conflicts of interest are not the sole preserve of GPs. LPs with co-investments, seats on the LPAC, and interests in series of funds have conflicts of interest of their own to manage. LPs do not seem to demonstrate their concerns with action.
Jason Scharfman	Is there room for improvement beyond the standard disclosures in fund legal documents?
Claire Wilkinson/ Ludovic Phalippou	There is actually no mandatory industry-wide training requirement on the management of conflicts of interest. Invest Europe's Professional Standards Handbook gives excellent guidance on conflict management and disclosure. However, I think there is room for improvement in how the messages in the Handbook are disseminated within both LP and GP organizations.

Jason Scharfman   What private equity compliance and regulatory trends
                       do you see going forward?

Claire Wilkinson/   Maybe a quasi-independent compliance function
Ludovic Phalippou   reporting to the LPAC or to the annual LPs meeting
                       will appear. While compliance culture is hard to mea-
                       sure, an annual qualitative analysis of key compliance
                       metrics would raise the profile of compliance both in
                       the GPs and with the LPs. On the flipside, what I see
                       all too easily happening is that senior management will
                       delegate compliance window-dressing to a compliance
                       function that meekly accepts the responsibility in
                       return for a quiet life and a small percentage of the
                       carried interest, to the detriment of all.

CHAPTER 12

Compliance Trends and Future Developments

12.1 INTRODUCTION

The private equity industry is an evolving one that has retained steady interest from both large institutional allocators as well as smaller investors. As part of this evolution, General Partners (GPs) have had to continue to adapt to the external demands of regulators, Limited Partners (LPs), and the broader asset management industry in general. This has included continuing to adapt from an investment standpoint, as well as developing more sophisticated compliance programs to keep up with these growing demands. In this final chapter, we look to the future of the private equity compliance landscape and analyze developing trends in this area.

12.2 SPECIALIZED REGULATORY FOCUS ON PRIVATE EQUITY

Recent regulatory enforcement actions, particularly in the United States, have demonstrated an increased specialized focus on the specific compliance practices of private equity managers. This is as compared to previous broader regulatory approaches that would generally group hedge funds and private equity fund managers together with little distinction between the two. As we outlined in Chapter 1, there are indeed a number of similarities in the regulatory obligations of both of these private funds; however, there are also a number of important distinctions as well. Based in part on the volume of recent enforcement actions against private equity managers, it seems that regulators are beginning to intensify their focus on private equity specific compliance practices.

Those in the fund management industry, however, have faced increased frustration in dealing with regulators who are still managing the process of overseeing the implementation of regulations that are not necessarily tailored specifically to the private equity industry. Additionally, concerns have been raised regarding the overall competence and knowledge of regulatory personnel with regard to the way private equity operates as compared to other fund types. The results of a July 2017 Practitioner Panel Survey conducted by the United Kingdom's Financial Conduct Authority (UK FCA), the primary UK financial regulator for private equity funds, highlights this point. Only 42% of those responding to the survey felt that FCA staff maintained sufficient knowledge to understand the practices employed at their firms.[1]

The comments of one survey respondent who works for what the FCA refers to as a *fixed portfolio firm* (i.e. larger firms for whom regulation has a greater impact on their business as compared to so-called *flexible firms*) further highlight this knowledge disparity. In the survey the FCA posed the question, "Do I trust that the FCA is capable of performing its duties adequately?" In response this individual stated, "Staff at FCA hardly know the difference between a hedge fund and a private equity fund. Most of them have never traded a financial instrument. They should be seconded to asset managers. Escalation of questions should bring back more educated answers."[2]

The survey further outlined that two other issues contributing to a lack of trust in the FCA's knowledge and experience were concerns relating to the assignment of relatively junior personnel who demonstrate a lack of experience to deal with fund managers as well as the continued high turnover among FCA staff.

As a result of feedback such as this, coupled with increased enforcement of US regulatory violations, regulators such as the FCA will likely continue to refine their process toward tailoring their oversight of private equity firms to more appropriately address the specifics of private equity fund managers.

12.3 FOCUS ON PRIVATE EQUITY FEE TRANSPARENCY

Another trend that has recently emerged is a movement by both regulators and LPs to push GPs for enhanced disclosures with regard to private equity fees.

---

[1]C. Wilson, "FCA Staff 'Lack Understanding' of PE," *Private Equity International*, August 7, 2017.
[2]Financial Conduct Authority, "FCA Practitioner Panel Survey," July 2017.

From the regulatory perspective, we can look to the July 2017 Asset Management Market Study conducted by the UK FCA.[3] This study in part focused on the transparency of fees and charges by various types of fund managers. While the study did not originally focus specifically on alternative investment managers, the study did note that comments by market participants indicated that so-called "complex fund structures" such as hedge funds and private equity funds were "particularly opaque" with regards to fees as compared to other sections of the asset management industry. Subsequent comments by the FCA suggested that in private equity the FCA would consider increasing transparency requirements in the area of fees.[4]

It should be noted that the interest in fee disclosures did not focus exclusively on fees related to investment transactions, but also on included proposals for enhanced transparency on other fees, including performance fees. The FCA study even contained a proposal of a single all-in-fee to impose more discipline on fund managers with regard to the management of fees, as well as to facilitate price competition in the asset management industry and provide further visibility of all fund fees and charges to investors.

This push toward increased private equity transparency by regulators has also raised the issue regarding the appropriateness of the level of fees charged by private equity managers. The FCA refers to this concept as the so-called *value for money* offered by an investment product, which has also been referred to as the manager's *alpha*. As a demonstration of the emphasis that regulators are placing on fee levels, the FCA implemented an enhanced responsibility for fund managers to deliver this value for money as part of the broader implementation of the Senior Managers and Certification Regime (SM&CR) to apply to asset managers in 2018.[5]

12.4 MiFID II AND PRIIPs PRIVATE EQUITY TRANSPARENCY CHANGES

Another key driver of private equity transparency coming from Europe stems from the implementation of two key regulations effective January 2018 across the European Union. They are the Markets in Financial Instruments

---

[3]Financial Conduct Authority, "Asset Management Market Study MS15/2.3 Final Report," June 2017.
[4]S. Ring and S. Jones, "U.K. Asset Managers Face Sweeping Shake-up of Fee Charges," *Bloomberg*, June 28, 2017.
[5]C. Flood, M. Marriage, and J. Thomson, "13 Takeaways from the FCA's Review into Asset Managers," *Financial Times*, June 29, 2017.

Directive II (MiFID II) and the Packaged Retail and Insurance-based Investment Products (PRIIPs) Regulation.

When PRIIP was first announced, many private equity managers believed that regulations would not directly apply to them because the regulation is primarily aimed at protecting retail investors, particularly during the initial fundraising process. The EU's definition of the term *retail investors* turned out to be broader than initially anticipated and effectively will be interpreted to apply to fund managers who raise capital not just from retail investors as they have been traditionally defined, but also from sophisticated institutional and high-net-worth investors.

There may also be applicability to staff co-investment and carried interest funds. This latter group is exactly the type of investors that are commonly targeted by private equity funds during the fundraising process, and as such PRIIP is applicable to those that seek to raise capital in the so-called European Economic Area (EEA).

Private equity firms that are subject to PRIIP are required to produce what is known as a Key Information Document (KID). The KID is a brief mandatory template that contains requests for information, including:[6]

- Information about a firm (referred to as the "manufacturer" of a fund in the regulations)
- Product (i.e. fund) specific information, including its objectives and to whom it is intended to be marketed
- Fund risk profile data, including an aggregated Summary Risk Indicator that is a combination of a quantitative Market Risk Measure (MRM) and Credit Risk Measures (CRM) as well as data on maximum possible losses of invested capital
- Anticipated fund returns through the use of scenario analysis as well as the dampening effects on performance such as taxes
- A detail of investment costs, including both direct and indirect costs
- Fund terms, including what is the ability for investors to cancel capital contribution commitments or redeem capital before the expiry of the stated term
- Details of how investors may submit complaints.

The KID guidelines further outline the specific ways in which this information must be presented. A private equity manager subject to these reporting requirements would also be required to review the KID at least annually

---

[6]Commission Delegated Regulation (EU) 2017/653 of 8 March 2017 supplementing Regulation (EU) No. 1286/2014 of the European Parliament, December 4, 2017.

if not more frequently should material changes occur that would require an amendment to the document on an intra-year basis.

These PRIIP KID requirements are effectively an outgrowth of a requirement from the Undertakings for Collective Investment in Transferable Securities Directive (UCITS) IV that was implemented in July 2011. Specifically, UCITS IV added the requirement for a Key Investor Information Document (KIID). Although there is a great deal of similarity between the UCITS KIID and PRIIP KID disclosure requirements, there are material differences as well, including requirements in the areas of fund costs breakouts and the aggregation of costs.

While MiFID II and PRIIP are each broad pieces of legislation covering a wide variety of topics, there are several areas of overlap between the types of data private equity managers are required to report under both regulations. A key goal of these increased disclosure requirements is to provide investors with more uniform information from fund managers, including private equity funds, in areas relating to fees, risks, and fund performance. This overlap was effectively endorsed by the European Securities and Markets Authority (ESMA) in a June 2017 document they produced on MiFID II.[7]

New regulatory disclosure and reporting requirements such as the PRIIP KID have presented a number of logistical, data management, and operational challenges. Private equity managers in particular who may take an approach that much of these types of regulations are geared more heavily toward retail funds must take extra care to focus on both the applicability of these regulations and accompanying reporting requirements to their organizations. GP compliance departments in particular are having to devote more and more time to the growing scope of regulations to which private equity managers are subjected. This includes revising compliance budgets upwards and better managing existing resources to handle an increasing private equity compliance workload.

12.5 REGULATORY FOCUS ON PRIVATE EQUITY DATA SECURITY

In addition to increased regulatory demands for more transparency from private equity GPs, there is also a trend for GPs to bear increased accountability for the oversight and security of data. The best example of this is the General Data Protection Regulation (GDPR).

---

[7]European Securities and Markets Authority (ESMA), "Questions and Answers on MiFID II and MiFIR Investor Protection and Intermediaries Topics ESMA35-43-349," October 3, 2017.

GDPR, also known as Regulation (EU) 2016/679 of the European Parliament, is a new regulation that comes out of Europe that is leading the charge with regard not only to the above-referenced private equity transparency initiatives, but also on the GP data front. The EU GDPR replaces the former Data Protection Directive 95/46/EC and was designed to harmonize data privacy laws across Europe as well as to protect EU citizens' data privacy across the region. The new GDPR regulations bring many revisions and stricter obligations over the previous regulations. GDPR was adopted on April 14, 2016, and came into effect in May 25, 2018. As the law continues to be implemented it will institute major changes for both hedge funds and private equity managers with regard to the way they store and protect data.

Key features of GDPR include:[8]

- *Increased territorial scope*
- *Increased penalties.* Those organization in breach of GDPR can be fined up to 4% of annual global turnover or €20 million (whichever is greater).
- *Consent.* The EU has strengthened the conditions surrounding the requirement for the disclosures regarding the consent given for the use of data to be in plain language and not full of complex legal terminology. Also strengthened are the rules surrounding the ease with which consent can be withdrawn.
- *Breach notifications.* Notification of any data breaches must be provided within 72 hours of a fund manager first becoming aware of the breach.
- *Right to access.* Expanded rights for individuals to be able to obtain clarification as to whether personal data concerning them is being utilized, where, and for what purpose.
- *Data erasure.* Investors in a fund also will have a right under GDPR to have their data forgotten. Investors may also even have the ability to request that third parties that the funds work with stop processing their data.
- *Data portability.* GDPR introduces a new concept known as data portability, which is the right for an investor, sometimes referred to as a *data subject* in the regulations, to receive the personal data concerning them. Investors may also have the right to transmit that data to another entity such as a different fund manager.

---

[8] EU's FAQ on GDPR.

- *Privacy by design and data minimization requirements.* These privacy and design concepts are integrated into GDPR and call for data privacy controls to be implemented as part of the initial design of a fund manager's systems. An additional theme of GDPR is to collect and retain only the minimum amount of data required and to limit access to only essential personnel.

GDPR contains a number of technical terms which GPs must be familiar with in designing their policies and procedures to comply with this legislation. One key term is *controller*. This is the entity that determines the purposes, conditions, and means of the processing of personal data. A data "processor" is an entity which processes personal data on behalf of the controller. Using this terminology, under most situations a GP would likely be the controller and third-party fund service providers would be processors.

There is also a requirement under GDPR for a private equity fund manager in the majority of cases to appoint an individual to a position known as a data protection officer (DPO). There are a number of similarities between the role of a DPO and compliance-related roles such as a money-laundering reporting officer (MLRO), as well as the chief compliance officer (CCO) position. Similar to the role of the MLRO and CCO, the DPO may be either an employee of the fund manager or a third-party service provider. Another similarity to the practices typically employed for CCOs under GDPR is that the DPO role must report directly to the highest level of management, must avoid conflict of interest, and must have appropriate resources to carry out their tasks.

In preparing for GDPR, private equity fund managers must likely integrate their initial and preparatory compliance work as well as ongoing oversight with various departments, including compliance, information technology, risk management, and senior management. The ways in which a fund manager has begun to make these preparations will likely be a useful source of information to signal whether the manager is aware of the intricacies of GDPR and has begun to make the appropriate preparations.

Similar to the initial implementation of Form PF in the United States, there have been a number of information technology vendors and other fund third-party service providers including law-firms that have offered GDPR consulting services to private equity funds. The wide variety of services range from technology-based data solutions to more traditional compliance and law-based consulting. The GDPR-related services offered by these firms may overlap with services a private equity manager is currently utilizing from an existing provider. Sorting all this out so as to avoid a duplication of efforts, either internally at the fund or among multiple service providers, should be part of a fund's pre-GDPR implementation game plan.

Private equity managers are increasingly utilizing cloud-based solutions in part for their ease of accessibility, enhanced security, and cost efficiency. A consideration for fund managers under GDPR would be if data is stored by a manager on their own cloud or more likely using third-party-based cloud solutions. Additionally, a fund's service provider, such as an administrator or information technology vendor, may store fund-related data on the cloud. Alternatively, a vendor engaged by a fund to assist with GDPR as part of this process may also store fund data on the cloud. This use of the cloud could expose not only the third-party vendor to risk, but also the fund itself to enhanced data security and oversight obligations under GDPR.

There are also considerations for UK-based fund managers facing uncertainty surrounding whether the UK will retain GDPR in a post-Brexit environment. While the situation is uncertain, in part based on a history of similar previous UK legislation, such as the UK Data Protection Act of 1998, the UK government has suggested that any legislation they implement will largely follow GDPR.

When considering GDPR obligations, a GP should first question whether GDPR will be applicable to them. If not, have they confirmed this with external counsel? It should also be noted that GDPR applies not only to EU-based fund managers, but also to those that offer funds to EU investors. For example, a US-based fund manager marketing its funds in the EU would likely be subject to elements of GDPR.

If GDPR is indeed applicable to a GP, key questions that should be considered include:

- What steps has the GP taken to prepare for GDPR implementation?
- Has the GP worked with any third-party vendor such as compliance consultants or external legal counsel to evaluate their level of GDPR preparedness?
- How has the information technology department been involved in preparing for GDPR implementation?
- Is there a plan for GDPR considerations to be integrated into ongoing compliance, technology, and internal audit testing?
- How will GDPR influence your cybersecurity plan, including ongoing data breach testing?
- Who will be/is the GP's DPO? Have they considered the pros and cons of outsourcing this role?

Another related GDPR consideration for LPs would be if they intend to pass through any of the compliance expenses surrounding GDPR implementation directly to any underlying funds. Such direct pass-throughs will likely be frowned upon by investors, but still the increased costs of GDPR compliance may be passed through as a result of increased overall fund expenses for items such as shared servers or software to assist with compliance, which a fund's investors may end up paying part of.

12.6 INCREASED SCRUTINY ON PRIVATE EQUITY RESEARCH DATA COMPLIANCE

Private equity fund managers have become increasingly creative in their attempts to collect and mine what some call "alternative data" for investment research purposes. Examples of these new types of data collection techniques that have replaced or augmented the traditional store channel checks have included the use of drones and satellite imagery to monitor retail establishment parking lots, analyzing credit card transaction data, and the monitoring of cell phone signals for geodata to track the volume of visits to locations including hospitals and stores.

This data is often utilized as part of a larger predictive analysis and may also be combined with big data analysis techniques. These new technology-based data collection techniques have raised a number of potentially concerning gray areas with regard to the privacy implications surrounding this data, including potential implications for violations of insider trading laws.

Under regulations such as GDPR, fund managers will have to ensure that the ways in which they collect and store this information comply with GDPR requirements. Many fund managers may not be collecting this data themselves but instead purchasing it. If that is the case, there are considerations under regulations such as GDPR relating to the ways in which this data must be made anonymous in a GDPR-compliant manner.

12.7 FURTHER SCRUTINY OF POTENTIAL PAY-TO-PLAY VIOLATIONS

In 2010 the U.S. Securities and Exchange Commission (US SEC) adopted Rule 206(4)-5 of the Investment Advisers Act of 1940, which is also referred to as the "pay-to-play" rule. The term *pay-to-play* effectively refers to *quid pro quo arrangements*, which effectively amount to the intentional bribery of government officials in exchange for business for a fund manager. Specifically, this Rule prohibits RIAs from managing funds for a government client for two years after a campaign contribution by the firm or certain employees.[9]

A notable case against an investment adviser by the US SEC under the pay-to-play rules was brought in June 2014 against a private equity firm with a venture capital strategy, TL Ventures Inc. The SEC Press Release dated June 20, 2014 described the situation as follows:[10]

> An SEC investigation found that TL Ventures violated pay-to-play rules by continuing to receive compensation from two public pension funds – Pennsylvania's state retirement system and Philadelphia's pension plan – within two years after an associate made a $2,500 campaign contribution to a Philadelphia mayoral candidate and a $2,000 campaign contribution to the governor of Pennsylvania. The mayoral position appoints three of the nine members of the Philadelphia Board of Pensions and Retirement. Therefore, a mayor can influence the hiring of investment advisers for the public pension fund. The 11-member board of Pennsylvania's state retirement system includes six gubernatorial appointees. Therefore, a governor can influence the hiring of investment advisers for the public pension fund. After the contributions, TL Ventures improperly continued to receive compensation from the pension funds for those advisory services.

The specific donations in this case were made by Robert Keith, co-founder of the Firm, to Philadelphia Mayor Michael Nutter and Pennsylvania Governor Tom Corbett.[11] It is interesting to note that the TL Ventures funds into which capital the pensions were invested were past their 10-year initial terms and were in wind-down mode. However, as is common for many private equity funds, the funds had the ability to request an extension

---

[9]Further details regarding the specific technicalities of the Rule can be found in the US Securities and Exchange Commission's "Staff Responses to Questions About the Pay to Play Rule," updated August 18, 2017, and available at: https://www.sec.gov/divisions/investment/pay-to-play-faq.htm, as well as in the Securities and Exchange Commission release on the final rule, "17 CFR Part 275 Release No. IA-3043; File No. S7–18-09 RIN 3235-AK39, Political Contributions by Certain Investment Advisers," available at: https://www.sec.gov/rules/final/2010/ia-3043.pdf.

[10]US Securities and Exchange Commission Press Release, "SEC Charges Private Equity Firm with Pay-to-Play Violations Involving Political Campaign Contributions in Pennsylvania," June 20, 2015.

[11]W. Alden, "Venture Capital Firm Settles S.E.C. Charges Over Pay-to-Play," *Dealbook*, June 20, 2014.

in the initial term of the fund through two one-year extensions, subject to approval by a majority of the LPs of the fund.[12] As the SEC determined in this case, this potential extension, coupled with the fact that fee payments may have continued beyond the 10-year period, subjected the firm to the requirements of the pay-to-play rules.[13]

Compliance violations such as these can also have direct financial consequences. In this instance, TL Ventures was ordered to pay disgorgement of $256,697, prejudgment interest of $3,197, and penalty of $35,000.[14] These are significant penalties when compared to the relatively low dollar amounts of the campaign contributions made.

12.8 CHAPTER SUMMARY

This chapter provided an overview of emerging trends in private equity compliance. The trend of an increased specialized regulatory focus on private equity fund managers was discussed. Next, the ways in which regulatory agencies such as the UK FCA have focused on GP fee transparency were addressed. The impact on the private equity industry of new legislation such as MiFID II and PRIIPs was examined. We then discussed the regulatory focus on data security through GDPR. Finally, the continued focus on pay-to-play violations in the private equity industry was addressed.

---

[12]United States of America Before the Securities and Exchange Commission, Investment Advisers Act of 1940 Release No. 3859/June 20, 2014 Administrative Proceeding File No. 3-15940, In the Matter of TL Ventures Inc.

[13]D. Primack, "How a Zombie VC Firm Broke Pay-to-Play Rules," *Fortune*, June 23, 2014.

[14]J. DiStefano, "UPDATE: Pension Manager Broke, 'Pay-to-Play' Ban, Gave $ to Mayor Nutter, Gov. Corbett, SEC Says," http://Philly.com, June 20, 2014.

About the Author

Jason Scharfman is the Managing Partner of Corgentum Consulting, a specialist consulting firm that performs operational due diligence reviews and background investigations of fund managers of all types, including hedge funds, private equity, real estate, and long-only funds on behalf of institutional investors, including pensions, endowments, foundations, fund of funds, family offices, and high-net-worth individuals.

He is recognized as a leading expert in the field of due diligence, and is the author of Hedge Fund Governance: Evaluating Oversight, Independence, and Conflicts (Academic Press, 2014), Private Equity Operational Due Diligence: Tools to Evaluate Liquidity, Valuation, and Documentation. (John Wiley & Sons 2012), and Hedge Fund Operational Due Diligence: Understanding the Risks (John Wiley & Sons, 2008). He has also contributed to the Chartered Alternative Investment Analyst (CAIA) curriculum on due diligence and has served on the organization's Due Diligence, Risk Management, and Regulation Committee.

Before founding Corgentum, Mr. Scharfman previously oversaw the operational due diligence function for a $6 billion alternative investment allocation group called Graystone Research at Morgan Stanley. While at Morgan Stanley, he was also a senior member of a team that oversaw all of Morgan Stanley's hedge fund operational due diligence efforts, allocating in excess of $13 billion to a firm-wide platform of more than 300 hedge fund managers across multiple investment strategies. Before joining Morgan Stanley, he held positions that primarily focused on due diligence and risk management within the alternative investment sector at Lazard Asset Management, SPARX Investments and Research, and Thomson Financial.

Mr. Scharfman received a BS in finance with an additional major in Japanese from Carnegie Mellon University, an MBA in finance from Baruch College's Zicklin School of Business, and a JD from St. John's University School of Law. He is admitted to the practice of law in New York and in New Jersey. In addition, he holds the Certified Fraud Examiner (CFE) and Certified in Risk and Information Systems Control (CRISC) credentials. He has consulted with the US House Judiciary Committee on hedge fund regulation. He has also provided training to financial regulators on hedge fund due diligence. Mr. Scharfman has served as a consultant and testified as an expert in litigation and arbitration proceedings and has lectured on the subject of hedge fund operations and operational risk as an adjunct professor at New York University. He is a member of several industry organizations, including the Information Systems Audit and Control Association, the American Bar Association, the New York State Bar Association, and the New Jersey State Bar Association. He has written extensively on the subject of operational due diligence and speaks worldwide on due diligence and operational risks.

Index

207